And the Rest Is History

And the Rest Is History

The Famous (and Infamous)
First Meetings of the World's
Most Passionate Couples

Marlene Wagman-Geller

A PERIGEE BOOK

A PERIGEE BOOK
Published by the Penguin Group
Penguin Group (USA) Inc.
375 Hudson Street, New York, New York 10014, USA
Penguin Group (Canada), 90 Eglinton Avenue East, Suite 700, Toronto, Ontario M4P 2Y3, Canada
(a division of Pearson Penguin Canada Inc.)
Penguin Books Ltd., 80 Strand, London WC2R 0RL, England
Penguin Group Ireland, 25 St. Stephen's Green, Dublin 2, Ireland (a division of Penguin Books Ltd.)
Penguin Group (Australia), 250 Camberwell Road, Camberwell, Victoria 3124, Australia
(a division of Pearson Australia Group Pty. Ltd.)
Penguin Books India Pvt. Ltd., 11 Community Centre, Panchsheel Park, New Delhi—110 017, India
Penguin Group (NZ), 67 Apollo Drive, Rosedale, North Shore 0632, New Zealand
(a division of Pearson New Zealand Ltd.)
Penguin Books (South Africa) (Pty.) Ltd., 24 Sturdee Avenue, Rosebank, Johannesburg 2196,
South Africa
Penguin Books Ltd., Registered Offices: 80 Strand, London WC2R 0RL, England

First edition: February 2011

Library of Congress Cataloging-in-Publication Data

Wagman-Geller, Marlene.
    And the rest is history : the famous (and infamous) first meetings of the world's most passionate
couples / Marlene Wagman-Geller.
        p.   cm.
    "A Perigee book."
    Includes bibliographical references.
    ISBN 978-0-399-53641-0
    1. Couples—History.   2. Paramours—History.   3. Man-woman relationships—History.   I. Title.
    HQ801.A2W34   2011
    306.7092'2—dc22   [B]   2010038244

PRINTED IN THE UNITED STATES OF AMERICA

10 9 8 7 6 5 4 3 2 1

To J—

And the rest was my history

CONTENTS

INTRODUCTION

Did my heart love till now?
Forswear it, sight!
For I ne'er saw true beauty till tonight.

—From *Romeo and Juliet*, by William Shakespeare

One of life's most significant moments is being able to say, "I've met The One." Such a statement is invariably followed by the question, "How did you two meet?" *And the Rest Is History* is a look at how history's most famous lovers first laid eyes on each other: through fate, setups, and plain old blind luck. The first meetings shared in this book give us a look at what makes that one grand passion.

In some instances, lovers' destinies changed the world. When a weary traveler spied a girl at a well, it led to the birth of a people; an encounter outside the British Parliament sounded the death knell to Ireland's independence. A Prague ball led to a great war, a fox hunt to a royal abdication.

Although other encounters did not etch new lines on the face of history, they nevertheless left their calling cards on the arts. One love affair led to the crown jewel in the world's architecture; a visit to a

London home resulted in immortal poetry; a backstage exchange brought together the king and queen of country music.

The stories in *And the Rest Is History* also focus on how the lovers parted. Often it is only in the moment of farewell that people truly look into the face of love. Before Abelard left for his Benedictine monastery, Héloise said, "Farewell, my only love." Napoleon's last words were "France, the army, the head of the army, Josephine." Queen Victoria's final breath was spent whispering, "Bertie."

In some cases, farewells were caused not by death but by an inability to remain together. Although many of the liaisons did not end with a happily-ever-after, this does not make them any less romantic; indeed, it can make them more so. The stories that touch us most deeply are often born of human frailty. Just because it ended doesn't mean it wasn't love.

Like others reared on tales beginning with "Once upon a time," I am an out-of-the-closet romantic. Growing up, I eagerly read about how fictional characters met their loves. Romeo's life was inextricably bound with that of Juliet, whom he first spied when he crashed the Capulet ball. Sleeping Beauty awoke from a hundred-year slumber with a kiss from a stranger who just happened to be a handsome prince. Catherine was introduced to Heathcliff when her father brought home a foundling from the streets of Liverpool. However, as I was unlikely to be invited to Verona, I'm not adept with a spinning wheel, and no orphan was ever adopted in my childhood home, I turned from fictional forays to nonfictional ones to discover how people met their *beshert*, Yiddish for "preordained soul mate."

It is love that makes us want to live, or makes us want to die. Shakespeare's Antony said of his Cleopatra, "Age cannot wither her, nor custom stale / Her infinite variety." The same can be said of the immortal love stories. Together these make a treasure trove of the romance of the ages, for both armchair romantics and those who can say of their own life-changing encounter, "And the rest is history."

Marlene Wagman-Geller
San Diego, California, 2010

Author's note: There are always new stories of the ways couples met. Harrison Ford and Calista Flockhart, who tied the knot in Santa Fe, New Mexico, in 2010, revealed that they met when Calista accidentally spilled wine on the *Indiana Jones* star at the 2002 Golden Globes. Please feel free to email me about other interesting first encounters at onceagaintozelda@hotmail.com or go to my website, www.onceagaintozelda.net.

Jacob and Rachel

1759 BC

*T*he Old Testament tells the tale of a lost paradise, a great flood, a promised land; it also features one of the world's first love stories.

The biblical Jacob's life was the antithesis of uneventful—he wrestled an angel, had four wives and dozens of children, and christened a country. Yet one of his greatest struggles involved his years of toil—all for the woman he loved.

Jacob's life was tumultuous, even in the womb. When his mother, Rebekah, asked God why her pregnancy was so agonizing, she was told her twins were wrestling and were to do so all their lives. In fact, when Jacob was born, he came out clutching his twin Esau's heel, which led to his being named Jacob, Hebrew for "the supplanter." One fateful day, Esau, a hunter, returned home with a voracious appetite, and Jacob decided to exploit his brother's hunger. Jacob told his starving sibling that he would feed him a "mess of pottage" (the biblical vernacular for a meal of lentils) in exchange for Esau's inheritance of the family wealth, which was his birthright as the elder sibling. Their father, Isaac, old and blind, mistakenly conferred his blessing on the wrong son. Infuriated, Esau swore to kill his brother upon their father's death. To protect Jacob, Rebekah sent him to her brother's country; it was where he was to fall in love and, in the process, leave his imprint on the millennia.

The life of Rachel, Jacob's destiny, was calm before the arrival of her lover. She lived with her father and siblings; her task was to water their flock of sheep at a well near Haran, an outpost of the ancient city of Ur.

Yet one day, her family had a visitor, and the family's tranquillity was to become a thing of the past. Her first cousin Jacob arrived in a state of extreme exhaustion; he had just fled from his home, five hundred miles away, desperate not to become the victim of a fratricide, and had experienced an out-of-body experience in which he saw angels ascending and descending a ladder. He was relieved when he spied a well and sat down to rest. There he met a number of shepherds who were waiting for others to join them, because it took several men to lift the heavy stone that covered the well.

The first time Jacob met Rachel she was approaching the watering hole with her sheep. She was "beautiful of form and face," with mesmerizing eyes, and Jacob was immediately smitten. In an astounding feat of strength, exhaustion forgotten, he single-handedly removed the huge stone. Genesis states, "Then Jacob kissed Rachel, and lifted his voice and wept." She was suitably impressed with the combination of masculine strength and tears, and she hurried home with her newfound love interest in tow.

Within a month the couple desired to wed, and Jacob approached Rachel's father, Laban, to ask for the hand of his daughter. Laban agreed, with the caveat that Jacob would have to labor seven years without pay for the privilege. Jacob, the trickster, was to discover he was a rank amateur in comparison to Laban.

Jacob was so enamored of his fiancée that the seven years "seemed to him but a few days because of his love for her" (Genesis). Indeed, those words are some of the loveliest ever penned of a man's devotion to the woman he loved.

At last, the longed-for day dawned. After the ceremony, the groom took his veiled bride to his tent. He was ecstatic to finally be with his love after his seven years of labor. To his extreme consternation, in the light of dawn, he found not his intended, but her older sister, Leah. In a fury he approached his father-in-law for an explanation. Laban justified the switch by saying he had promised Jacob his daughter; he had just not specified which one. (Perhaps this was karma for the deception Jacob had practiced on his father; he had pretended to be his brother, Esau, and Leah had pretended to be her sister, Rachel.)

Laban pointed out that in Haran it was protocol for the older sister to marry first. Rather than bemoan love's labors lost, Jacob again sued for the hand of his beloved. Laban agreed, with the provision that he had to agree to another seven-year tour of duty—though, in compassion, he conceded that the marriage could take place after the ceremonial week of the first wedding. Jacob, understanding that great love was synonymous with great sacrifice, consented. Hence Rachel became Jacob's second wife, though she was always first in his heart.

After the nuptials, the feelings between the two sisters were akin to the ones between the two brothers. Rachel did not forgive her sister for her part in the deception, and Jacob referred to Leah as the "unloved" one. However, despite her unloved status, Leah bore several children; after each one she prayed for her husband's affections, which were never forthcoming. On the other hand, Rachel, the wife of Jacob's heart, remained barren.

One day, Leah's son Reuben brought home mandrake roots as a present for his mother. His aunt desperately desired them, as they were a popular aphrodisiac in the ancient world. Leah agreed that her sister could have them in exchange for promising that Rachel would command Jacob to have intercourse with Leah that night. The result was that Leah again conceived while Rachel did not.

Trying another tactic, Rachel arranged for her maidservant Bilhah to serve as her surrogate, and through this means she became the mother of two. In retaliation, Leah gave her maidservant Zilpah to Jacob, which resulted in another two sons.

Jacob and Rachel's greatest joy was when she finally conceived and gave birth to Joseph, who would become his father's favorite. Jacob would one day show his preference by distinguishing Joseph with the special gift of a multicolored coat.

Wanting his mother, Rebekah, to meet her new grandson, Joseph, Jacob decided it was time to depart Haran and return to Canaan, in the hope that with time Esau's hatred had abated. Jacob gathered his four wives, dozens of children, and flocks of sheep and set his eyes toward home. Before they left, Rachel stole her father's idols, which represented the protective deities of his home and served as a property deed. Her plan was to secure the property for her husband. She figured that years ago, on what should have been her wedding night, Laban had stolen her happiness; it was time to return the transgression.

The clan had crossed the Euphrates when Laban arrived and accused Jacob of theft. His innocent son-in-law denied knowledge of wrongdoing with the curse, "With whoever you find your gods, he will not live" (Genesis). Not convinced, Laban searched every inch of all the tents; however, he neglected to look under the camel seat cushion where Rachel was sitting—the spot where the idols were hidden. She explained, "Let not my lord be angered that I cannot rise up before you, for the way of women is upon me" (Genesis). This was a lie; she was not menstruating and was actually pregnant with her second son. Laban departed, but Jacob's curse remained.

During the odyssey, Jacob, despite his four wives and innumerable children, found time for solitude, wherein he had his second out-of-body experience. In it he encountered an angel who wrestled with him throughout the night. In the course of the struggle the angel informed him that he was no longer Jacob, the supplanter; henceforth he would be known as Israel, meaning "ruling with God." He was told that a great nation would be named after him, and his twelve sons would give rise to twelve tribes.

When Canaan was in sight, ever protective of his first love, Jacob placed her at the rear of his family (the place of the greatest safety) in the contingency of an attack by Esau, who he still feared. Jacob was overjoyed when his brother not only forgave him but welcomed him; however, his elation was short-lived. At this juncture Rachel went into an excruciating labor, and after giving Jacob his twelfth son, Benjamin, she passed away: "And Rachel died, and was buried on the way to Ephrath, which is Bethlehem. And Jacob set a pillar upon her grave: that is the pillar of Rachel's grave unto this day" (Genesis).

Her husband was devastated at the loss of the woman he had adored since he had laid eyes on her, the one who was to be revered as the biblical matriarch. Jacob continued on his journey, his heart left behind.

Postscript

→ Rachel's Tomb is considered the third-holiest site in Judaism. It is visited by thousands annually.

➔ Jacob (then known as Israel) passed away in Egypt, in the Land of Goshen. His son Joseph returned his father's body to his homeland, Canaan, where he gave him a stately burial and interred him in the Cave of Machpelah to join those of his grandparents Abraham and Sarah; his parents, Isaac and Rebekah; and his first wife, Leah.

2

Abelard and Héloise

1118

The relationship scandal of the twelfth century is the tale of Abelard and Héloise, star-crossed lovers whose passion survived calamity and continues to echo throughout the millennia.

Medieval depictions of women are stylized: they wear chastity belts, weave tapestries, and watch their knights jousting. However, Héloise d'Argenteuil was not cut from the cloth of her time; she was an accomplished linguist, versed in Latin, Greek, and Hebrew. Her uncle and guardian, Fulbert, served as the canon of Notre Dame University, a position of respect; however, his greatest source of pride was his beautiful and accomplished niece. Because Héloise's greatest pursuit was knowledge, the canon decided to procure the most revered teacher in France.

Héloise's destiny, Peter Abelard, was the most renowned thinker of his age, the son of a noble family from a village in Brittany. Although he had been destined for knighthood, he forfeited that path for academia, and thousands of students converged on Notre Dame

University (which later became the University of Paris) to hear the high priest of philosophy. He became so venerated that he prided himself on being the most eminent living theologian.

In the twelfth century, the position of teacher was similar to one of cleric in that both had to take vows of chastity, as those professions demanded single-minded devotion. This caveat did not bother Abelard, because he had dedicated his life to learning—that is, until temptation made its appearance.

The first time Héloise met Abelard was when he became a lodger at her uncle's home in exchange for his services. On that first encounter, Abelard discovered that the life of the body was as vital as the life of the mind. Divesting himself of his religious vow of chastity as well as his moral code, Abelard was soon tutoring Héloise in more than Socrates. Abelard took a break from philosophy and penned love songs for Héloise. He later wrote of his earliest moments with her, "Her studies allowed us to withdraw in private, as love desired, and then with our books open before us, more words of love than of reading passed between us, and more kissing than teaching. My hands strayed oftener to her bosom than to the pages; love drew our eyes to look on each other more than reading kept them on our texts." Abelard's attraction to Héloise transcended the merely physical; it was also the meeting of minds. He said of Héloise that she was *"nominatissima"*—"most renowned" for her brilliance.

The course of true love went smoothly for eighteen months, until Canon Fulbert caught the two making love on Good Friday. Fulbert was infuriated and saw the situation as a teacher taking sexual advantage of a teenager twenty years his junior. As further salt in his wound, it had been conducted covertly in his own home. A final public twist of the knife occurred when he discovered that Héloise was pregnant.

The enraged canon demanded that the couple be immediately

married to prevent family shame and public scandal. Although Abelard readily agreed, Héloise was reluctant; she had her own theology of love that did not allow her to put public censure over Abelard's eminent post. Abelard wrote of Héloise's altruism, "She, however, most violently disapproved of this, and for two chief reasons: the danger thereof, and the disgrace which it would bring upon me. . . . What penalties, she said, would the world rightly demand of her if she should rob it of so shining a light!" Héloise wrote of her impending nuptials, "Then there is no more left but this, that in our doom the sorrow yet to come shall be no less than the love we two have already known."

After the clandestine wedding, the canon spread the news that his niece was married and their baby, Astrolabe (named after an astrological instrument), was therefore legitimate. However, Héloise, ever protective of her husband's career, continued to deny her marriage. The situation became so volatile that Abelard, fearing for his new wife, placed her in a convent in Argenteuil, on the outskirts of Paris. Ironically, this act of protection led to the couple's tragic destiny.

Fulbert, acting under the erroneous assumption that Abelard had put Héloise in the abbey to abandon her, decided to exact a fitting revenge. When Abelard was asleep, Fulbert, with the assistance of one of Abelard's servants who had been bought off, broke into his room. As Abelard later wrote of their violent attack, "They cut off those parts of my body with which I had done that which was the cause of their sorrow." The castration was, so to speak, Fulbert's variation of "an eye for an eye." To lesser loves this act would have served as the death knell, but Abelard and Héloise's devotion remained constant.

No longer able to live as Héloise's husband, Abelard took his vows in the St. Denis monastery; similarly Héloise, in her heart still married to Abelard, stayed on at her convent and eventually became a nun. She later explained that she agreed to devote her life to religion only because it was Abelard's will: "It was your command, not love of God, which made me take the veil."

Although the violent act had forced their lives asunder, Abelard never abandoned his love. When Argenteuil was taken over by the abbey where Peter had been ordained, he arranged for Héloise and her fellow nuns to enter the Oratory of the Paraclete. Héloise, by channeling the energy she had once expended on Abelard to her religious calling, rose to the position of abbess.

For years, the couple lived their separate lives, though their thoughts were always of one another. They eventually reconnected when Peter penned a twenty-thousand-word account of his tragedy in deference to the medieval genre of the "letter of consolation," whereby, in order to console a fellow pilgrim in pain, one wrote of his or her own sorrow, demonstrating the democracy of agony. Héloise received a copy of the confession and immediately composed a letter to her estranged husband clarifying that not even time, vows, or God had been able to extinguish the flame of her feelings. Thus began a twenty-year correspondence.

In her letters, Héloise encouraged Abelard in his quest for knowledge and exhorted him to share with her every detail of his life, making sure not to spare any unpleasant aspects. In one she wrote, "I will finish a long letter with a brief ending: Farewell, my only love." In turn, his missives are filled with endless pages of his steadfast feelings. Between the lines one can read the message of what could have been. Their love affair became material for troubadours and medieval minstrels and remains poignant today.

Héloise's reaction to the cruelty of fate was always to bemoan her cruel loss and long for the physical intimacy which had made her feel alive. Throughout her life she questioned God for permitting the horror inflicted on Abelard and for her role as a nun. The only thing she never questioned was her unwavering feelings for her lost love. She wrote to him, "I should be groaning over the sins I have committed, but I can only sigh for what we have lost." At the end, even when Héloise was wrapped in the robes of a nun, earthly romance was her true religion. Abelard, on the other hand, stricken in conscience, viewed his castration as divine retribution for his flouting of morality. He perceived their tragedy as one orchestrated by the Almighty, as the means for him to embrace the love of God over the love of the flesh. He explained his philosophy in a letter: "See then my beloved, see how with the dragnets of His mercy, the Lord has fished us up from the depths of the dangerous sea."

In 1142, on his way to Rome to plead a theological question, Peter fell ill and collapsed at the Abbey of Cluny, where he lingered for several months. From there he was taken to the priory of St. Marcel, where he passed from this world to the one with which he was always absorbed. His last words were, "I don't know."

Héloise survived Abelard for more than twenty years, without even the comfort of his written words. Her last words were of her first love: "In death, at last, let me rest with Abelard."

The treatises of the scholar Abelard have been consigned to the dustbin of history; what survives is the tale of two martyrs to romance who, although they were the playthings of fate, managed to transcend physical love for an immortal one.

Postscript

➤ Peter Abelard was buried in St. Marcel; however, Héloise arranged for his remains to be secretly removed to the Paraclete so they could be under her care. When she passed away, her body was placed next to his.

➤ Six hundred years later, the empress Josephine Bonaparte, enamored of the star-crossed lovers' passion, arranged for their removal from their original resting place to the Pere-Lachaise Cemetery in Paris, so they could be entombed together in the city where they had first kindled their romance. The crypt has become a mecca for romantics and the lovelorn, who leave notes at the burial ground.

3

Antony and Cleopatra

41 BC

*T*he romance between the Roman general Antony and Cleopatra, his Egyptian queen, has captured the imagination of artists, poets, and playwrights since antiquity. The reason for their timeless appeal most likely lies in their last desperate acts, history's most famous suicides—undertaken because they preferred death to life without each other.

Controlling the land of the Nile since the reign of Alexander the Great, the Ptolemy family and their royal line of succession decreed that a brother and a sister marry and jointly share the throne. With the death of Pharaoh Ptolemy XII, power passed to his eighteen-year-old daughter Cleopatra and his twelve-year-old son Ptolemy XIII. Although the dynasty is to be commended for not favoring male heirs over female ones, the brother-sister/husband-wife rulers often engaged in more than mere sibling rivalry. Driven by a desire to be the sole ruler, Cleopatra embarked in a civil war against her brother; as a result she was driven from her palace in Alexandria by an army loyal to Ptolemy.

In the thick of the royal family feud Julius Caesar arrived from Rome in pursuit of his enemy Pompey; however, with the discovery that the Egyptians had assassinated his rival, he turned his attention to arbitrating the bloodbath that was tearing apart the land of the Nile. In one of the great iconic meetings in world history, Cleopatra, barred entry to her palace, had her servants roll her up in a Persian carpet and smuggle her into the palace, where the rug was laid at Caesar's feet. When the seductively clad Egyptian queen tumbled out, Julius was charmed both by her gesture and her allure, so much so that they soon became intimate.

The following morning Caesar let it be known that Cleopatra's enemies were now his enemies. The ruler who was to proclaim *"Veni, vidi, vici"* ("I came, I saw, I conquered") was himself conquered by the femme fatale with the kohl-rimmed eyes, and nine months later she bore his baby, Ptolemy Caesar, nicknamed Caesarion. Ptolemy XIII (conveniently for his sister) ended up drowned in the Nile, thanks to Julius's machinations.

When Caesar returned to Rome, he did so with his paramour and their son in tow. To the disgust of his wife, Calpurnia, and his people, in the Temple of Venus he erected a golden statue of Cleopatra, depicted as Isis. Although Hollywood portrayed the queen as a great beauty, coins bearing her likeness prove the contrary. Plutarch writes of her, "For her beauty was in itself not altogether incomparable, nor such as to strike those who saw her." In other words, she was plain. What made Cleopatra attractive were her wit, charm, and intelligence. The only claim she had to looks was a large nose, which was considered a mark of beauty in her epoch.

In 44 BC, Julius Caesar was assassinated on the steps of the Forum on the ides of March. His death would change the course of history as well as Cleopatra's own life.

After Caesar's death, the general Marcus Antonius (Marc Antony), became, along with Octavian, one of the three leaders of Rome. Fearing an eventual power struggle with Octavian, Marc arranged for a meeting with the Egyptian queen, hoping to gain a powerful political ally. He was to gain far more.

When Cleopatra received Antony's summons for an interview, she vowed to seduce him in the same fashion as she had done her former Roman general. She needed the protection of the ruler of the most powerful nation in the world to safeguard her throne and secure the succession of Caesarion. She staged the entrance of the millennium.

Cleopatra sailed down the river in a gilded barge, adorned with swelling sails of Tyrian purple. The ship was filled with such a quantity of rose petals that the Romans knew of her arrival before she appeared on their horizon. The oars were silver, drawn by servant girls clad as nymphs. The boat drew near the shore to the accompaniment of the music of flutes and harps. Against this frame, Cleopatra lay on a divan beneath a canopy of gold, dressed in the garb of Venus, fanned by boys clad as Cupid.

The first time Cleopatra met Antony was when he came to dine on her palace barge. He was immediately enraptured by the seductress. The queen, who had most likely given herself to Caesar only for political expediency, became the paramour of Antony—but this time, it was for love. The couple spent all their time together, which led to Antony's neglect of his legions.

When Cleopatra returned to Alexandria, she did so with Antony, who abandoned his military campaign to follow her. According to Plutarch, Cleopatra "played at dice with him, drank with him, hunted with him. At night she would go rambling with him to disturb and torment people at their windows, dressed like a servant-woman, for Antony also went in servant's disguise . . . However, the Alexandrians in general liked it all well enough, and joined good-humoredly and kindly in his frolic and play."

Not so the Romans. They viewed her as a lustful seductress who employed sex and sorcery to seduce their two greatest generals. Marc Antony had fallen far from the magnificent orator whose eulogy for Caesar had made him the most celebrated of his countrymen.

Finally, after a year Antony pulled himself away from Cleopatra to rejoin his legions in Rome. When he arrived, to help make amends, he agreed to wed Octavian's sister, Octavia, though his heart lay in Egypt. The messengers who conveyed this information to Cleopatra probably did so with the greatest of trepidation, as she was known to kill those who brought disturbing news (giving birth to the expression "Don't kill the messenger"). She was particularly unhappy with the timing of her lover's nuptials, as she was pregnant with his twins, Alexander Helios ("The Sun"), and Cleopatra Selene ("The Moon").

In his own country, Antony was caught in an emotional tug-of-war, endlessly torn between his two mistresses: Rome and Cleopatra. Unable to deny the latter, he headed to Asia Minor and sent for Cleopatra to join him. There he married her under Egyptian law, which allowed polygamy, and announced the paternity of his son and daughter. As a wedding present he presented her with the Roman dominions of Syria, Phoenicia, Cyprus, and Crete. She was delighted with the gifts; Octavian, however, did not share the sentiment.

The couple began presenting themselves as divine and bedecked themselves as Osiris and Isis. Disgusted with these actions, Rome, as much as it once idolized Antony, now vilified him. Antony, by falling into Cleopatra's arms, had placed his neck in Octavian's hands. The latter decided to destroy Antony to advance his own means. By obliterating his enemy he would avenge his slighted sister; moreover, he could set himself up as Augustus Caesar and become his country's first emperor. He asked the Senate to declare war against Egypt.

In 31 BC, Antony's forces faced Octavian's in a high-stakes naval battle off the coast of Actium in Greece. The victor would become the undisputed leader of the most powerful country in the world. Cleopatra, in a ship with a gold sail, anxiously awaited its outcome. At a crucial stage in the battle, Cleopatra suddenly gave a signal that signified retreat. At this point Antony had a choice: follow his heart and Cleopatra, or follow his duties as a Roman general. He immediately set off after her, proving that to him power was nothing; his queen was everything. When his legions saw that their leader had abandoned the battle, they did likewise and joined forces with Octavian. Shakespeare, in his play *Antony and Cleopatra*, wrote of Antony's action, "The triple pillar of the world transform'd into a strumpet's fool." The legions of Rome marched to Alexandria.

During the ensuing land battle, Cleopatra took refuge in a mausoleum. When Antony heard this news, he assumed his queen was dead. He had made his love the world; without her, there was nothing. No longer willing to go on, in the Roman fashion of suicide, he fell on his own sword. As he lay dying, he was informed that she was merely in hiding. His last order as a general was for his soldiers to carry him to Cleopatra; he died in her arms. The Queen of the Nile had but one course of action: to show how a descendant of kings could die. Ten years earlier she had made a grand entrance to meet Antony; now it was the occasion to make a grand departure.

She wrote a letter for Octavian, with a plea that she be buried alongside Antony. Cleopatra also ordered her servants to bring her a basket of figs, inside which was concealed a poisonous asp. Dressed in full royal regalia, replete with the pharaoh's Uraeus headdress, she put the cobra to her breast. She then lay down on a couch of gold to join her ancestors, to join Antony.

Antony and Cleopatra flung away the two greatest empires of the world and committed suicide for one another, ensuring that their tale would pass from an individual story to an iconic one.

Postscript

➤ Plutarch wrote that Cleopatra was found dead, with her handmaiden Iras dying at her feet while another handmaiden, Charmion, was discovered adjusting her queen's crown before she too succumbed to poison. Octavian honored the couple's last wish, interring them together in one tomb in Alexandria.

➤ Egypt's top archaeologist, Zahi Hawass, who sports an Indiana Jones hat, believes that a temple located thirty miles from Alexandria contains the tomb of the doomed lovers.

4

Prince Khurram and Mumtaz Mahal

1607

*T*he man who was renowned as king of the world achieved immortality not through empire, but rather through the monument he erected as an immortal tribute to the woman he loved.

The eastern fairy tale began in India with the birth of Prince Khurram Shihab-ud-din-Muhammad, the third and favorite son of Emperor Jahangir and his second wife. The name Khurram, Persian for "joyful," was bestowed by his grandfather. As a youth he distinguished himself in martial arts, as a military commander, and in architecture. His destiny, Arjumand Banu Begum, was born in Agra, in what was then the Mogul Empire, which stretched from Russia to China and included modern India, Afghanistan, and Pakistan.

The first time Khurram met Arjumand was when the fifteen-year-old prince was strolling in the Meena Bazaar, the private market attached to the harem. Every female at the marketplace held a torch for the handsome, fabulously wealthy son of Emperor Jahangir. However, it wasn't until he passed an exquisitely beautiful girl whose stall was filled with silk and glass beads that his attention was caught. Khurram asked the girl the price of the largest of the trinkets, and, in the age-old language of flirtation, she replied it was a precious diamond, one he could not afford. He paid her the fantastic sum of ten thousand rupees and left carrying the glass bead, as well as the heart of the girl—Arjumand.

That evening he asked his father's permission to marry Arjumand, the daughter of the prime minister, and the emperor raised his right hand in assent, as his son was his favorite, and as he too was in awe of Arjumand's dazzling allure. However, the emperor declared that the marriage could not take place for five years, and that his son could not see his intended for that period and would have to first marry another wife, a Persian princess, for political reasons. The emperor's word was law, and the prince was obliged to wed two times and to carry out his conjugal duties with each one; his unions produced two children.

In 1612, the court astrologers agreed on an auspicious date for the royal union, and the couple, now nineteen and twenty, still madly in love, could finally be together. The emperor arranged for the wedding of the millennium, and he himself adorned his new daughter-in-law with a wedding wreath of pearls. He also changed her name to Mumtaz Mahal, meaning "ornament of the palace." The couple headed the wedding procession, surrounded by the officials of state wearing robes of spun gold, slaves shooing off flies, servants carrying torches, and dervishes reciting from their prayer beads. Behind them followed musicians and dancers, acrobats, exotic animals in cages, slaves, and priests.

The ceremony was a fitting prelude for their gloriously happy union. During their years of marriage, Khurram built Mumtaz Mahal sumptuous palaces, showered her with jewels, ignored his polygamous rights with his two other wives, and even entrusted her with the royal seal. Full-time poets were employed at court to extol the beauty of the empress. However, all was not charmed.

In the Mogul Empire, the throne was not passed down through primogeniture; rather the royal inheritance dictated that the male heirs had to compete with one another for the scepter. This, of course, created fraternal ties similar to the ones shared by Cain and Abel. Upon Emperor Jahangir's death, a war of succession ignited among his five sons. After years of fighting, during which his brothers all died under highly suspicious circumstances, twenty-five-year-old Prince Khurram was victorious. He was crowned king and given the title Shah Jahan, which translates to "king of the world."

Because of the shah's conquests, his empire grew in size, power, and opulence and was the superpower of its epoch. In true megalomaniac fashion, he built monuments to his power. Immediately following his coronation in 1628, he commissioned the creation of a gold-and-jewel-encrusted Peacock Throne. It took seven years to complete and had as its centerpiece the famous Koh-i-Noor diamond, once valued at half the wealth of India. Today, the fabled jewel is among the crown jewels of Queen Elizabeth. Inscribed on the arches of the ceremonial chair were the words *If there be paradise on earth, it is here.* However, for the shah, paradise did not come from his boundless wealth, but from the queen who was his ever-faithful companion, Mumtaz Mahal.

The shah and the empress loved each other to such an extent that throughout their twenty years of marriage they were inseparable. Not willing to be parted from her husband, she was always willing to forgo the pleasures of their palace for the rigors of his military campaigns. Tragically, on one of these, after giving birth to her fourteenth child in nineteen years, she became seriously ill from complications stemming from the delivery. On her deathbed, she asked her husband to erect a monument to their love.

The shah was consumed with grief at her death and went into a weeklong seclusion during which he refused all food. The only sound his ministers heard coming from the locked room was a low, continuous moan. When he emerged, he was a changed man: His black hair had turned white, his back was bent, and his spirit was gone. He ordered his empire to observe two years of mourning; all music, public amusements, perfumes, cosmetics, jewelry, and brightly colored clothes were forbidden. The "king of the world," after all, was essentially just a man.

He declared his life's mission: to create the most magnificent structure in the world to immortalize his lost love. The shah placed all his resources into his passion to leave a monument fitting for Mumtaz Mahal. Because Islamic belief forbids graphic representations of the divine, his vision of eternity had to be symbolized: His wife's mausoleum was to be one of divine geometry, symmetry, and grace. From the four corners of his far-flung empire, transported on the backs of a thousand elephants, came priceless treasures of marble, gold, and jewels. A labor force of twenty thousand men toiled on erecting the tomb for twenty years. The finished mausoleum combined Hindu, Persian, Turkish, and Buddhist elements so that its design was entirely unique. The marble building clad in white was covered with designs, each inlaid with precious jewels created by the greatest artisans of the day. The entire edifice was reflected in a pool so its beauty could be seen on a shimmering surface. The crowning touch of the structure is its dome, reminiscent of a giant pearl floating above the building's four minarets, recalling the prophet Muhammad's vision of the throne of God as a pearl surrounded by four pillars. It was the shah's most fervent prayer that one day he would stand before this throne, where God would usher him into paradise, to a reunion with Mumtaz.

In a story that may be urban legend, the shah ordered the blinding of his chief architect so he would never again be able to create such magnificence. Another tale is that during the rainy season, only one droplet of rain falls on the queen's tomb, which is why the poet Rabindranath Tagore described it as "one tear-drop . . . upon the cheek of time."

Soon after the mausoleum was completed, Shah Jahan was to receive another sword in his already broken heart. Seeing their father's weakened state, his children began fighting in a vicious power struggle for the Peacock Throne. Eventually his son Aurangzeb proved himself the most skilled in fratricide, after which he deposed the king. He imprisoned the shah in his own palace, the Red Fort, which became his cell. He was allowed every luxury except freedom. In contrast to his son's perfidy, his daughter, Jahanara, volunteered to remain at his side for his remaining years, although that too made her a virtual prisoner.

For most of the eight years he was under palace arrest, Shah Jahan gazed out the window at the building he had created, inspired by the woman he had treasured beyond all else. To those who see with their eyes, the emperor was merely indulging in vanity, reflecting that he had given birth to something immortal. However, to those who see with their hearts, he was merely looking at the place where his wife waited for him to lie by her side once more.

In 1666, Khurram fell ill with dysentery; after reciting verses from the Qur'an, he slipped from this world to the next. The embodiment of an emperor's devotion for his "ornament of the palace" was the Taj Mahal—the jewel in the crown of world architecture, rendered more beautiful when one knows that within its depths lie entombed those whose love story caused its creation.

Postscript

➤ Mumtaz died in 1631; her body was temporarily interred in a walled garden. She was later disinterred and transported in a golden casket to Agra. The casket was placed in a small building until its final resting place in the Taj Mahal.

↪ The reigning shah, not eager to draw attention to the old, refused Jahanara's request for an elaborate funeral. Khurram's body was washed in accordance with Islamic rites and transported to the Taj Mahal, to rest for eternity at the side of Mumtaz Mahal.

5

Napoleon Bonaparte and Josephine Beauharnais

1795

*I*t is common knowledge that France's most acclaimed general possessed the ambition of the Scottish general Macbeth. What is less well known is that Bonaparte also possessed the romance of a Romeo and the jealousy of an Othello. These latter characteristics became manifest when he fell in love with the Rose of Martinique.

Napoleone di Buonaparte was born in Corsica (which had recently come under the dominion of France) in 1759, the second of eight children. At age sixteen he was sent to the elite École Militaire in Paris, where he trained to become an artillery officer. The British general Wellington, when asked who was the greatest general of his day answered, "In this age, in past ages, in any age, Napoleon."

Napoleon's destiny, Marie Josephe Rose Tascher de la Pagerie, proves that one can never foretell where the spotlight of fame will cast its beam. The girl from a sugar plantation in Martinique was to one day stand on the center stage of her epoch.

When hurricanes destroyed his crop, Marie's financially strapped father arranged an advantageous marriage between his sixteen-year-old daughter (then called Rose) and Viscount Alexandre de Beauharnais. Upon meeting her fiancé, she was ecstatic; he was young, wealthy, well connected at court, and reputed to be one of the best dancers in Paris. On the other hand, she was provincial and barely literate. Another legacy of her birthplace was rotting and blackened teeth, a direct result of the sugar-saturated cuisine of her childhood. Self-conscious, she tried her best to keep from smiling. Rose and Alexandre had two children, Hortense and Eugene, whom he left to court glory in the American War of Independence. However, renown was not all he courted. The ever-energetic Alexandre left a number of mistresses and illegitimate children in his wake.

The young viscount's enthusiasm was finally halted during the Reign of Terror, when he was guillotined. As a nobleman's spouse, Rose was similarly incarcerated, and she shared a cell with Marie Grosholtz. Both women had their heads shaved, awaiting their appointment with the guillotine. The latter was to survive and achieve fame as Madame Tussaud; the former was to achieve fame in a far different fashion.

Following an outbreak of violence, a law was passed in France forbidding any citizen to possess weapons. Eugene de Beauharnais, unwilling to surrender his father's sword, beseeched General Bonaparte to let him keep his precious memento. He acceded to the child's request, and the rest was history.

The first time Napoleon met Josephine was on October 14, when Rose went to thank the general for his kindness. He was instantly smitten and remarked to a friend, "She had that certain something that was irresistible. She was a woman to her very fingertips." The only quality he disliked was her name, and, in the spirit of "a rose by any other name would smell as sweet" (or in this case, sweeter), he called her Josephine. Napoleon was brought to his knees.

Rose, on the other hand, was less enthusiastic, but destitute and a spendthrift, she agreed to become Josephine Bonaparte. For a wedding present he presented his bride with a gold medallion inscribed with the words *To Destiny*. On their wedding night he received a scar from Josephine's dog, Fortuna; while in bed the pug had viciously bit his ankle.

Forty-eight hours after their marriage, Napoleon left for Italy to embark on a war against the Austrians; Josephine stayed in France and embarked on an adulterous affair with Hyppolyte Charles. Devastated at their separation, Napoleon penned dozens of letters to his wife: "Come and join me, that at least, before death, we may be able to say, 'We were many days happy.' A thousand kisses, and one even to Fortuna, notwithstanding his spitefulness. BONAPARTE."

When word reached the general regarding his wife's affair, he threatened divorce. Josephine always referred to her husband's discovery of her infidelity as the "day of the catastrophe." The unsavory revelation marked an abrupt shift in their relationship; Josephine never took another lover, whereas Napoleon was never without one. However, these liaisons stayed within the realm of physical and not emotional adultery. As he said, "My mistresses do not in the least engage my feelings. Power is my mistress." After a stormy reunion, the couple reconciled and took up residence in the Tuileries Palace. As Josephine played her role as the wife of the most powerful man in the continent, her charm won over the populace. Napoleon recognized her as a political asset when he said, "I only win battles; Josephine wins hearts for me."

Ironically, in 1884, the upstart Corsican, who had fought a revolution whose purpose was to end monarchy, was in Notre Dame Cathedral for his coronation ceremony, presided over by Pope Pius VII. At the last moment, Bonaparte took the crown from the pontiff's hand and placed it on his own head, thereby signifying that his power surpassed the Church's own. The kneeling Josephine was crowned Empress of France.

For the next two years, while Bonaparte was not subjugating Europe and Josephine was not on a ravenous spending spree, the two spent passionate days together. However, Bonaparte's meteoric rise proved the demise of their marriage. As emperor, he was desperate to have an heir. Initially Napoleon believed that their failure to have children lay with him, as Josephine was already a mother; however, when his mistress became pregnant, it became apparent that Josephine, either because she was in her late thirties or because her time awaiting execution had triggered an early menopause, was infertile. Napoleon declared that he had to obtain a divorce for "reasons of state," as the throne was his main paramour. He began to compile lists of eligible princesses. Afterward, while the Bonapartes were dining, from the next room, Napoleon's secretary heard screams; Josephine did not take the news well of her forthcoming divorce.

The following day, servants took her possessions to the Château de Malmaison, a magnificent mansion near Paris, where her chief interest was strolling in her gardens. Eventually Josephine, now the Duchess of Navarre, admitted defeat. She knew that against another woman, she would win; against Napoleon's ambition, even she did not have a chance. At the divorce proceedings they declared their mutual love, despite the breaking of their hearts. Napoleon stated, "She has adorned thirteen years of my life; the memory will always remain engraved on my heart." Josephine stated, "I am pleased to offer him the greatest proof of attachment and devotion ever offered on this earth." Three months later Napoleon married the nineteen-year-old Austrian Archduchess Marie Louise, and within a year Napoleon had his long-awaited heir, to whom he gave the title "King of Rome." Two years after the birth, Napoleon arranged for Josephine to meet the young prince "who had cost her so many tears."

When Napoleon tore himself from Josephine, his once-charmed life became cursed. The erstwhile invincible general suffered military defeats, was eventually forced to abdicate, and was exiled to the island of Elba. There he attempted suicide, but the pill he had long carried had lost its potency. Marie Louise had taken a lover and refused to join him with their son. However, Josephine wrote to Napoleon telling him of her plans to leave for Elba, but destiny had another plan. While walking in her garden with Tsar Alexander, she became ill and passed away shortly after. Her dying words were, "Elba! Marie Louise, Napoleon." When news of her death reached the defeated general on his island prison, he locked himself in his room for two days, refusing to see anyone.

With Josephine's death, Napoleon was left with his only remaining love, France, and he managed to escape and return to Paris. When the soldiers saw him, the air rang with shouts of *"Vive l'Empereur!"* After regaining control of his troops, Napoleon visited his shrine of Malmaison and went to the room in which his beloved had died. Before he departed, he retrieved some violets, Josephine's favorite, from her garden.

Napoleon reigned once more, for a hundred days, until his defeat at the Battle of Waterloo. This time he was placed under an even heavier guard on the island of St. Helena. There he finally met an opponent even history's greatest general could not defeat: death. In 1821 he passed away holding a picture of Josephine. In a locket around his neck were the crushed violet petals from her garden. Bonaparte's last words were to his first love: *"France, armée, tête d'armée, Josephine"* ("France, the army, the head of the army, Josephine").

Postscript

→ King Louis-Philippe obtained permission to retrieve France's famous son, and his remains were transported to France. The procession stretched from the Arc de Triomphe (which Bonaparte had commissioned) down the Champs-Élysées until it reached its destination, where he was interred next to his son.

➤ Bonaparte's tomb lies in the gold-domed magnificent edifice of Les Invalides; in the midst of its grandiose room is a life-sized white-and-gold statue of Napoleon. As if he were a French pharaoh, his remains are entombed in a series of coffins of tin, mahogany, lead, ebony, and oak. He lies in the last one, dressed in military attire, his hat spread over his legs.

➤ Josephine was buried in a church near Château de Malmaison, Saint Pierre-Saint Paul in Rueil. Her daughter, Hortense, is interred nearby.

6

Prince Albert and Queen Victoria

1836

*I*n nineteenth-century England, the country's greatest boast was, "The sun never sets on the British Isles." In like fashion, the sun never set on the couple who steadfastly referred to themselves as "we two."

Alexandrina Victoria Hanover was born in Kensington Palace in London; there, when she was eighteen, the Archbishop of Canterbury informed her that with the death of her uncle, King William IV, she was to inherit the throne of England. Her response, "I beg Your Grace to pray for me." However, Victoria, unlike her famous predecessor Queen Elizabeth I, did not want to bear the splendid burden of royalty alone.

Victoria's destiny, Francis Albert Augustus Charles Emmanuel of Saxe-Coburg, was born to a family whose main claim to fame was its connection to many of Europe's monarchs. His life was supposed to be a mere footnote in German history, but fate arranged otherwise.

The first time Victoria met Albert was on May 18, 1836, in London, where he arrived as the result of a royal matchmaker. King Leopold I of Belgium decided to try to arrange a marriage between his nephew and niece. However, Victoria was not impressed with her chubby, self-absorbed cousin; similarly, Albert, who was extremely serious, found her to be too frivolous for his taste. No tears were shed when Albert returned to Germany, but Cupid's arrow did leave an impression, and although she was introduced to the most eligible bachelors of Europe, three years later the queen invited her cousin for another visit.

It was love at second sight. She wrote to their Uncle Leopold to thank him "for the prospect of *great* happiness you have contributed to give me, in the person of dear Albert . . . He possesses every quality that could be desired to render me perfectly happy." As a monarch, she had to be the one to propose, which she did three days later, and on February 10, 1840, they were wed in the Chapel Royal of St. James's Palace. She decided to forgo the traditional bridal dress color of the day: silver for the upper classes and blue for the lower ones. Instead she chose white, a tradition that became an established one. The ring that the queen slipped on her beloved's finger was engraved with the date she had proposed. Victoria's own ring was a diamond-encrusted snake with ruby eyes biting its tail, which in its era was a symbol for eternity. On her dress, over her heart, she wore a present from her groom, a sapphire and diamond brooch. Her dress had a six-foot train; her wedding cake measured nine feet. The next day, Victoria wrote, "What I can do to make him happy will be my greatest delight."

Despite the saying that opposites attract, their union was based on commonalities: Victoria and Albert were born in the same year with the assistance of the same midwife; their families had royalty in their blood, and, as Victoria's mother was from Germany, they spoke the same language. Moreover, they were both victims of un-happy childhoods: When Albert was five his parents divorced and his exiled mother never saw him again; Victoria's father passed away when she was an infant, and her mother was comparable to any Brothers Grimm fairy-tale villainess. The couple found the affec-tion, companionship, and trust that neither had experienced while growing up. Victoria's first act as queen, when she moved into Buck-ingham Palace, was to symbolically give her mother a bedroom far from her own. In response, her mother gave her as a nineteenth-birthday present a copy of *King Lear*.

The popular view of Queen Victoria is the embodiment of sexual repression; urban legend has it that she ordered all the piano legs in her palaces to be covered with skirts because of their suggestive-ness to female anatomy. Similarly, her advice to her daughters on their wedding nights was, "Lie back and think of England." The quo-tation most associated with her is, "We are not amused." However, she bore nine children in seventeen years, and their conception was as much a result of her love for her husband as it was duty to her country.

Prince Albert's position when he came to live in his adopted homeland was difficult. He was a foreigner in the British castle and thus vulnerable to suspicion. Moreover, in the male-dominated epoch he was in a subservient role, as it was his wife who was one of the most powerful leaders in the world. She was the marquee attraction; he was merely her understudy. His lesser status was reflected in his title of prince consort, rather than king. Three months after his mar-riage he wrote to a friend, "I am only the husband, and not the master of the house."

Given his situation, Albert could have taken the path of indolence and idleness, but in her choice of husband, as in most else, Victoria proved astute. Instead of partaking in ale and fox hunting, Albert became a hands-on father to his nine children. Although he possessed the silver spoon since birth, he had empathy and campaigned for those who did not share his good fortune. Because he earned the respect of his adopted countrymen, he was able to introduce the German tradition of the Christmas tree, its decorations, and the placing of wrapped presents under it. In a sense, he eventually became the power behind his wife's throne as well as her steadfast companion. In the eyes of their court he walked a step behind her, but as husband and wife they were equals. They referred to themselves as "we two," in the sense of two souls as one.

Those with blue blood are not inured to horror, and this held true with the queen and her consort. During Victoria's first pregnancy, seventeen-year-old Edward Oxford attempted to assassinate the queen as she was riding in London in her carriage. Before he had time to fire a second shot, Prince Albert pushed her down so that the bullet again missed its mark. Undaunted, days later the queen attended an opera; the audience's cheering for their monarch delayed the performance for several minutes. The newspapers praised the prince for his courage and coolness during the attack; he did not lose his head even when faced with losing his heart. There were eventually seven unsuccessful attempts on Victoria's life.

On December 12, 1861, Albert fell ill with typhoid fever. When he came out of his delirium, his last words to his Victoria were *"Gutes Frauchen"* ("Good woman"). In turn she replied, *"Es ist das kleine Frauchen"* ("It is the little woman"). Her trademark expression was never truer; she was not to be truly amused again. Albert died in the private apartments at Kensington, where Victoria had first gazed upon the man whose countenance she cherished above all else. He left this world in the presence of the queen of his heart and five of his children.

The room was kept as a shrine to her beloved; in addition, hot water was brought there each morning and its linen and towels were changed daily, as if Albert were due back momentarily. For three years after Albert's death, Victoria refused to go out in public, and for the next forty years she never wore any color but black. When she traveled she did so with a huge portrait of Albert, which she had positioned on an easel at the foot of her bed, with a smaller one by her pillow. In this way, when she awoke, it was to him. She said of the hole he left, "Can I—can I be alive when half my body and soul are gone?" She became convinced that she would shortly follow where her prince had gone, but fate had other plans.

Throughout the years without her essential half, Victoria spent Christmas at Osborne House on the Isle of Wight, where she died in 1901, at age eighty-two, after being on the throne for sixty-three years, a longer reign than any other British monarch. In contrast to her lengthy title of Victoria, Queen of the United Kingdom of Great Britain and Ireland, and Empress of India, her final farewell was brief. Her last word was to her first love: "Bertie." For the world it was the passing of an epoch; for the queen it was reunion with her beloved.

Postscript

➤ Albert's body was entombed in the magnificent mausoleum at Frogmore. Over the entrance Victoria had inscribed, "Farewell best beloved, here at last I shall rest with thee, with thee in Christ I shall rise again."

➤ When Queen Victoria passed away she was clothed in a white dress and her wedding veil; by her side was one of Albert's dressing gowns. Also enclosed was a cast of Albert's hand by her side. After lying in state, she was interred beside Prince Albert. In the crypt are marble effigies of Victoria and Albert; the queen's likeness is slightly turned to gaze upon the prince consort. Because of her distaste of black-themed funerals, London was festooned in purple and white.

7

Robert Browning and Elizabeth Barrett Moulton

1845

One never knows where Venus's capricious son is going to leave his calling card. Elizabeth Barrett Moulton was a reclusive, middle-aged morphine addict under the dominion of a tyrannical father when she met a fellow poet. Their romance gave rise to some of literature's most immortal poetry.

Elizabeth was born on a five-hundred-acre estate in Hertford-shire. The source of her family's fortune was a Jamaican sugar planta-tion that relied on slave labor. As a child Elizabeth enjoyed riding her pony on the extensive grounds, tending her garden of white roses, and arranging theatrical productions with her eleven younger sib-lings. Her father, recognizing her brilliance, allowed her an education and encouraged her writing; when she was fourteen, he published fifty copies of her narrative poem.

Elizabeth's happiness was sharply curtailed in the mid-1820s, when she contracted a mysterious illness. She described her symp-toms as if a cord were tied around her stomach "which seems to break." Her doctors were unable to diagnose the cause of her distress, which eventually rendered her bedridden; however, they prescribed morphine for the pain, which ultimately exacerbated her problems when she became addicted. Because of her physical frailness and overprotective father, she became agoraphobic.

When she was twenty-two, she was devastated by the death of her mother; her passing for a time left Elizabeth without the power to concentrate. A few years later, because of ill health, Elizabeth traveled to Torquay, in the hope that the seaside would restore her health. She was accompanied by her favorite brother, who drowned in a boating accident. She stayed there for another year and recalled that the sound of the sea always was like the "moan of a dying man." Added to her emotional bereavement was financial hardship; the abolition of slavery marked the end of her family's lucrative Jamaican plantation, and they were forced to relocate to London, where they bought a house at 50 Wimpole Street.

During several reclusive years, Elizabeth's diversions were family and a golden-haired cocker spaniel named Flush. Her other emotional life jacket was what had sustained her since childhood: poetry. As an adult she had achieved acclaim when she published her works in both a book and in magazines. Her only contact with the outside world was when John Kenyon, a distant cousin, introduced her to the luminaries of the literary world such as William Wordsworth; Samuel Taylor Coleridge; Walter Savage Landor; Alfred, Lord Tennyson; and Thomas Carlyle. Though she'd never experienced romantic love, she wrote of it often, such as in "A Woman's Shortcomings": "Unless you can die when the dream is past— / Oh, never call it loving!"

Elizabeth's destiny, Robert Browning, was born in London into a liberal environment; his father was an abolitionist and intellectual whose vast library contained six thousand volumes. He was an ardent admirer of the Romantic writers, especially his idol Percy

Bysshe Shelley. When he read the poetry of Elizabeth Barrett, he was extremely impressed and wrote to her, "I love your verses with all my heart, dear Miss Barrett . . . I do, as I say, love these verses with all my heart." He asked John Kenyon to secure an invitation to 50 Wimpole Street.

The first time Elizabeth met Robert was in May 1845. He immediately became as enamored of the woman as he was of her poetry. For her part, Elizabeth found it difficult to believe that a worldly man six years her junior would have an interest in a thirty-nine-year-old reclusive, bedridden, morphine-addicted spinster; however, he was able to convince her that his interest was genuine. Thus, passion entered Elizabeth's life.

Over a twenty-month courtship, Elizabeth found a way to make "death less deader" whereby the couple exchanged 574 letters in which they poured out their emotions to each other. Unfortunately, their meetings were clandestine because Elizabeth's father would not permit any of his twelve children to marry. (One theory behind this odd edict is that he believed that his forebears, who had lived in Jamaica, had cohabited with slaves, which he feared might come out in the birth of a dark child.)

At first, Elizabeth, feeling guilty that Robert should have an ailing partner, decided against a relationship "with all her will, but much against her heart." However, love, as is sometimes the case, conquers all, and on September 12, 1846, the couple had a private marriage at St. Marylebone Parish Church. After the ceremony, the bride was forced to return to Wimpole Street. Her romantic bliss is summed up in her poem "First Time He Kissed Me": "A ring of amethyst I could not wear here, plainer to my sight / Than that first kiss . . ."

A week later, Elizabeth left Wimpole Street for the last time. Like his hero Shelley, Browning whisked his bride off to Italy; he hoped the sunny region would do more for his wife's health than England's wet climate. Whether it was indeed the weather, his love, or the fact that her life had a new purpose, the new Mrs. Browning, though still frail, was no longer confined to bed. The couple spent time in various locales, which was especially welcome for Elizabeth, who had spent so many years confined to one room.

In Pisa, Elizabeth first showed her husband *Sonnets from the Portuguese*, her collection of poems inspired by their courtship and marriage. The title came from Robert's nickname for her; he called her "Portuguese" as a term of endearment because of her dark hair. She explained that because of their personal nature, she did not intend to publish them. He, on the other hand, thought otherwise. As he said, "I dared not reserve to myself the finest sonnets written in any language since Shakespeare's." The first two lines of the soon-published Sonnet 43 became her most famous: "How do I love thee? Let me count the ways." The sonnets are the autobiographical revelation of one of the greatest poets, who once believed love had overlooked her.

The couple eventually settled in Florence in a home, Casa Guidi, where they lived for twenty years. Robert was enthralled with his adopted country and once remarked, "Italy was my university." Their home became the spiritual and physical mecca for the expatriate English and American communities. Their drawing room was fitted with large bookcases, constructed of Florentine carving and selected by Robert. Tapestries, pictures of the saints, and portraits of Dante, Keats, and Robert Browning hung on the walls. Eventually there was another portrait of a beloved family member. At age forty-three, despite ill health, two miscarriages, and a morphine addiction, Elizabeth gave birth to a blond-haired, blue-eyed baby, Robert Wiedemann Barrett Browning, nicknamed Penini or Pen. His middle name came from Robert's mother's maiden name.

During these happy years in Florence, the only blight was that Elizabeth's father refused to acknowledge her; his silence made it clear that she had forever forfeited her old family.

Later in life, Elizabeth, always socially conscious, wrote about other issues than affairs of the heart. She turned her pen to women's tribulations and championed Italy's unstable political troubles.

However, the Brownings' pens truly flowed when they turned to romance. Kenyon wrote, "With the single exception of Rossetti, no modern English poet has written of love with such genius, such beauty, and such sincerity as the two who gave the most beautiful example of it in their own lives." And Robert summed up their happiness in his poem "Pippa Passes":

The lark's on the wing,
The snail's on the thorn;
God's in his heaven—
All's right with the world!

In 1861, Elizabeth again suffered from ill health, eating little and turning more and more to morphine for relief. As she lay dying, she uttered her last word to her first love: "Beautiful."

Postscript

➳ Browning buried his wife in Florence in an elaborate Carrara marble tomb in the English cemetery in Piazzale Donatello.

➳ In 1889, Robert Browning passed away in Venice. He was buried in the poet's corner in Westminster Abbey, adjacent to Alfred, Lord Tennyson.

8

Sir Richard Burton and Isabel Arundell

1850

*T*he Victorian era gave birth to some of the most colorful personalities in world history, and yet Sir Richard Burton's larger-than-life personality managed to eclipse most of his colorful contemporaries. It took an extraordinary woman to win the heart of the restless wanderer, and he found it in the woman who followed him throughout the world.

Richard Francis Burton was born in Devon, England; however, he spent most of his childhood traveling with his family throughout Europe. He attended Oxford University, where he pursued his genius for language, and took up the pursuits of falconry and fencing. He was expelled for attending a steeplechase, as well as for antagonizing both faculty and students. Before departing, as his final calling card, he trampled the college's flower beds with his horse and carriage. After his expulsion, he enlisted in the army of the East India Company, because, as he explained, he was "fit for nothing but to be shot at for six pence a day."

Burton had many habits that set him apart from other soldiers. One was his flawless command of twenty-nine languages. Another oddity was that he kept a large menagerie of tame monkeys in the hopes of understanding their communication. He was also well known for his proficiency in sexual practices, especially ones from foreign countries. However, Burton did not care what others thought of him, as he said, "Do what thy manhood bids thee do, from none but self expect applause."

Richard's destiny, Isabel Arundell, came from an old and distinguished Catholic family and was educated at a convent near her home. Although raised in a traditional fashion, from a young age she did not want to play the role of a typical upper-class woman. As a debutante, she was far different from the shallow, husband-seeking females of her class. When introduced to eligible young men at dances, she referred to them as "mannikins" or "animated tailors' dummies." She wrote, "'Tis man's place to do great deeds!" She determined she would rather spend her life in a convent than as a country squire's wife. In her diary she confided, "As God took a rib out of Adam and made a woman of it, so do I, out of a wild chaos of thought, form a man unto myself. He is a gentleman in every sense of the word; and of course he is an Englishman. He is a man who owns something more than a body; he has a head and a heart, a mind and a soul." A few months after her entry, in Essex, she met a Romanian gypsy, Hagar Burton, who foretold that her life would be bohemian: "Your life is all wandering, change and adventure. One soul in two bodies, in life or death, never long apart. Show this to the man you take for a husband."

The first time Richard met Isabel was in Boulogne, France. Isabel had traveled there (the first time she had left England) for a family vacation; Richard was on leave to visit its fencing school. Their first glimpse of one another was when Isabel and her sister were on a stroll and she saw the man whom she was forever to refer to as "my destiny." Of their meeting she wrote, "He looked at me as though he read me through and through in a moment, and started a little. I was completely magnetized, and when we got a little distance away I turned to my sister, and whispered to her, 'That man will marry me.'" The next day when he saw her he chalked on a wall, *May I speak to you?* and then left the chalk beside his message. Isabel wrote as her response, *No, Mother will be angry.* However, she never lost an opportunity of making her path cross his. Later they met at a British colony party; afterward, because he had put his arm around her waist when they waltzed, she treasured the sash he had touched.

When it was time for the Arundells to return to London, Isabel did so with a sinking feeling in her heart; she was hopelessly in love with Richard. However, he made no professions of his affection. He was already looking forward to the horizon of future adventures. Hence, when they parted they did so as friends, though Isabel yearned for far more. While she was out of sight and out of mind, he embarked on the journey that was to make him one of the most celebrated of Victorians.

Richard's seven years in India had made him familiar with the customs of Islam, a necessary step for him to attempt a hajj, a pilgrimage to Mecca. For verisimilitude, he dressed, spoke, and acted like a Muslim; in addition, he stained his skin with henna. Even more extreme, he underwent a circumcision to lessen his chance of discovery. This was essential, as the penalty for detection was death. He became the first non-Muslim European to enter the Islamic forbidden city, which he accomplished under the guise of Abdullah of Afghanistan.

His adventures were eagerly devoured by the British public, especially Isabel. She was horrified to read about his misadventure in Somalia, where warriors attacked his contingent. A javelin had impaled Richard's cheek and exited from the other, leaving a lifelong scar. He made his escape with the weapon still embedded in his face. When the newspapers reported that Burton's next venture was in the Crimea, the ever-faithful Isabel tried three times to join Florence Nightingale's nurses, but was told she was too young and too inexperienced.

However, in 1855, two months after Burton had arrived in England, he ran into Isabel where she was reading in London's Botanical Gardens. For the next two weeks they met there every day, and finally Richard embraced her and asked if she would give up civilization for him. Isabel did not hesitate in her acceptance. "I would rather have a tent and a crust with you than be queen of all the world. And so I say now: Yes, yes, yes!" They sealed their engagement with a passionate kiss. Later she recalled that she "trod on air." However, they decided to keep their romance a secret, as the Royal Geographical Society had engaged him to explore the east of Africa, where he was to lead an expedition which was to result in the discovery of Lake Tanganyika.

Four years later when he returned, the impediment to their marriage was Isabel's mother. She was a fervent Catholic and didn't want her daughter marrying an atheist who would drag her beloved daughter off to some "heathen" outpost. Moreover, while Richard had achieved fame he had not gained fortune; his sole assets were his charisma and adventurous life. In addition to these concerns, there was the matter of his well-known fascination with sexuality. If all this were not enough, she did not appreciate his sense of humor. When she had confronted him regarding his intentions toward Isabel he had answered, "Strictly dishonorable, Madam. Englishmen who are restricted to one wife cannot be too careful."

In 1861, the couple married in a private ceremony without family, attended only by a handful of friends at the Bavarian Catholic Church. Afterward they retired to Richard's bachelor quarters. Isabel recalled that although they had only a few pounds, "we were as happy as it is given to any mortals out of heaven to be." Because of

Burton's fame, the prime minister hosted a dinner party to honor the newlyweds, and Queen Victoria, contrary to all precedent, allowed the bride of an elopement to be presented at court.

Unfortunately, immediately after their marriage Burton entered the Foreign Service and was stationed in Guinea. As the climate was considered extremely unhealthy for Europeans, Isabel could not accompany him. She wrote of their separation, "I am neither maid nor wife nor widow." However, they were reunited when Richard was transferred to Brazil.

When Richard received a post in Trieste, then part of the Austro-Hungarian Empire, he was able to engage in one of his other interests: writing. His best-known contribution to literature was when he translated foreign works into English, thereby giving the Western world *The Kama Sutra*. Its sexual content was considered the epitome of pornography. Another masterpiece he added to literary lore was his translation of *The Arabian Nights*, thereby introducing to the western world stories from the east: *Sinbad the Sailor*, *Aladdin's Magic Lamp*, and *Ali Baba and the Forty Thieves*.

Many felt that Burton's travel books that delineated exotic sexual practices were based on primary sources. This aspect of her husband's nature pained the extremely Catholic Isabel, as did his premise that polygamy was not immoral. Isabel was aware of the gossip bandied about that her conjugal bed was used to test Oriental sexual practices. However, she never regretted her destiny. As she wrote her mother, "I want to live . . . I want a wild, roving, vagabond life . . . I wish I were a man. If I were I would be Richard Burton: but, being only a woman, I would be Richard Burton's wife." Their marriage, despite her absorption with piety and his with pornography, was one of unending devotion.

Public recognition and respect for Burton culminated with his knighthood: In 1886, they became Sir Richard and Lady Burton.

In Trieste, in 1890, death found the man who had evaded it for so long when Burton passed away from a heart attack. By his side was his partner in wanderlust, his ever-devoted Isabel. During his final moments he used his wife's nickname and made his final request. His last words were to his first love: "Quick, Puss, chloroform—ether—or I am a dead man."

In death, as in life, Isabel remained devoted to Richard. She commissioned a mausoleum in the shape of a stone reproduction of a Bedouin tent. On its wall hang two portraits of husband and wife on their wedding day. When Isabel passed away she was buried beside her knight in the Arab-styled stone tent, under the British sky.

Postscript

➤ The atheist Burton had three church services performed over him and 1,100 masses said for the repose of his soul. Four days later, Trieste gave the legend a full military funeral "such as is only accorded to royalty." All the flags in the city were lowered to half staff and most of the 150,000 inhabitants turned out to view his coffin, draped in a Union Jack. Richard's body was shipped to England, where it was temporarily laid to rest in a crypt under the altar in St. Mary Magdalene's Church until his stone tent mausoleum (and six years later, Isabel's as well) was completed.

9

Charles Parnell and Katharine O'Shea

1880

*T*hroughout history, women have been portrayed as femmes fatales whose sexuality brought about the fall of great men: the mythological Pandora, the biblical Eve, the Egyptian Cleopatra, the Shakespearean Lady Macbeth. Ireland has its own such femme fatale; when Charles Parnell took Katharine O'Shea into his arms he brought his country to its knees, and thus, she was viewed as responsible for the downfall of the one she loved.

Charles Stewart Parnell was born in Avondale, County Wicklow. His parents separated when he was six, and he was sent to school in England, eventually attending Cambridge. As an adult, he returned to Ireland and, as a landowner, his interests aligned with the nationalist political agenda: home rule—freedom from England's yoke. He was elected president of the newly founded Irish National League and traveled to raise funds for famine relief. He was so well received in Toronto that he was dubbed "the uncrowned king of Ireland."

Parnell also became president of the Land League, which encouraged the Irish to protest against unfair rent by the mainly British landlords. The first English victim of this policy was Captain Charles Boycott, whose name has become part of the English lexicon. Parnell was known not only for his ability to lead men but also for the magnetic effect he had on women. However, he had no interest in the latter; his only mistress was his country.

Parnell brought dignity and power to a people who for centuries had been robbed of it. Yet when the Irish looked to their leader to make home rule a reality, the man who had been faithful only to his cause realized that he had a greater love than Ireland.

Charles's destiny, Katharine, was born in England, the youngest of thirteen children of Lady Emma and Sir John Page Wood, an Anglican vicar. She was raised to acquire a husband, as were other proper Victorian girls. "Look lovely and keep your mouth shut," a brother advised her, voicing the common wisdom of the age. Although they had the trappings of wealth (such as a mansion in Riverhall), the family lacked money. The only one who was well-to-do was Emma's oldest sister Maria, who, when she married a man named Benjamin, was affectionately dubbed "Aunt Ben."

When Katharine went to visit her brother's regiment, she met the Irish captain William O'Shea, whom she married at age twenty-two. He was chiefly known for his velvet jackets and his passion for get-rich-quick schemes. The childless Aunt Ben lavished a £5,000 dowry on her niece, but it quickly evaporated in William's spendthrift hands.

The O'Sheas had three children, and to support his family William abandoned business for Irish politics and became a member of parliament for County Clare. Cracks soon erupted in their marriage. William preferred a bachelor's life with constant absences and excessive gambling, and his moderate income left the family in dire straits. As their finances deteriorated, Katharine made an arrangement with Aunt Ben to move into her home with the children. She would look after the now-elderly woman in exchange for room and board. She said this period was "narrow, narrow, narrow, and so deadly dull." It was not how she had envisioned her life, and she desperately wished for another.

In 1880, William O'Shea, eager to make the acquaintance of the man who was dominating the Irish political scene, urged Katharine to invite Charles Parnell to a dinner party. However, Parnell, a committed loner, was not one to socialize and ignored their letter. In the spirit of "if Muhammad will not go to the mountain, the mountain must go to Muhammad," Katharine decided to attend Parliament.

The first time Katharine met Charles was when she approached him as he was leaving the House of Commons and inquired why he had not responded to her invitation. Katharine recorded her first impression of Parnell: "He looked straight at me smiling, and his curiously burning eyes looked into mine with a wonderful intentness that threw into my brain the sudden thought: *This man is wonderful—and different.*" Her impression on Parnell was just as startling, and he later told her that from the first moment he gazed into her eyes he had known she was his destiny. As she was departing, Katharine leaned out of her carriage and a rose on her bodice fell. Parnell picked it up, kissed it, and placed it in his buttonhole. This rose was discovered years later by Katharine in an envelope with her name and the date on which they first met.

After the encounter, the man who rarely wrote personal missives was constantly penning love letters. He also attended her next dinner party, which was followed by an evening at the theater, where they were engrossed in each other rather than the stage.

Katharine knew the risks of an affair: Aunt Ben's inheritance, the anger of her husband, and Victorian condemnation. Charles, knowledgeable about politics but naive about the dangers of gossip, believed there should be no "impediment to the marriage of true minds." However, it was the marriage of bodies that courted disaster.

The O'Shea relationship was a tightrope that Parnell walked for a decade. When in England, he lived with Katharine; when in Ireland, he wrote her countless letters that began "My Dearest Wifie." In one he stated, "For good or ill, I am your husband, your lover, your children, your all. And I will give my life to Ireland, but to you I give my love, whether it be your heaven or your hell."

A year later, Parnell was arrested by the order of English prime minister William Gladstone for his continued disruption of Parliament and placed in Kilmainham Jail. However, instead of getting rid of the "Irish problem," the plan backfired and Parnell was viewed as a martyr, which elevated him to hero status in Ireland.

On the domestic front, Katharine was devastated by Charles's absence. She was pregnant with his child and worried that his always-precarious health would suffer. When their daughter was born, Katharine sent him a snippet of the baby's hair, which he placed in a locket that contained his lover's portrait.

Ireland had erupted into violence over Parnell's arrest, so Gladstone reluctantly released the only man who could quell it. The Emerald Isle considered this a victory, and hopes for recognition as a sovereign nation reached a fever pitch. For his part, Parnell rushed to the side of Katharine, who was inconsolable at the loss of her baby six weeks after birth.

For the next eight years, Charles and Katharine lived together in perfect propriety (other than their marital status). The three O'Shea children were joined by two more babies, both girls. Initially infuriated, Captain O'Shea challenged his rival to a duel. However, his anger abated when he learned he stood to inherit money from his wife's aunt and Parnell could advance his political career. In 1886, he was given a position representing Galway City. His appointment caused one member to comment, "The candidate's wife is Parnell's mistress and there is nothing more to say."

By 1889, Ireland was ecstatic; it seemed that victory was imminent, and Irish home rule would be theirs. However, the house of cards began to collapse; William O'Shea filed for divorce on the grounds of his wife's adultery, and Charles Parnell was cited as co-respondent. William's breaking point was the death of Aunt Ben, who had left her inheritance in trust only in her niece's name. William attempted to blackmail his wife and demanded £20,000. When she refused, he retaliated with divorce. The fallout was steeped in such drama that it could have been lifted from the pages of a Victorian novel. As Parnell was reduced to a running joke, his enemies took out their knives and went for blood. James Joyce wrote of his fall, "In his final desperate appeal to his countrymen, he begged them not to throw him as a sop to the English wolves howling around them. It rebounds to their honor that they did not fail this appeal. They did not throw him to the English wolves; they tore him to pieces themselves."

The Irish Roman Catholic Church withdrew its support for Parnell; he also lost the majority of his own party, which felt that a man who could sacrifice his career for a woman was not fit to hold the reins of power. The bitterness of the split would tear Ireland apart. Parnell's enraged countrymen took to calling his love "Kitty," slang for a prostitute. Joyce referred to her as "that bitch, that English whore." She became the most reviled woman in Irish history.

On June 25, 1891, Katharine and Charles married in the Steyning registry office in Sussex, as the Church would not sanction their union. The bride's bouquet consisted of white roses chosen by the groom. When they returned home, they were confronted with hordes of reporters. Charles told them to stand back and allow Mrs. Parnell to pass.

Four months later, in an attempt to regain power, Parnell traveled to Dublin even though he was suffering from rheumatism. The fury of his erstwhile supporters was evidenced when local coal miners threw lime at his eyes. Undeterred, he gave a speech on a rainy day and began to feel even sicker, but he determined to carry on for Ireland's sake. He returned to Katharine at the earliest opportunity. By the time he arrived home, he was so frail that his wife of four months had to help him from his carriage. A few nights later, lying in bed, he said his last words to his first love: "Kiss me, sweet wifie, and I will try to sleep a little."

The Irish vilify Kitty O'Shea for barring their entry to the Promised Land; however, for Charles, she was the one who had allowed him to experience love, a love that passed into legend.

Postscript

➝ Katharine placed the rose that had fallen from her dress when they first met in Charles's coffin. When it was sealed, a wreath was placed on top with the inscription *To my own true love, my husband, my king*. In Ireland (where Katharine was not welcome), Charles's coffin bore a banner bearing his false last words: *Give my love to my colleagues and the Irish people*. On the coffin's final journey to Glasnevin cemetery, it was drawn by six horses, with Parnell's own horse, Home Rule, following immediately behind, boots and stirrups reversed. His interment was attended by more than two hundred thousand people. His gravestone, made of unhewn granite, bears just one word in large letters: *Parnell.*

➤ When Katharine Parnell died, her hearse passed unnoticed through the streets of Sussex to the municipal cemetery. A simple cross was erected over the grave by her daughter. Its inscription: *To the beloved memory of Katharine, widow of Charles Stewart Parnell. Fide et Amore.*

10

Nicholas Romanov and Princess Alix

1884

*I*n most fairy tales, the handsome prince falls in love with the beautiful princess, they overcome the force of evil, and live happily ever after. In true-life love stories, however, the prince and princess don't always get their happy ending.

Princess Alix Victoria Helena Louise Beatrice was born in 1872 in a palace in the German Empire. She was the fifth of seven children born to Queen Victoria's second daughter, Princess Alice. Her otherwise happy childhood was marred with the deaths of her brother, who passed away from hemophilia, and her mother and youngest sister, who succumbed to diphtheria.

Alix's destiny, Nicholas Alexandrovich Romanov, was born in the palace Tsarskoye Selo in Russia, the son of Tsar Alexander III—a six-foot-four man who cast his giant shadow over his hundred million subjects as well as his family. As tsarevitch, the young heir to the throne as well as the greatest fortune in the world was happy with his role as playboy prince, relishing having the best of everything without any attendant responsibilities. However, his life was forever altered when he met the princess for whom he would at last defy his father.

The first time Alix met Nicholas was in St. Petersburg at the marriage of her older sister Elizabeth to Tsar Alexander's brother, the Grand Duke Serge. During the wedding ceremony in the chapel of the Winter Palace, the twelve-year-old Alix stole side glances at the sixteen-year-old Nicholas. He reciprocated her interest and soon after gave her a small brooch, which she did not accept. However, this refusal was due to propriety rather than disinterest. After the ceremony, Alix scratched their names on the window of the Peterhof Palace.

The two did not see each other again for five years, when she returned to Russia to visit her sister. They fell in love and spent all their time together, ice skating and attending balls; before she departed he threw her a party in Tsarskoye Selo. He wrote in his diary, "My dream is some day to marry Alix. For a long time, I resisted my feeling that my dearest dream will come true." Alexander did not share his enthusiasm, declaring that a minor German princess was not a sufficient matrimonial prize to the heir to the Russian empire. Everything changed when the tsar became gravely ill at age forty-nine. The result was that the new tsarevitch received permission to marry the woman he loved. It also meant he had impossibly giant boots to fill.

In 1894, the royal heads of Europe traveled to Germany for the wedding of Alix's brother Ernest. When Nicholas arrived at the station, Alix was waiting for him and that night they went to dinner and an operetta. The following morning he proposed; however, although she loved him (it was why she had turned down a proposal from the Prince of Wales), she refused as she was committed to her Lutheran religion. Finally, realizing she had adored him for a decade, she capitulated and they both broke down in tears. After ten days he was obliged to leave and wrote, "What sadness to be obliged to part from her for a long time. How good we were together—a paradise."

Their separation did not last long. As his father lay dying, Nicholas, with a tremendous duty hovering, was desperate for the support of his beloved, and Alix hastened to Russia where she converted to Russian Orthodoxy, thus becoming Alexandra Fedorovna. To each other, however, they were Nicky and Alicky.

Although they were to be married in the spring, Nicholas changed the date to the week following the funeral, which took place on November 26, 1894, in the Grand Church of the Winter Palace in St. Petersburg. Mourning obscured their sumptuous Orthodox wedding. The superstitious peasants took this as a bad omen and repeatedly crossed themselves while murmuring, "She comes to us behind a coffin." On their wedding night, the bride wrote in her husband's diary, "Never did I believe there could be such utter happiness in this world, such a feeling of unity between two mortal beings. I love you, those three words have my life in them."

The royal couple's main residence was Tsarskoye Selo, an enchanted fairyland comprising two hundred rooms on eight hundred acres, replete with artificial lake. There the tsar and tsarina lived in a cocoon of preposterous protocol unchanged since the reign of Catherine the Great. Their rarefied world was protected from the real one by a high iron fence and five thousand guardsmen. One of its most famous rooms was the empress's mauve boudoir, so named because everything in it was of that hue.

Soon the area above the Mauve Room became the nursery for four daughters: the Grand Duchesses Olga, Tatiana, Maria, and Anastasia. Dwelling in their domestic idyll, the girls proclaimed their unity by referring to themselves as the OTMA, derived from the first letter of each of their names. Much as Nicholas and Alexandra adored their daughters, they desperately desired a son, as only males could inherit the throne. Therefore, they were ecstatic with the arrival of Alexei. Little could they have imagined that his arrival would result in the fall of the three-hundred-year reign of the House of Romanov.

Soon after his birth, the new tsarevitch had a bleeding episode from hemophilia. When the doctors proved powerless, the desperate mother turned to a peasant holy man, Grigory Rasputin. She became convinced he was her son's sole hope of survival, and, consequently, he began to wield great influence in the royal inner circle. This infuriated the Russian nobles, who were aghast that a low-born man, one given to drinking and womanizing, wielded more power than they did. He also further antagonized the peasants; they might have accepted their monarch's wealth, but the sinner masquerading as a saint was too much. Nicholas wanted to dismiss the mad monk but, realizing that his presence gave his wife hope, refused to do so.

Nicholas and Alexandra also made a fatal mistake in hiding Alexei's illness; they did so in the belief that the next tsar should display no weakness. Ironically, this plan had the opposite effect, as the populace, had they been privy to the truth, would probably have been empathetic to the family's pain. The Romanovs became increasingly the subjects of innuendo.

Archduke Franz Ferdinand was assassinated in Sarajevo in 1914. Nicholas, as part of an alliance, brought his country into World War I, and, as commander of the army reluctantly left his family to be at the front with his troops. He took with him a metal pocket case with his wife's portrait. Unfortunately, Nicholas was as bad a leader as he was as loving a husband and father. The ill-equipped Russian soldiers suffered devastating casualties, and the mismanaged government resulted in widespread hunger; the country was on the verge of revolt.

To make matters worse, Nicholas had placed the reins of government with his wife, who was viewed with extreme suspicion, as she was German and the first cousin of Kaiser Wilhelm II, and she relied heavily upon Rasputin.

In 1916, to help stem the tide of horror sweeping across their country, Russian nobles murdered Rasputin; because of his prodigious strength the killing necessitated poison, gunshots, clubbing, and drowning. In fairy tales, the demise of the evil sorcerer meant the salvation of the prince and princess; not so with the reign of the Romanovs. The only effect of the assassination was to drive Alexandra into despair over Alexei's fate. She believed that without her holy man, her son would succumb to his hemophilia

In 1917, besieged on all sides, Tsar Nicholas was forced to abdicate, and the Romanovs were transformed from absolute monarchs to virtual prisoners. They were removed to the Urals, where the family, who had always lived as gods, were subject to endless indignities. The guards rifled through their belongings, food and heat were rationed, and the sentries scrawled lewd drawings to offend the four daughters. Further compounding their anguish, Alexei suffered an accident and became unable to walk. The only source of comfort was the fact that the close-knit family was allowed to remain together and their hope that the royal heads of Europe, their relatives, would come to their rescue.

On July 16 at ten thirty p.m., the Romanovs retired to their rooms; Yakov Yurovsky, the Bolshevik in command, on orders from Lenin, awakened them at midnight and told them to dress quickly. Nicholas came down the stairs first, carrying Alexei. In the basement, he sat with his arm around Alexandra, Alexei on his lap. As they waited, men carrying revolvers entered. Yurovsky stated, "Your relations have tried to save you. They have failed, and we must now shoot you."

Nicholas began to rise from his chair to protect his wife. He had just time to say, "What?" before Yurovsky shot him in the head. Alexandra began to raise her hand to make the sign of the cross before she too was killed. The OTMA huddled together for the last time. The sisters survived the first hail of bullets, as they had sewn priceless jewels into their clothes; it took countless rounds of ammunition before they met their excruciating end. Alexei, who had always been protected by the phalanx of his family, perished clutching his father's coat.

Although their love had destroyed their family and brought ruination to their empire, perhaps the words that Alexandra had written in Nicholas's diary on her wedding night could serve as their epilogue: "At last united, bound for life and when this life is ended, we meet again in the other world and remain together for eternity. Yours, yours, Alexandra."

Postscript

↦ The Romanov bodies were thrown down a disused mine shaft. In 1979, the remains of Nicholas, Alexandra, and three of the daughters were discovered. They were interred in Saint Petersburg, with great ceremony, on the eightieth anniversary of their execution.

11

Franz Ferdinand and Sophie Chotek

1895

O ne of the events that drastically altered the course of history
was World War I, a calamity that led to endless rows of white
crosses in graveyards across Europe. The nightmare began with a
Black Hand, one that cruelly crushed a Balkan love story.

The historic equivalent of "What came first, the chicken or the
egg?" is "Do the times make the man or does the man make the
times?" In the case of Franz Ferdinand, the answer is the latter. His
life was forever altered with the execution of his uncle, Ferdinand
Maximilian, emperor of Mexico, and the murder-suicide of his cousin
Crown Prince Rudolf and his lover, Baroness Marie Vetsera, in his
Mayerling hunting lodge. With their passing, he became the heir to
the throne of Austria-Hungary. His chief passion in life was hunting;
on the walls of Artstetten Castle hung the heads of five thousand
deer. However, his passion for the hunt was to be replaced by a passion of his heart.

Franz's destiny, Sophie Chotek, was born in Stuttgart, the fourth daughter of an aristocratic yet impoverished count. Because of financial need, she was compelled to take the position of lady-in-waiting to the Archduchess Isabella. Little did she imagine that she was to become, for a period, a contemporary Cinderella.

The first time Franz met Sophie was at a ball in Prague. At the soiree his eyes bypassed all the suitable princesses who were paraded before him; he contemptuously referred to them as *piperl*, "chicks." However his interest, and ultimately his heart, was to fall captive to Sophie. Because she was not of royal parentage, she was ineligible to wed into the imperial family. Their relationship, to which both were fiercely committed, had to be clandestine.

Franz started to make regular trips to the home of the Archduchess Isabella, who took the royal visits as a sign that the heir was interested in one of her six daughters; she assumed his love interest was her eldest, Marie Christine. However, the cat was let out of the bag when a servant discovered the archduke's gold watch, left behind at the tennis court. Isabella opened it, expecting to see Marie Christine's portrait. Instead, she was infuriated to discover the photograph of her lady-in-waiting. Sophie was immediately dismissed, and the archduke's secret love became a public scandal.

Franz Ferdinand, now that his heart had become an open book, was determined to marry Sophie; however, the emperor was equally determined that the match would not take place and berated his nephew for his lack of dynastic discipline. Franz Joseph's antipathy was founded on the premise that the only proper consort for the future king was a princess from the House of Habsburg or a princess from one of the other reigning European dynasties. The tug-of-war between uncle and nephew escalated to such a degree that Pope Leo XIII, Tsar Nicholas II, and Kaiser Wilhelm II argued for a compromise, as the royal battle of wills was undermining the stability of the monarchy. The impasse was resolved when the king agreed to the match; however, there was a caveat: The marriage had to be morganic. This meant that none of their issue could ever wear the crown; moreover, Sophie would not be entitled to share her husband's rank, title, or other privileges, such as appearing beside him in public. She was not permitted to ride in the royal carriage, dine with him at state functions, or sit beside him in the royal opera box. When entering a room for a formal function, Sophie would have to wait until all of the higher-ranking women made their entrance.

The wedding took place on July 1, 1900, at Reichstadt in Bohemia. Emperor Franz Joseph, to show his royal displeasure, did not attend. All other archdukes, including the groom's brothers, likewise stayed away. The only members of the imperial family who were present were Franz's stepmother and her two daughters. Upon her marriage, Sophie received the title of Princess of Hohenberg; she could never attain the rank of archduchess. European royals accorded Sophie little respect, with the exception of King George V and Queen Mary, who welcomed her to Windsor Castle in November 1913.

Although tensions existed between the couple and the court, inside Artstetten Castle Sophie was Franz's undisputed queen. Soon, in contrast to the dead animals lining the walls, the house came alive with the birth of children: Sophie, Maximilian, and Ernst. Because of the nature of their marriage contract, the children did not carry their father's name of Habsburg; their surname was von Hohenberg. After the birth of his youngest, Franz wrote to his stepmother, "The most intelligent thing I've ever done in my life has been the marriage to my Soph. She is everything to me: my wife, my adviser, my doctor, in a word: my entire happiness. Now, after four years, we love each other as on our first year of marriage, and our happiness has not been marred for a single second." However, even the enclave of their home could not keep the bitterness at bay. Franz named one of the pathways in their estate's magnificent garden *Oberer Kreuzweg* ("The Upper Stations of the Cross"), a bitter nod to the degradations his wife had to endure at court.

In 1914, General Oskar Potiorek, governor of the Austrian provinces of Bosnia-Herzegovina, invited the archduke to watch his troops on maneuvers. Franz decided to accept as a fourteenth-anniversary present for Sophie. Away from the Austrian court, strict protocol was not enforced, which meant on their visit Sophie could accompany her husband everywhere. Franz was warned that the visit might be potentially dangerous; many of the people living in Bosnia-Herzegovina were angry over Austrian imperialism and wanted their independence from the crown. In answer the archduke replied, *"Mann ist überall in Gottes Hand"* ("It's all in God's hands"). It was an attitude that would decide their fate.

In 1910 a secret terrorist organization, the Black Hand, whose motto was "Unification or Death," formed with the intent to rid the Balkan states of the yoke of Austria. When they discovered that the archduke was on his way to their country, they planned their vengeance on the hated House of Habsburg.

The military exercises went off well and were followed by an official visit to the capital city of Sarajevo on Sunday, June 28, to round off the trip. Franz and Sophie traveled the short distance from their hotel to the capital by a special train. There they joined a convoy of six cars to drive through the streets to an official welcome at the town hall. Franz was dressed in full military regalia; Sophie beamed with joy at riding alongside her beloved husband for a state event, in a street lined with spectators. The car had its roof down so the crowds could have a better view of the waving royal couple. At the same time, seven young members of the Black Hand, assassins who had been trained in neighboring Serbia, were waiting to move into action, thereby altering world history.

When the royal procession passed the central police station, Nedjelko Cabrinovic hurtled a hand grenade at the archduke's car. The driver accelerated when he saw the object flying toward them, and the grenade exploded under the wheel of the car behind the royal one. Two of its occupants were seriously wounded, and a dozen spectators were hit by bomb splinters. In anger Franz shouted, "So you welcome your guests with bombs!" Although badly shaken, they attended the official reception at City Hall. Afterward the archduke inquired about the members of his party who had been wounded. Upon learning that they had sustained serious injuries, he insisted on visiting them in the hospital. Baron Morsey suggested that this step might be dangerous; Oskar Potiorek retorted, "Do you think Sarajevo is full of assassins?" Nevertheless, Potiorek did concede that it would be better if Sophie remained behind at City Hall. However, she refused to do so, with the words, "As long as the archduke shows himself in public today I will not leave him."

In order to avoid the densely packed center of the capital, General Potiorek decided that the royal car should travel straight through the Appel Quay en route to the hospital. However, through an oversight, no one informed the driver of the change of plans. On the way, at the Latin Bridge, the driver took a right turn into Franz Joseph Street. At this point Potiorek told the driver he was going the wrong way, so the chauffeur put the car in reverse. In doing this, he slowly moved past one of the conspirators, nineteen-year-old Gavrilo Princip, who, having heard of the botched assassination, had gone into the Moritz Schiller Café for a sandwich. He was shocked that his targets had appeared directly in front of him.

Princip rushed to the car, drew his pistol, and at a distance of five feet, fired several times—shots that were to ultimately claim seven million lives. A bullet hit Franz Ferdinand in the neck, and another lodged in Sophie's abdomen, whereby she collapsed on her husband's legs. He then said his last words to his first love: *"Sopherl, Sopherl, stirb nicht . . . Bleib am Leben für unsere Kinder!"* ("Little Sophie, little Sophie, don't die! . . . Stay alive for our children!")

Princip's actions ignited World War I, which would turn Europe into a graveyard. Viscount Edward Grey wrote of the catastrophe triggered by a fateful shot, "The lamps are going out all over Europe; we shall not see them lit again in our lifetime."

When historians analyze the causes of World War I, they point the finger of blame at a blood-soaked street in Sarajevo. However, when romantics recall the fateful last ride, they view it as an immortal Balkan love story.

Postscript

➺ The bodies of Franz Ferdinand and Sophie provided silent proof of the archduke's devotion. The bullets that had pierced his wife had passed through his body first, as he tried to shield her from harm. The slain couple were returned to Vienna, followed by a joint funeral mass; Franz Joseph did not attend.

➺ The archduke, as a Habsburg, was buried in an ornate coffin, with pomp and circumstance befitting royalty.

➺ Sophie, because of her lesser status, was placed on a bier eighteen inches lower than her husband. On her casket was placed a pair of white gloves and a black fan, symbols of a lady-in-waiting.

➺ Their morganic marriage precluded her burial in the Habsburg imperial crypt; however, in deference to their love, they were interred in the crypt of their Austrian castle, Artstetten.

12

Leonard Woolf and Virginia Stephen

1903

*T*he adjective *uxorious* is defined as "slavishly devoted to one's wife." Leonard Woolf could definitely be thus described, as he was Virginia's lighthouse throughout all her emotional storms and provided her with the light she needed to navigate through her darkness.

Adeline Virginia Stephen was born into a family that would never remotely have qualified as typical. Her father, Sir Leslie, was an eminent man of letters (the widower of William Makepeace Thackeray's daughter), and her mother, Julia (the widow of Herbert Duckworth), was a renowned beauty, a descendant of one of Marie Antoinette's attendants. The Stephen household consisted of offspring from three marriages: Laura Makepeace Stephen; George, Gerald, and Stella Duckworth; and the four children Sir Stephen and Julia had together: Vanessa, Thoby, Virginia, and Adrian. Their home was also filled with guests whose names graced the most literary books of the times: Henry James and George Henry Lewes. Adeline (who preferred the name Virginia) described it as a place of "books, writers and literary gossip." The Stephens summered in Cornwall, where their dwelling overlooked the Godrevy Lighthouse.

Virginia's happy and literate childhood did not presage the tragedies that were to shadow her life. Her mother passed away in 1895, followed by her sister, who died two years later. Always psychologically fragile, she was shattered at the specter of death. Before she could recover, her father succumbed to his illness and she lost him in 1904. Her grief culminated with her first mental breakdown at age twenty-two. She was briefly institutionalized and would struggle for the rest of her years to maintain mental and emotional equilibrium. A further contributing influence to her psychological instability was the sexual abuse she suffered at the hands of her half-brothers George and Gerald Duckworth. Upon the passing of her parents, the siblings moved to a new home in Bloomsbury, close to the British Museum. It was to become the meeting place of London's intellectuals, and where Virginia fell in love.

Virginia's destiny, Leonard Sidney Woolf, was born in London, the third of ten children of a barrister, Solomon Rees Sydney and Marie (de Jongh) Woolf. As a Jew in anti-Semitic England he developed what he called his "carapace," a hard shell, to shield himself from the "outside and usually hostile world." A brilliant student, he won a scholarship to Cambridge, where he met some of the great thinkers of the era: Lytton Strachey, Rupert Brook, Clive Bell, John Maynard Keynes, Bertrand Russell, and E. M. Forster. He also became friendly with Virginia's brother Thoby, whose nickname was "the Goth." Upon graduation Woolf took a position in the Ceylon Civil Service; accompanying him were seventy volumes of Voltaire and a fox terrier, Charles.

The first time Virginia met Leonard was when she and her sister Vanessa went to Cambridge to visit Thoby. Leonard later recalled,

"She was a vision in white—resplendent in a summery dress, large hat and parasol. Her beauty literally took one's breath away."

After graduation he would see them again every Thursday evening when he attended their literary salon. Enraptured with her beauty and intellect, Leonard proposed twice; however, she rejected him with the comment that he was a "penniless Jew." Undeterred, he wrote her, "If I try to say what I feel, I become stupid & stammering: it's like a wall of words rising up in front of me & there on the other side you're sitting so clear & beautiful & your dear face that I'd give everything in the world to see now." Upon his third proposal, she accepted, and Virginia and Leonard were married on August 10, 1912, at a registry office in London. The newlyweds honeymooned in France, Spain, and Italy.

Leonard greatly encouraged his wife to write, as both a form of therapy and something to engage her interest. She had already penned a piece on Hayworth, the Brontës' parsonage, and had contributed to the Sunday *Literary Supplement*. She said of her passion, "I am ashamed, or perhaps proud, to say how much of my time is spent in thinking thinking, thinking about literature." Cognizant of his wife's ever-fragile psyche, Leonard suggested starting their own printing press. He felt this would not only give his wife a project; it would also promote controversial literary works that otherwise would not have made it into print.

In 1917 the Woolfs founded the Hogarth Press, named after their London home. The original machine, small enough to fit on their kitchen table, published Virginia's novels as well as Katherine Mansfield's short stories and T. S. Eliot's *Waste Land*. They also printed nonfiction, such as the complete twenty-four-volume translation of the works of Sigmund Freud. When Virginia met the psychoanalyst in 1939 when he had fled Nazi Germany, she wrote in her diary, "A screwed up shrunk very old man: with a monkey's light eyes, paralyzed spasmodic movements, inarticulate: but alert."

During the 1920s Virginia became the high priestess of the Bloomsbury Group, and the Hogarth Press also published her soon-to-be classic novels: *Mrs Dalloway*, *To the Lighthouse*, and *Orlando*. Leonard, an aspiring writer, never envied the success that eluded him; his entry into literary immortality was as Mr. Virginia Woolf.

However, despite Virginia's professional acclaim and adored husband, she was never able to keep at bay "the hairy black devils" of her mental instability. On and off, Virginia struggled with anorexia, insomnia, and headaches. What always presaged a complete nervous breakdown was when she began hearing birds singing in Greek. Leonard's sign of the horror to come was when his brilliant wife began to talk, nonstop, in gibberish. He said of these precursors, "She talked almost without stopping for two to three days, paying no attention to anyone in the room or anything said to her . . . Then gradually it became completely incoherent, a mere jumble of dissociated words." Had it not been for his support, she would have been placed in an asylum. Instead, he ministered to her in her madness, and, when obliged to work, hired nurses.

The 1920s also saw the birth of Virginia's affair with the similarly married writer Vita Sackville-West, whose aristocratic family could trace their lineage to William the Conqueror. This relationship resulted in Woolf's novel *Orlando*, which she dedicated "to V. Sackville-West." Vita's mother was enraged at the book, which exposed what she had tried so hard to conceal—her daughter's fondness for women. She referred to Virginia as "the Virgin Woolf." Leonard hailed his wife's book as a groundbreaking literary masterpiece. He was also there to pick up the pieces of his wife's heart when Vita cast Virginia away for another woman.

Leonard never condemned his wife's affairs. He remained committed to his tenet that Virginia's happiness was his greatest good. Virginia also reciprocated his affection. She wrote in her diary,

"Love-making—after 25 years can't bear to be separate . . . you see it is enormous pleasure being wanted: a wife. And our marriage so complete."

While the 1920s brought literary fame and Vita into Virginia's life, the 1930s brought ever mounting depression. In 1935 Leonard and Virginia, along with their pet marmoset Mitzy, who liked to perch on Leonard's shoulder, drove through Germany and saw the growing horrors of Nazism. Virginia had relinquished her earlier anti-Semitism and wrote to a friend, "My Jew has more religion in one toenail—more human love, in one hair."

In 1940, while the Woolfs were staying in their country home, Monk's House, near the village of Rodmell in Sussex, they received the devastating news that their London home had been destroyed by the *Luftwaffe*. They were forced to remain in Sussex, which exacerbated Virginia's psychological frailty, cutting her off from her circle of friends and the distractions of London. Moreover, the two realized that if the Nazis took over England, Leonard, as a Jew and an intellectual, would be sent to a concentration camp. The couple made a suicide pact: If Leonard was ever in danger of imprisonment they would shut their garage door, take a lethal dose of morphine, and end their lives together.

The specter of world events, ones that threatened Leonard, her only emotional life jacket, contributed to Virginia's ever-evolving web of depression. As with all the other onsets of her breakdowns, her words and writing began to slip away; the birds once more began to sing in Greek. In 1941, Virginia Woolf, her pockets laden with stones, journeyed into the River Ouse near her country home. After Virginia's death, Leonard wrote, "I know that she is drowned and yet I listen for her to come in at the door. I know that it is the last page, and yet I turn it over." In her suicide note Virginia wrote her last words to her first love:

Dearest, I feel certain I am going mad again. I feel we can't go through another of those terrible times. And I shan't recover this time. I begin to hear voices, and I can't concentrate. So I am doing what seems the best thing to do. You have given me the greatest possible happiness. You have been in every way all that anyone could be. I don't think two people could have been happier till this terrible disease came. I can't fight any longer. I know that I am spoiling your life, that without me you could work. And you will I know. You see I can't even write this properly. I can't read. What I want to say is I owe all the happiness of my life to you. You have been entirely patient with me and incredibly good. I want to say that—everybody knows it. If anybody could have saved me it would have been you. Everything has gone from me but the certainty of your goodness. I can't go on spoiling your life any longer. I don't think two people could have been happier than we have been. V.

Leonard's words from his letter proved as true after her death as those from before their wedding: "your dear face that I'd give everything in the world to see now."

Postscript

➤ Leonard arranged for his wife to be cremated; her ashes were scattered at Monk's House, under its elms. Below a bust of Virginia, Leonard inscribed a quote from her novel *The Waves*: "I meant to write about death, only life came breaking in as usual."

➤ When Leonard Woolf passed away in 1969, his ashes were scattered at Monk's House, under its elms.

13

Gertrude Stein and Alice B. Toklas

1907

*T*he years between the two world wars can be viewed as the French Renaissance, as the greatest creative minds of the century congregated in Paris. The luminaries indulged in a meeting of minds in a famous salon dominated by Gertrude Stein and the woman she considered her wife, Alice B. Toklas.

Gertrude Stein was born in Pennsylvania into a wealthy Jewish family. After a European sojourn the Steins relocated to Oakland, California, about which Gertrude wrote, "There is no there there." Her closest confidante was her brother Leo, and when he went to Harvard, she followed him to Boston. However, as the school would not admit women, she attended Radcliffe. The pivotal event of her university years was being tutored by the psychologist William James, whose influence would later emerge in her subsequent novels' stream-of-consciousness style.

Later Gertrude transferred to Johns Hopkins; there, although intellectually stimulated, she felt emotionally bereft. Her notebooks of this period reveal a troubled and depressed young woman unable to envision herself fitting into the prescribed roles as wife and mother. Her "red deeps," as she termed her inner turmoil, were exacerbated when she fell in love with May Bookstaver, who, involved with another woman, did not reciprocate Gertrude's feelings. Distraught, Gertrude dropped out of medical school and once more followed Leo, this time to Europe.

Gertrude's destiny, Alice Babette, was born in San Francisco in 1877, the only daughter of middle-class Jewish parents, Ferdinand and Emma (Levinsky) Toklas. After Alice's mother passed away (a few weeks before Alice's twentieth birthday), her life had evolved into the role of housekeeper for her father and brother.

In 1906 Michael Stein (Gertrude's eldest brother) and his wife, Sarah, paid a visit to his friend Alice when they arrived in San Francisco to check on the earthquake's damage to their properties. They brought along with them three Matisse paintings and tales of Parisian life. When Michael extended an invitation to visit him in France, Alice accepted, to escape the drudgery of her current life and in the hope that the trip would provide an exciting interlude.

The first time Gertrude met Alice was on Alice's first day in Paris on September 8, at the home of Michael and Sarah Stein. When she was introduced to Gertrude, she said a bell went off in her head, a sound signifying that she was in the proximity of a genius. Gertrude had been quite fond of declaring herself a genius long before Alice heard bells, and that became the first thing they agreed upon. A similar note resounded in her heart; she wrote of that initial meeting, "She was a golden brown presence, burned by the Tuscan sun and with a golden glint in her warm brown hair. She was dressed in a warm brown corduroy suit. She wore a large round coral brooch and when she talked, very little, or laughed, a good deal, I thought her voice came from this brooch. It was unlike anyone else's voice—deep, full, velvety, like a great contralto's, like two voices."

The two women were quick to fall in love, and their attraction to each other was immediate. In her memoir Alice wrote, "It was Gertrude Stein who held my complete attention, as she did for all the many years I knew her."

Although both were horizontally challenged (Gertrude was five feet one, while Alice was four feet eleven), they adopted very different styles. Gertrude, rotund, wore her hair in a Roman emperor cut and favored severe, mannish outfits. Alice knitted for her the shapeless garments and heavy woolen stockings she felt most comfortable in. Alice, who was extremely slight, favored couture outfits (though she wore them badly) and gypsy earrings, and chain-smoked Pall Malls. Gertrude's term of endearment was "Pussy," while Alice called her "Baby."

Gertrude expressed her love in words. Alice, an early riser, often woke to notes that Gertrude, who wrote late at night, left on her pillow. These were often signed "Y. D." ("Your Darling"). The couple was inseparable; if Ms. Stein appeared at a café, by her side would be Ms. Toklas. The high-profile women also liked to stroll the streets of Paris and browse flea markets, walking their enormous white poodle, Basket, who, upon his passing, was replaced by Basket II.

In 1908, on a hillside outside Paris, Gertrude proposed to Alice and presented her with a ring. Stein wrote of the day, "It happened very simply that they were married. They were naturally married."

When Alice B. Toklas first hitched her heart to Gertrude's star, little did she imagine that by doing so she was destined to become half of one of the most famous lesbian couples of the twentieth century. Alice and Gertrude's Left Bank apartment became the living room for all the great artists living in Paris between the two world wars. Their salon's walls showcased the avant-garde painters of the day: Picasso, Matisse, Toulouse-Lautrec, Cezanne. These stars orbited Stein, the grande dame of her salon, and Pablo Picasso painted Stein's portrait, which currently hangs in the Metropolitan Museum of Art. When Toklas commented on it, he responded, "Yes. Everybody says that she does not look like it but that does not make any difference, she will." Not to slight Ms. Toklas, he rewarded her with a needlepoint pattern, which she used to make tapestries for two Louis XVI chairs.

The writer closest to Stein was Ernest Hemingway, who had arrived on her doorstep armed with a letter of introduction from Sherwood Anderson. Gertrude and Alice became the godmothers of his first child, John. His parents' nickname for him was Bumby; the two ladies called him Goddy, as they were his godparents. (John became the father of actresses Margot and Mariel.) It was about Hemingway that Stein coined her famous expression: "You are all a lost generation." Toklas, fanatically possessive when it came to Gertrude, banned Hemingway from their home when she felt he was getting too close to Stein. Perhaps in retaliation, in his memoir *A Moveable Feast*, he recounted an argument between the two hostesses: "I heard (Miss Toklas), speaking to Miss Stein as I have never heard one person speak to another, never, anywhere, ever."

Toklas, in a similar jealous vein, in reference to Gertrude's youthful crush on May Bookstaver, forced the author to replace every instance of the word *may* with *can* in Stein's 1932 epic poem "Stanzas in Meditation."

The conversation during Gertrude and Alice's Saturday night soirees always revolved around art. While Gertrude entertained the men, Alice gossiped with their wives and girlfriends. She also provided fragrant, colorless liquors that she made herself from plums and raspberries. While Gertrude shone in the drawing room, Alice excelled in the kitchen, as she was one of the finest chefs in Paris. Later she wrote a cookbook of her famous recipes, which included her specialty: brownies with a dash of hash. (Some believe that the term *toke* when referring to marijuana is derived from the surname Toklas.) However, Alice's main task was to ensure that nothing disturbed the flow of Gertrude's genius. Thornton Wilder called Alice "the dragon protecting the treasure." Without Alice, Gertrude would not have been Gertrude.

When the Nazis goose-stepped into Paris, Gertrude and Alice's friends encouraged them to return to America; Stein refused by explaining, "America is my country, but Paris is my hometown." As lesbians and Jews, they managed to escape by moving to Bilignin, their country retreat in the south of France, where they were aided by a collaborator. After liberation, Stein wrote to Toklas, "I love you so much more / every war more and more and more and / more."

In 1946, Stein began to experience stomach pain and was diagnosed with cancer. When the end was near she was taken to a hospital in Neuilly-sur-Seine. On vigil was Alice, already grieving the remaining empty years. However, like Rick and Ilsa, they would always have Paris.

As Gertrude died, Alice listened to her "deep, full, velvety, contralto's voice for the last time," ask, "What is the answer?" Alice did not reply. Gertrude then said her last words to her first love, "Then what is the question?"

Postscript

→ Gertrude Stein was buried in the Pere-Lachaise Cemetery in Paris.

→ Not long before Alice died in 1967, she converted from Judaism to Catholicism. She had asked her priest, in reference to her new religion, "Will this allow me to see Gertrude when I die?" Toklas was interred in the adjoining grave to Stein's.

14

William Randolph Hearst and Marion Davies

1916

S tanding high above the sea and close to the sky, a California castle stands silent sentry. If its walls could talk, it would recall the glory days of yesteryear when Hollywood's elite rushed to San Simeon for a coveted invitation to William Randolph Hearst's pleasure dome. However, its most riveting tale would be of the romance of the tycoon and his showgirl.

Marion Cecilia Douras, born in 1897, was the youngest of five children. At a young age she was bitten by the showbiz bug as she watched her sisters perform in local stage productions. She determined that she would stand on stage one day, and she was not going to let her stutter be an impediment. In order to reinvent herself, after seeing a Brooklyn realty sign, Davies Real Estate, she adopted the name as her own. With her eye on the prize, she traded her native Brooklyn for Broadway. In the end, Marion achieved immortality not for what she did in front of the bright lights, but for her love affair with the man who sat in front of them.

William Randolph Hearst was born with the silverest of spoons as the only son of a millionaire miner. When he was a child, his adoring mother, Phoebe, took him to Europe, where he developed a lifelong passion for fine art and antiques. He attended Harvard (with a ten-thousand-a-month allowance), until his expulsion for presenting several of his professors silver chamber pots engraved with their names. This did not trouble him, as his aspiration lay not with academia but with publishing. His foray into the arena he would come to dominate began when he persuaded his father, Senator George Hearst, to let him run the family-owned *San Francisco Enquirer*. He transformed it into the city's most popular daily, partially through publicity gimmicks such as marching bands, oyster dinners, firework displays, and free boat rides. After he acquired the *New York Journal*, the publishing industry would forever bear his imprint.

His empire grew to encompass dozens of newspapers and magazines (the latter included *Cosmopolitan*, *Town and Country*, and *Harper's Bazaar*). In 1903, the day before his fortieth birthday, William married a twenty-one-year-old chorus girl, Millicent Wilson, with whom he had five sons.

When his adored mother passed away in 1919, William inherited 168,000 acres on a hilltop, La Cuesta Encantada ("The Enchanted Hill"), in San Simeon, California, on which he spent $37 million to build a castle. The walls of its 165 rooms were graced with his $50 million art collection (a quarter of a billion dollars in modern currency); its grounds included a Roman-style pool where *Spartacus* was filmed as well as the largest private zoo in the country. Hearst called San Simeon his "little hideaway." When he lived on the East Coast his form of relaxation was the theater, where he was to meet the greatest love of his life—one for whom he was to risk his reputation.

The first time Marion met William, the eighteen-year-old

Marion was working as one of the chorus girls in the Ziegfeld Follies. As she was cascading down the steps on the stage, she caught the eye, and eventually the heart, of the publishing baron who occupied the front two seats (one was reserved for his hat)—William Randolph Hearst. Afterward, he had bouquets, gloves, candies, and silver boxes delivered to her dressing room and arranged to have her photographed at his studio. During the session, however, she caught only a glimpse of him, as he slipped away before they could talk.

The two crossed paths again a few months later in Palm Beach, when, on the way to an amusement park, she lost control of the brakes on her bicycle and crashed, just missing the car in which William, coincidentally, was sitting. Stunned, as she was lying flat on her back, he asked if he could help. He tied her broken bike to his car and told his chauffeur to take her to the Royal Poinciana Hotel. They recognized each other from the photography session, but no mention of it was made, as Mrs. Hearst would not have been amused. He then stuck his head in the car and asked his wife to walk with him.

Soon after, Marion was at a party in New York City; as she turned to leave, Hearst shook her hand. When he departed, she opened her palm; on it was a diamond wristwatch.

Eventually the fifty-eight-year-old tycoon and the teenaged showgirl began a romantic relationship. When he asked her why she was going with a married man twice her age and the father of five, she replied, "Because I'm a gold digger." Hearst, forever surrounded by sycophants, found her forthright words refreshing. Besides, he was in the throes of infatuation.

As time went by, despite their huge differences, the two fell in love. William felt pain that he could not make her Mrs. Hearst; to comfort W. R., as she called him, she said, "Love is not always created at the altar. Love doesn't need a wedding ring." She felt they were together and that was all that mattered. William became Marion's Svengali, and his tabloids praised her skills as an actress; she was once described as the bubbles in champagne. Marion's comment on her lover's promotion was, "With me it was 5% talent and 95% publicity." In her autobiography she stated that had it not been for Hearst, she would have ended up as a Bertha, a sewing-machine girl.

Soon the newsman himself became the news, and the public felt Ziegfeld's folly had become Hearst's own.

Mrs. Hearst was enraged at her husband's public display of adultery, which had become Hollywood's worst-kept secret. However, the former showgirl had established herself as the grande dame of Manhattan and felt that her social position would not be enhanced with a divorce. Soon she absented herself from the West Coast, and Marion became the official belle of Hearst's castle, which drew European blue bloods such as Winston Churchill and American royalty such as Carole Lombard, Mary Pickford, Charlie Chaplin, Clark Gable, John F. Kennedy, and Charles Lindbergh. Marion would later immortalize these heady days in her autobiography, *The Times We Had*.

Hearst was a generous man, and when it came to Marion his largesse knew no limit. After spying a photograph of St. Donat's Castle in Wales, he bought the property in 1925 and presented it as a token of his love. George Bernard Shaw told Hearst that his castle was "what heaven would be like if God had your money." The titan also purchased for Marion a 118-room Santa Monica home, Ocean House (dubbed "the Versailles of Hollywood"), which today is worth $165 million. Anybody who was anyone, such as Charlie Chaplin and Greta Garbo, coveted invitations to Marion's three-day, on-the-beach, stop-the-band-at-four-a.m. soirees. Hearst showered her with jewels, perhaps in guilt over never being able to give her the one jewel they both wished she could have worn: a wedding band.

Unlike most "other women," Marion never demanded that the mistress become the wife. She told him, "You are one of the most important men in the world. Now it's all right for you to have a blonde ex-Follies girl for your mistress. That's all right. But you divorce the wife and mother of your five sons to marry a much younger blonde, and you're an old fool." Marion knew she was W. R.'s wife of his heart; with that she was content.

Although Hearst was omnipotent in his publishing empire, there were some things that even the Chief (the name his employees called him) could not control. Orson Welles's movie *Citizen Kane* was a roman à clef based on the mogul; it portrayed his love interest as Sally, a talentless, drunken opportunist whose own ambitions were curtailed by her tycoon's megalomania. Herman J. Mankiewicz, co-writer of *Citizen Kane*, heard the name Rosebud from the actress Louise Brooks at San Simeon; apparently it was Hearst's pet name for a certain part of Marion's anatomy. Citizen Hearst was not impressed. Marion was equally defensive; she told a reporter, "I don't care what you say about me, but don't hurt him. He's a wonderful man." Welles later commented on his film, "Kane was better than Hearst but Marion was better than Susan."

In 1937, the unthinkable happened: Hearst had run out of money. However, Marion came to his rescue. She liquidated everything she owned and presented W. R. with a check for a million dollars. Overcome with emotion, he asked why she made the sacrifice. Her answer was that the gold digger had fallen in love. Not only did Marion make the sacrifice of money; she also gave up her career to be with the man who now needed her more than ever. She explained, "I thought that the least I could do for a man who had been so wonderful and great . . . was to be a companion to him." She proved that her love had not been merely dollars deep.

In his eighth decade, Hearst rebounded financially, and the couple returned to the castle. In their evenings in the home, they sat together in their screening room, where tears came to William's eyes as he watched Marion's movies. In the morning she woke up to poems he had penned for her; a cherished one ended, "But no beauty of earth is so fair a sight / As the girl who lies by my side at night."

In 1951, the unthinkable happened once more; Hearst had run out of time. In failing health, he was taken to his Beverly Hills home to be near medical care. His mansion's bedroom was emptied of all the treasures he had spent a lifetime acquiring; they all remained at the only place Hearst cared about, the home on the Enchanted Hill. His only personal effect was a photograph, on a desk beside his massive canopied bed, of Marion, who had been his faithful companion for thirty-four years. On it she had written a quotation from *Romeo and Juliet*: "My bounty is as boundless as the sea / My love as deep; the more I give thee / The more I have, for both are infinite."

Citizen Kane's final whispered word, "Rosebud," held the elusive key to the life of the prince of publishing. Hearst departed the world with no recorded last words; however, if he had, there is no doubt which name would have been on his lips.

Postscript

➻ When Hearst passed away, his body was flown to San Francisco. The funeral was fittingly ornate; however, Marion Davies was barred from attending by Millicent and her children. Hearst was entombed with his parents at Cypress Lawn Cemetery outside San Francisco.

➤ Marion died in Hollywood in 1961 of cancer of the jaw. Her funeral was attended by former president Herbert Hoover, Bing Crosby, Mary Pickford, Mrs. Clark Gable, and Joseph Kennedy. Patricia Lake was later buried beside her. She was Marion's niece; there are persistent rumors that she was the daughter of Marion Davies and William Randolph Hearst.

15

F. Scott Fitzgerald and Zelda Sayre

1918

S cott and Zelda, after nine decades, remain the golden couple of a golden age, their romance immortalized in Fitzgerald's flawless prose. They serve as legends of their era, the embodiment of the triumph and tragedy of the Roaring Twenties, dwelling, for a time, this side of paradise.

Zelda Sayre was born in Montgomery, Alabama, into a prominent family; her father was a justice of the supreme court of Alabama. Her indulgent mother named her after a gypsy princess from a romance novel; it was to prove an apt moniker. She had an unappeasable appetite for attention; for example, the teenager (the antithesis of Southern propriety) wore a tight, flesh-colored bathing suit to fuel rumors that she swam nude. Not surprisingly, she and her childhood friend Tallulah Bankhead left Montgomery with no shortage of gossip. Her high school yearbook encapsulated her philosophy: "Let's think only of today and not worry about tomorrow." Even the imaginative girl could not have envisioned what a roller coaster her tomorrow would hold when her life merged with a self-proclaimed romantic egotist.

Zelda's destiny, Francis Scott Key Fitzgerald, was born into an Irish Roman Catholic family in St. Paul, Minnesota. A disinterested student, he dropped out of Princeton to enlist in World War I, hoping the experience would provide material for the novels he aspired to pen. Ironically, his stint in the army introduced him to the passion that would drive his books, many of which were to become American classics.

The first time Zelda met Scott was when he was stationed at Camp Sheridan and received a coveted invitation to an exclusive country club, where he saw a "golden girl." She was swaying to the song "Dance of the Hours," and the twenty-one-year-old first lieutenant was mesmerized. He asked her to dance, of which experience she would later say, "He smelled like new goods ... being close to him with my face in the space between his ears and his stiff army collar was like being initiated into the subterranean reserves of a fine fabric store."

Scott attempted to impress her by telling her that one day he would be a famous writer and she his novel's heroine, and that he was named after his famous second cousin twice removed, Francis Scott Key, who had composed "The Star-Spangled Banner." However, as Zelda thirsted for more material tangibles, Scott departed for New York City to establish a career. Before he left, Zelda presented him with a silver hip flask engraved with the words *Forget-me-not*.

After obtaining employment at an advertising agency, Scott sent Zelda his mother's ring. Zelda, however, did what mice do when the cat's away and resumed her flirtations, one with a university star quarterback. Involved with the two men, she sent them both her autographed picture; however, she placed them in the wrong envelopes and Scott was enraged to receive her photograph inscribed to another. Zelda claimed she had done so accidentally; however, it may have been a ruse to incite jealousy. The result was a violent argument, and they ended their relationship. He told his friend, "I wouldn't care if she died, but I couldn't stand to have anyone else marry her."

Nevertheless, desperate to win her back, Scott revised his manuscript *The Romantic Egotist* and recast it as *This Side of Paradise*. The twenty-three-year-old author wrote his publisher, Maxwell Perkins, imploring for its immediate release: "I have so many things dependent on its success—including of course a girl." Their engagement was resumed, and Zelda wrote her fiancé, "Both of us are very splashy, vivid pictures, those kind with the details left out. But I know our colors will blend."

On April 30, 1920, before a small wedding party in St. Patrick's Cathedral, Scott finally possessed the embodiment of his ideal. He told a reporter, "I married the heroine of my stories." They honeymooned in the city's Biltmore Hotel, where, because of noise complaints, they were asked to leave.

After their nuptials, the Fitzgeralds became the enfants terribles of the Jazz Age because of their hedonistic lifestyle, unconventionality, and commitment to the pursuit of happiness. As literary celebrities they rubbed shoulders with Gloria Swanson and Douglas Fairbanks. Every one of their outrageous, drunken escapades (despite Prohibition) became tabloid fodder, such as the time Zelda jumped into the fountain at the Plaza Hotel. When Dorothy Parker first met them, when they were sitting atop a taxi (which is how they often rode down Fifth Avenue), she said, "They did both look as though they had just stepped out of the sun; their youth was striking." William Randolph Hearst enlisted a reporter to write solely about them. Actress Lillian Gish said, "They didn't make the 20s;

they were the 20s." For a time, the Fitzgeralds basked in the lime-light; always at Scott's side was the woman he had termed "the first American flapper."

On Valentine's Day, 1921, while Scott was working on *The Beautiful and the Damned*, their only daughter, Frances Scott ("Scottie") was born. This did not turn Zelda into a domestic diva. When a magazine asked her to contribute an article for *Famous Recipes from Famous People*, she supplied one for burnt toast. Her lack of household skills posed no problem, as the Fitzgeralds employed a cook, a housekeeper, and a nanny.

Tragically, the Fitzgeralds' relationship began to unravel, as they were beset by problems. Although *This Side of Paradise* brought in staggering royalties, they spent it as quickly as it came in. The situation was exacerbated by their chronic drinking: Scott employed his own personal bootlegger, and Zelda did her utmost to keep up. Soon, instead of riding atop taxis, inebriated they were brought home in one. Their relationship no longer blended; instead, it had become a folie à deux. Desperate for money, Scott, though he felt he was prostituting his talent, took to writing for magazines.

Of their mounting marital tensions Zelda stated, "When we meet in the hall, we walk around each other like a pair of stiff-legged terriers spoiling for a fight." Still devoted to each other despite their tensions, they decided to join the American expatriate community in France, which Gertrude Stein christened the Lost Generation. Zelda was thrilled at the prospect. Their daughter Scottie later said of her mother that she "never liked a room without an open suitcase in it."

In Paris the pair socialized with Pablo Picasso and Cole Porter and were frequent visitors in Gertrude Stein's salon. Scott and Hemingway forged a bond as writers and fellow drinkers and frequented the American Bar. Hemingway, after meeting Zelda, in his customary terse style, pronounced her insane. His advice to Scott was to forgo his emotionally draining marriage for an alternative agenda of "hard drink and easy sex." For her part, jealous of his time with her husband, she accused Hemingway and Scott of being lovers and goaded Scott by calling him a fairy.

Despite the domestic turbulence, Scott was able to complete his magnum opus, *The Great Gatsby*, thereby fulfilling his initial pledge to Zelda to one day make her the heroine of his novel. Its dedication: *Once Again to Zelda*. She, however, felt he had exploited her to create his characters and told a magazine that apparently "plagiarism begins at home." Moreover, bored while he was writing, Zelda began an affair with a young French pilot, Edouard Jozan. Scott responded by locking her in the house; bereft, he wrote, "That September of 1924, I knew that something had happened that could never be repaired."

Zelda matched her husband in jealousy as well as alcohol. One evening, while dining, Scott was introduced to Isadora Duncan. Ever dramatic, he dropped to his knees at her feet, whereby she began to stroke his hair and called him "my centurion." This was too much for Zelda, and she threw herself down a series of stone steps. Of the unreal haze that hovered over their lives, Scott wrote, "Sometimes I don't know whether Zelda and I are real or whether we are characters in one of my novels."

Finally perceiving what was apparent to all else, a devastated Scott admitted Zelda into a series of psychiatric hospitals, where she would spend most of the remainder of her life. Her sorrow is laid bare in her words, "Nobody has ever measured, not even poets, how much the heart can hold." Scott's heartache was evident: "I left my capacity for hoping on the little roads that led to Zelda's sanatorium." While in one of the hospitals, Zelda wrote *Save Me the Waltz*. Two years later Fitzgerald wrote *Tender Is the Night*; the two books provide contrasting portrayals of their legendary marriage.

Although they were never to live together again, their bond

remained strong. Scott moved to Hollywood and wrote screenplays he despised to keep Zelda from the horror of state-run institutions. He visited regularly and sent a letter calling her "the finest, loveliest, tenderest, most beautiful person I have ever known." She described him as "the best friend a person could have been to me."

In 1940, Scott was a recovering alcoholic, unemployed screenwriter, living with gossip columnist Sheilah Graham. While taking some notes, he suddenly rose from his chair, clutched the mantelpiece, and fell to the floor, victim of a heart attack. Zelda, who during their courtship had written to him, "We will die together," received the devastating news in her sanatorium, while living three thousand miles away, in the Southern city where their love story had begun.

Eight years later, Zelda perished in a hospital fire; in her room were all of Scott's love letters. As much as she had been able, Zelda had always saved Scott the waltz.

Postscript

➤ During Scott's visitation Dorothy Parker reportedly said, "The poor son of a bitch," a quotation from *The Great Gatsby*. He was interred in the Rockville Union Cemetery.

➤ In 1948 Zelda passed away and was buried in the same cemetery as Scott. In 1975 Scottie arranged for her parents to be transferred to the Fitzgerald family plot in Saint Mary's Catholic Cemetery. They were laid to rest under a single headstone; its inscription bears a quotation from *The Great Gatsby*: "So we beat on, boats against the current, borne back ceaselessly into the past."

16

Diego Rivera and Frida Kahlo

1922

*F*rida Kahlo served as Diego Rivera's muse; he acted as her maestro, and together they became Mexico's most colorful couple. Their romance was a magnet; they were alternately attracted and repelled by one another. Despite, or because of, their love-hate relationship, they managed to create some of the most compelling visual images of the twentieth century. In the process, their love story possessed all the exoticism and eroticism of a Frida Kahlo canvas.

In a house symbolically named La Casa Azul ("The Blue House"), Magdalena Carmen Frieda Kahlo y Calderón, referred to as Frida, was born to a Hungarian-Jewish father and a devout Catholic mother. A poster child for Freud's theories, she adored her father and resented her mother. Her childhood was punctuated by gunfire outside her home from the Mexican Revolution as well as a bout of polio that left her confined to her room for nine months and resulted in a withered right leg. Her classmates taunted her by calling her "Peg-Leg Frida," and to disguise her deformity, she later took to wearing long, colorful skirts, which enhanced her exotic appearance, as did her trademark unibrow. At age fifteen she enrolled in the prestigious Escuela National Preparatoria, where she developed her passion for communism and met her larger-than-life love.

Frida's destiny, Diego Maria de la Concepción Juan Nepomuceno Estanislao de la Rivera y Barrientos Acosta y Rodríguez and his twin, Carlos, were born in Guanajuato, Mexico, in 1886. When his brother died less than two years later, Diego began drawing on every available surface, including the walls and furniture. In response, his father built him a studio with canvas-covered walls. In 1897 Diego began studying painting at the San Carlos Academy of Fine Art in Mexico City. Prior to graduation Rivera was expelled for leading a student protest against the reelection of President Porfirio Diaz, whose official title was a euphemism for a dictator, of the nonbenevolent variety.

In 1907, offered a scholarship by the Vera Cruz governor, Diego left to study art in Europe. In France he was befriended by the Impressionist painters and continued to pursue his leftist ideals. A man of gargantuan appetites (his six-foot-one frame carried three hundred pounds), his cravings extended to women. Angelina Beloff, a Russian artist, was his first wife, which resulted in the birth of his son Diego, who died at fourteen months in the influenza epidemic. During his marriage he had conducted an affair with another Russian artist, Marevna Vorobieff. The relationship ended when Marevna, then pregnant with their daughter Marika, cut Rivera's neck with a knife and then her own. Her action was the death knell of their union, and he refused all further contact with both mother and daughter. He later wrote of her, "She gave me everything a woman can give to a man. In return, she received from me all the heartache and misery that a man can inflict upon a woman." Diego returned to his native country, determined that his art should be for the many and not for the privileged few; his story would be told on murals.

The first time Frida met Diego was when he was commissioned for a work entitled *Creation* at the Preparatoria. Although students were forbidden to enter the auditorium while Rivera was painting, Frida was undeterred. Rivera later recalled that he was on a scaffold when he saw a girl who possessed "unusual dignity and self-assurance, and there was a strange fire in her eyes." Kahlo, who was sixteen, was infatuated with the thirty-six-year-old Mexican Michelangelo, and, ambivalent about her burgeoning sexuality, took to playing pranks on the artist. She stole his lunch and soaped the steps by the stage where he worked. After he departed, she did not forget him and confided in a friend that she would have his baby "just as soon as I convince him to cooperate."

Two years later, while Frida was riding the bus to school, the driver approached a risky intersection and decided to take his chances. Seconds later, an electric trolley rammed into their vehicle, launching bodies everywhere. Frida received a number of life-threatening injuries, including a broken spinal column and a crushed foot; in addition, an iron handrail had impaled her pelvis. She later described her injury: "The handrail pierced me as the sword pierces the bull." And while in the hospital she stated, "Death dances around my bed at night." During her months-long convalescence in a full body cast, her father gave her paint and her mother ordered a portable easel and attached a mirror to the underside of her bed's canopy so she could be her own model. For the rest of her life, her canvases, filled with innumerable self-portraits, became her visual diary. She turned from her medical studies to art as a form of recovery.

As Frida began to regain mobility, she joined the Communist Party, influenced in part by her friendship with the young Italian photographer Tina Modotti. It was at Modotti's 1928 gathering where Kahlo remet Rivera. With his towering physique, he was hard to miss, even more so when he took out his pistol and for some reason, fired at the phonograph. Frida found this appealing and re-called that it was at that moment "that I began to be interested in him although I was afraid of him."

Shortly afterward, Frida took three of her paintings to the Minis-try of Education where Diego was working on a fresco; her tactic was equal part as an artist and as a woman. When she arrived, she called up to the scaffold on which he was standing and, with characteristic boldness, commanded Diego to come down. Diego's version of the encounter in his autobiography, *My Art, My Life*, states, "Just before I went to Cuernavaca, there occurred one of the happiest events in my life." He remembered the girl he had met earlier and said of her, "Her hair was long; dark and thick eyebrows met above her nose. They seemed like the wings of a blackbird, their black arches framing two extraordinary brown eyes." His assessment of her work was that she was an authentic artist. She countered that she had been warned Rivera would compliment her as a segue to seduction. They parted with Diego's promise to visit Casa Azul the following Sunday.

The next week, when he knocked at its door, he heard someone over his head; it was Frida, perched high in a tree, whistling "The Internationale." Years later, when separated in a crowd, Diego whis-tled the first bar of the song and from her whistling the second bar, they found each other. Rivera recalled, "I did not know it then, but Frida had already become the most important fact in my life. And she would continue to be, up to the moment she died, twenty-seven years later."

During the subsequent visit they kissed for the first time and he became a regular visitor. Her father, in the spirit of "Forewarned is forearmed," took Diego aside and cautioned him that his daughter was a devil, to which Rivera responded, "I know." Diego's second wife, Guadalupe Marin, with whom he had two daughters, was infuriated by Frida, whom she disparaged with the comment that the girl "drank tequila like a real mariachi." Her husband did not share her contempt and asked Frida to be his wife as soon as he was free of Guadalupe, of whom he had grown tired.

Frida's father approved of her match to the rich Rivera, especially as he knew she would have lifelong medical expenses. Her mother, however, was against Frida's marriage to a man twice her age, the father of three, and an avowed atheist. She refused to attend their August 21, 1929, wedding, declaring it a match between an elephant and a dove. The ceremony was conducted by the town mayor, who doubled as a pulque (a Mexican alcoholic drink) dealer, and through it Frida held a cigarette. During the festivity that followed, a vengeful Guadalupe appeared, lifted Frida's long skirt, and cried out, "You see these two sticks? These are the legs Diego has instead of mine!" The groom, in a drunken tequila-fueled binge, went on a rampage and the bride went home alone. A few days later he came for his wife. The events were to foreshadow the stormy, passionate relationship that followed, serving as the catalyst for many of Frida's portraits.

At the onset of their marriage Frida was content to be the great genius's spouse and brought him lunch in a basket decorated with flowers and love notes—both to show devotion and to ward off any alluring models, always prime temptations for Diego. She also later agreed to a San Angel residence that consisted of two separate homes connected by a bridge, as Diego felt a painter needed privacy.

However, although they shared important commonalities such as art, communism, patriotism, and mutual devotion, in many arenas they only agreed to disagree. Frida wanted children and Diego did not; she desired him to be faithful and he subscribed to "machismo." The child conflict was resolved when Frida, as a result of the trolley tragedy, was unable to bring her pregnancies to term, a fact that tore at her soul. However, the faithfulness issue proved to be the rub.

In 1934, Frida's younger sister, Christina, whose husband had abandoned her and her two children, became Diego's favorite model, and she began appearing in his murals. She also began appearing in his bed. Kahlo began to suspect that Rivera was having an affair; however, she never imagined that the other woman was her sister. In her anguish she cut off her long hair, which she knew her husband loved; of the double betrayal she said she felt "murdered by life." She took her favorite pet spider monkey and moved out of the house. Kahlo stated, "I suffered two grave accidents in my life. One in which a streetcar knocked me down and the other was Diego. Diego was by far the worse." They eventually divorced in 1939 but, emotionally destitute without one another, remarried the following year on December 8 (Diego's fifty-fourth birthday) in San Francisco. However, the paradigm in their marriage had now shifted: Frida embarked on her own affairs, with both men and women. One of these liaisons was with the African American Josephine Baker; another with Leon Trotsky, who was eventually assassinated with an ice pick by order of Stalin. Diego tolerated her trysts with women but became enraged at those with men; at one point he threatened one of her male lovers with his pistol.

By this time, Frida had also become a celebrated artist, no longer merely Mrs. Diego Rivera. Her hand, bedecked with rings, appeared on a cover of *Vogue*, and her painting was the first the Louvre purchased from a Mexican artist. Picasso, entranced, gave her earrings in the shape of hands.

In the spring of 1953, Kahlo had at last her one-person show in Mexico City. Bedridden following surgery in which her leg was amputated below her knee, she wanted to stage her final appearance. She dressed in her native costume and jewelry and arrived at her exhibit in an ambulance. Attendants carried her to her canopied bed, which had been transported from her home. The headboard was decorated with photographs of Rivera and papier-mâché skeletons. Surrounded by admirers, the elaborately costumed Frida held court. In his autobiography Diego remembered the exhibition: "For me, the most thrilling event of 1953 was Frida's one-man show. Anyone who attended it could not but marvel at her great talent. Even I was impressed when I saw all her work together." He also recalled that his great love hardly spoke. "I thought afterwards that she must have realized she was bidding good-bye to life." It was indeed what she had done, in her own signature style.

In 1954, Kahlo passed away where she had been born, in the Casa Azul, from either an embolism or suicide. Her last diary entry read, "I hope the end is joyful—and I hope never to come back. Frida." However, as she remains Mexico's most famous artist and a half of a legendary love affair, in a sense she never truly left.

Postscript

➤ After she died, Frida's body, clothed in Tehuana attire and laden with her trademark jewelry, lay in state in the foyer of the Palacio de Bellas Artes, where Diego spent the night at her side. By noon the next day more than six hundred mourners had passed by her coffin. Kahlo had stated that she did not want to be buried as she had already spent too much time lying down. Led by Diego, the mourners sang "The Internationale." Before she departed, Rivera kissed her forehead and mourners held on to her hands and removed her rings as mementos. A pre-Columbian urn holding her ashes is on display in the Casa Azul.

➤ Rivera passed away from heart failure in his San Angel studio. He had requested that he be cremated and his ashes commingled with those of Frida. However, Diego's family refused to respect his last wishes; he was buried in the Rotunda of Famous Men in Mexico City.

17

George Burns and Gracie Allen

1923

Vaudeville was the ticket that allowed aspiring hams such as the Marx Brothers, the Three Stooges, and Charlie Chaplin to showcase their talent. However, there was one to whom vaudeville not only brought acclaim; it allowed the entertainer to achieve a state of grace—through love.

The man who was to entertain America for a century, Nathan Birnbaum, was born on Pitt Street in New York, the ninth of twelve children of Polish Orthodox Jewish immigrants. His father worked sporadically as a cantor, and when he passed away Nattie (his nickname) quit school at age seven. He and some friends started the Peewee Quartet and sang in saloons, in brothels, on street corners, and on ferryboats.

At thirteen, he opened a school of dancing; most of the clients came from Ellis Island. He told them one of the requirements of becoming a U.S. citizen was a $5 course of dancing lessons. When he recounted this story he agreed it was dishonest but added, "Have you ever been hungry?"

As a teen he entered the vaudeville circuit and decided he needed to come up with a more theatrical name than Nathan Birnbaum. An idolized sibling had been born Isadore and, hating his nickname Izzy, changed it to George. His younger brother followed suit. "Burns" came from the Burns Brothers Coal Company—a company he used to steal from in order to heat his home.

George's destiny, Grace Ethel Cecile Rosalie Allen, was born in San Francisco to an Irish Catholic family. Her father went AWOL when she was five, leaving his wife and five children destitute; Grace never spoke of him. Allen first performed at age three at an Irish dance at a church social. She fell in love with the audience's applause, and every day, on her way home from the Star of the Sea Catholic School, she would walk from theater to theater, dreaming of the time when her picture would be posted in one. Grace felt that her ticket to show business success would have to be her talent, as she was insecure about her looks. When she was a child, glass fragments from an exploding hurricane lamp had left her with one eye that appeared green and the other that appeared blue. Another childhood mishap, in which a boiling pot landed on her, resulted in a severely scarred left arm.

When Grace was eighteen, she and her sisters began to work professionally and billed themselves as the Four Colleens. The group disbanded and she became part of an act for which she was paid $22 a week. This too did not lead to success, and finding herself unemployed and destitute in New York City, she enrolled in a stenography course.

Grace would have led a life of silent desperation, joylessly taking dictation, but fate, in the form of her roommate, Rena Arnold, intervened. When Rena heard that two entertainers were looking for new partners, she suggested that she and Grace catch their show.

The first time George met Gracie was when she and Rena went backstage, and Grace said her first words to her last love: "I liked your act." Burns recalled in his memoir of their initial encounter, *Gracie: A Love Story*, "Like Grace herself, her voice was unforgettable." Allen chose to partner with George, which pleased him, as he found her attractive and she did not mind his cigar smoke.

They launched a comedy duo, and the audience loved Grace's "illogical logic." George did as well: "Next to Gracie, I was wonderful. All I had to do was stand next to her and imagine some of the applause was for me." He said of her Dumb Dora act that Grace was smart enough to become the dumbest woman in show business history.

George said that there wasn't one moment where he looked at Grace and suddenly realized he was in love. He stated in his memoir, "Love is a lot like a backache, it doesn't show up on X rays, but you know it's there." However, Grace was engaged to a fellow entertainer, Benny Ryan. In the vein of "Hope springs eternal," George bought a wedding ring that he kept in his pocket in case Grace changed her mind. He said of the $20 band that it was very special: "The metal actually changed colors as it aged in my pocket." Unfortunately for Burns, the ring was not enough to change Gracie's mind.

On Christmas Eve, George was serving as a party's Santa Claus but was in a far from jolly mood. The reason for his irritability: Grace had arrived late because she had been waiting for a call from Benny. Burns presented Allen with his gift of a silver bracelet with a small diamond; her gift was a lounging robe with a card inscribed, "To Nattie, with all my love." When he snarled, "You don't even know what love means," she raced to the bathroom in tears. At three a.m., he received a call from Grace agreeing to marry him. She explained that when he made her cry she realized how much she loved him. He opined that if he had made her miserable sooner, he could have won her earlier. George said that the call was the second-best

Christmas present of his life. The best was when they slept together Christmas night.

The couple married on January 7, 1926, in Cleveland, Ohio; because of their different religions they were wed by a justice of the peace. As the judge was in a hurry to go fishing, the newlyweds' taxi cost only fifteen cents for waiting time.

George wrote of their union, "I have to be honest, I was a lousy lover. But Grace married me for laughs, not for sex. Of course, she got both of them—when we had sex, she laughed." Allen endeared herself to her in-laws by adopting his mother's favorite phrase, used whenever her son aggravated her: "Nattie, you're such a schmuck."

George's main "schmuck" moment occurred when the couple got in an argument. Grace wanted to purchase a $750 silver table centerpiece; George didn't want to buy one at any price. He stormed out and ended up having a one-night stand with a Las Vegas showgirl. Grace knew of his indiscretion, and George was aware that his wife had found out. Burns felt the situation more intolerable than if they had engaged in a full-blown fight. Stricken with guilt, George bought the centerpiece as well as a $10,000 diamond ring. Grace didn't bring up the affair until seven years later when she was in the silver department at Saks with Mary Benny (Jack's wife). She found a centerpiece she liked and said to her friend, "You know, I wish George would cheat again. I really need a new centerpiece."

In contrast, George's finest moment occurred after he had been married for twenty-five years. They were in bed when Grace said that the nicest thing about him was that he had never mentioned her withered arm. His response, "Which arm is the bad one?"

While George was known as "Nattie," Grace too had a nickname. Once, in the middle of the night, she elbowed her sleeping spouse and asked him to make her laugh. Half asleep, he mumbled, "Googie, googie, googie." Henceforth that was his wife's pet name.

The couple's comedy success led to radio spots, and in 1940 the comedy duo's routine revolved around Allen running for president. In one of her "campaign speeches" she joked, "I don't know much about the Land-Lease Bill, but if we owe it we should pay it." Another line, "Everybody knows a woman is better than a man when it comes to introducing bills into the house." She actually drew votes in the November election.

During George and Grace's nineteen years in radio, they had an audience of 45 million and a salary of $9,000 a week. As always, George deflected fame from himself to his beloved: "I'm the brains and Gracie is everything else, especially to me." In 1950, they transitioned to television where they played themselves in a CBS series; in the wrap-up to each episode, Burns would look at Allen and say, "Say good night, Gracie," to which she would turn to the audience and simply respond, "Good night."

Unable to have children because of her health (she had a congenital heart condition), the Burnses adopted a daughter, Sandra Jean, and a son, Ronald John; they agreed to raise them as Catholics with the hope that when they were adults they would decide on which religion was the right one for them. With their two children, thriving career, and a stream of friends including Jack Benny and Fred Astaire visiting their home, 720 North Maple Drive was a happy place to be. George commented on his relationship, "She made me famous as the only man in America who could get a laugh by complaining, 'My wife understands me.'" Grace was never at a loss for the wisecrack herself. She said of her spouse, "My husband will never chase another woman. He's too fine, too decent, too old."

Grace suffered the first symptoms of a heart condition in the early 1950s, and eight years later, she retired. During her final performance, George said, "Say good night, Gracie," for the last time. The event made the cover of *Life* magazine. George remarked of their partnership, "The audience realized I had a talent. They were right. I did have a talent—and I was married to her for thirty-eight years." George tried to shoulder on alone, but the program folded within the year. He said, "The show had everything it needed to be successful, except Gracie."

After waging a battle with heart disease, Grace Allen suffered a heart attack in her home in 1964 at age sixty-nine. At the hospital the doctor asked Burns if he wanted to see Grace one last time. He replied, "Of course I did. I wanted to stand next to her onstage and hear the audience laugh. I wanted to hear that birdlike voice. I wanted her to look up at me with her trusting eyes."

Although they were millionaires many times over, at her death, Grace still wore the $20 wedding band that George had given her four decades earlier; like her spouse, it had been irreplaceable. George recounted of Grace's death: "For the first time in forty years I was alone. So I did the only thing there was to do. I leaned over and I kissed her on the lips." He said his last words to his first love: "I love you, Googie." George was left to shoulder on—sans Grace.

Postscript

➤ Gracie Allen was entombed in a mausoleum; the inscription on her crypt reads *Good night, Gracie.*

➤ In 1996, at age 100, Burns died in his Beverly Hills home of cardiac arrest. He was buried in his best dark blue suit, light blue shirt, and red tie. In his pocket were three cigars, his toupee, his watch that Grace had given him, his ring, his keys, and his wallet with ten hundred-dollar bills, a five, and three ones.

➤ Upon his interment with Grace, the crypt's marker was changed to read *Gracie Allen and George Burns—Together Again.* Grace is buried in the chamber above his because George said he always wanted Grace to have top billing.

18

Jean-Paul Sartre and Simone de Beauvoir

1929

*T*he existentialist "it" couple, Jean-Paul Sartre and Simone de Beauvoir, conducted their unorthodox romance against the backdrop of 1920s Parisian cafés, often with Picasso and one of his mistresses at the next table. During their tête-à-têtes the two discoursed upon events both personal and global. However, the topic upon which they most philosophized was their relationship, one of the most controversial in the history of literary lore.

The man who was to become renowned as half of France's greatest intellectual couple was Jean-Paul Sartre, the only child of a woman who, having lost her husband, lavished all her attention on her son. His wealthy mother was the former Anne-Marie Schweitzer, a great-niece of the famed Albert Schweitzer.

From an early age two traits were to define the boy's life: his genius and his appearance, which he felt was Quasimodo's own. He was five feet two and walleyed, and he wore thick glasses. Moreover, his skin and teeth indicated an indifference to hygiene. Not surprisingly, he identified strongly with the tale of Beauty and the Beast. As soon as Jean-Paul could, he escaped his school, where he was its outcast, and headed for Paris to study at the École Normale Supérieure, while simultaneously taking classes at the Sorbonne. In France's most eminent universities he distinguished himself as much by his brilliance as by his antics; he attended one student ball in the nude and another on the arm of a prostitute clad in a flaming-red dress.

Jean-Paul's destiny, Simone Lucie Ernestine Marie Bertrand de Beauvoir, was born in a Left Bank apartment in Paris to a *bas bleu* (bluestocking) family that had an aristocratic ancestry but very little in the way of finances. Another problem for the family was Simone's father, George, who began sleeping with his friends' wives and visiting brothels. His fanatically Roman Catholic wife abhorred his behavior, and violent fights ensued. From this situation Simone originated her philosophy, *"Chez l'homme, l'habitude tue le desir"* ("With men, habit kills desire").

Simone's lack of dowry made marriage uncertain and, needing to make her own way in the world, she enrolled in the Sorbonne. It would turn out to be an adventure that would shape not just her destiny, but that of her milieu. And in it, she'd meet the man who was to become the love of her life.

The two brilliant students heard of one another, and Sartre, in the hope of an introduction, sent Simone a drawing of Leibniz (the subject of her thesis) accompanied by an invitation to a group study session.

The first time Simone met Jean-Paul was on June 8 in Sartre's room at the Cité Universitaire. For the meeting, Sartre wore the least-soiled shirt he possessed and slippers; his room was in shambles. As soon as she started to expound on Leibniz, the group declared the topic boring and broke into a discussion on Rousseau. Nevertheless, the two had found their soul mates, which Simone was to refer to as "their twinness." So attuned were they to one another, they took to finishing one another's sentences. Sartre never forgot his first impression of Simone: "I think she's beautiful. I have always found her beautiful, even though she was wearing a hideous little hat when I met her for the first time. The miracle of Simone de Beauvoir is that she has the intelligence of a man and the sensitivity of a woman. In other words, she is everything I could want."

Despite their existentialist studies they were not beyond nicknames: Sartre was "the Kobra" and Simone was "the Beaver" (because of its similarity to the name Beauvoir). From her journal it was apparent that the Beaver was equally smitten: "Sartre corresponded exactly to the dream-companion I had longed for since I was fifteen: he was the double in whom I found all my burning aspiration raised to the pitch of incandescence."

A few days after their meeting, Simone and Jean-Paul raced to their universities to discover the results of their *agrégation*, the fiercely competitive exam. At age twenty-one, Simone was the youngest person ever to pass in philosophy and only the ninth woman to have done so. The only one whose results surpassed her own was Sartre. This was to set a pattern; for the rest of her life de Beauvoir believed she was second only to Sartre.

In October the inseparable couple strolled beside the pond in Paris's Luxembourg Gardens, which were graced with the stone statues of the queens of French history. However, Sartre's mind was not on the past, but on the future, which he wanted to spend with Simone. There, Jean-Paul, the more conventional of the two, proposed. Simone told him "not to be silly," and reminded him that he had condemned marriage as "a despicable bourgeois institution." Sartre, ever the thinker, came up with a "romantic" compromise. "What we have is an essential love; but it's good if we both experience contingent affairs." The crux of his offer was that they would both have the freedom to experience affairs with other people while remaining committed emotionally to each other. Moreover, as part of their arrangement they would conceal nothing of any liaisons from one another. His philosophical proposal had the same effect on Simone as a diamond ring has on other women. They pledged undying troth, existentialist style. The date of their agreement, October 14, 1929, became their "wedding anniversary"; the pact forever barred the door marked *normal*. Their legendary union made them pioneers of the sexual revolution, and although their unique pact lasted for half a century, it was to carry carnage in its wake. If the couple expected their arrangement to spare them the heartaches of a conventional marriage, they were sorely mistaken.

After graduation, Sartre obtained a teaching position in Le Havre and de Beauvoir obtained one in Marseilles, and the two lost no time in turning their pact into reality. It was at her post that Simone began an affair with a Jewish student, Bianca Bienenfeld, who had the misfortune of escaping from anti-Semitic Poland only to find herself in a France that was soon to be occupied by the Nazis. Simone subsequently introduced Bianca to Jean-Paul, who ended up taking her to a hotel, and, after some resistance, as Bianca had never slept with a man, she succumbed to his advances. Soon after, at Simone's prompting, they both broke up with Bianca, which, when compounded with the Nazi invasion, led to a major nervous breakdown. De Beauvoir and Sartre justified their actions as part of their ideology, which was embodied in Dostoyevsky's quotation, "If God is dead, than everything is permitted." Inevitably the two would always gravitate to one another, wherein they subjected their sexual escapades to a postgame analysis over drinks at a café.

In between their numerous couplings, the couple turned their philosophies into books, which were always edited with each other's help. De Beauvoir's greatest work was *The Second Sex*. In it she argued, *"On ne nait pas femme; on le deviant"* ("One is not born, but rather becomes, a woman"). With its publication, de Beauvoir's scandalous reputation was sealed. She was considered even more outrageous than her cross-dressing female author predecessors George Sand and Colette. The book was promptly blacklisted by the Vatican.

However, it was in her memoirs where she truly entered the confessional of her and Sartre's relationship, and they proved that the woman who publicly declared she was immune to jealousy actually writhed in it in private. It would have been far better for Simone's emotional equilibrium had Sartre left much unsaid; honesty did not prove their best policy.

Sartre's first published book was titled *Nausea*. Its dedication read: *To the Beaver*. In 1964 he was awarded the Nobel Prize for literature on his book titled *Words*; however, he declined the award on the premise that the award was too bourgeois and would therefore compromise his intellectual integrity. His public statement on his refusal: "The writer must refuse to allow himself to be transformed into an institution."

Together de Beauvoir and Sartre traveled the world and met the famous: Roosevelt, Khrushchev, Camus, Picasso, Castro, and Che Guevara. Despite the ever-changing carousel of partners, the couple remained committed to their pact and one another. In tribute to them, the Hotel Mistral on France's Rue de Cels has a large plaque in front, stating that the legendary couple stayed there on several occasions during the war. Under Sartre's name is a quotation from a letter he had written to de Beauvoir: "There is one thing that hasn't changed and cannot change: that is that no matter what happens and what I become, I will become it with you." De Beauvoir made a statement that is equally emotionally revealing: "Our relationship was the greatest achievement of my life." At the end, the only thing that could sever their souls was death.

For years Sartre had subsisted mainly on a regime of vast quantities of coffee, whiskey, cigarettes, sleeping pills, and the drug corydrane (a combination of aspirin and amphetamines), which enabled him to maintain his frenetic regime of writing, and in March 1980, when Simone went to wake up Jean-Paul, she found him gasping for breath. He was diagnosed as suffering from pulmonary edema, caused by hypertension, and was rushed to the hospital. As de Beauvoir was hovering over his bed, while his eyes were closed, Sartre took her by the wrist. He then said his last words to his first love: "I love you very much, my dear Beaver." The twin was left alone.

Simone crawled under the sheet to spend one final night with Jean-Paul. The epitaph she wrote for the burial plot they would one day share said, "His death separates us, my death will not unite us. This is how things are. It is enough that our lives were in harmony for so long."

Postscript

↠ After Jean-Paul passed away, the streets of Montparnasse and Saint-Germain were packed with fifty thousand people who had come to pay their last respects. De Beauvoir was chewing on Valium tablets as if they were throat lozenges.

↠ When the casket arrived at Montparnasse Cemetery, Simone, dressed in black trousers and a sunset-colored turban, climbed out of her car, at which the onlookers burst into applause. Because of the crush of the crowds, someone fell into the open grave. For ten minutes de Beauvoir sat beside the grave staring at the coffin, clutching a rose and weeping. When the undertakers picked up their shovels, she dropped the rose onto the coffin. On the way out she collapsed onto a tombstone.

↠ This was not Sartre's final resting place; five days later he was taken to the Pere-Lachaise Cemetery to be cremated. Then his ashes were returned to the Montparnasse Cemetery. De Beauvoir was too weak to attend the cremation.

→ Simone passed away on April 14, 1986, six years after Sartre, almost to the day, also from pulmonary edema. More than five thousand people followed her hearse through the streets of Montparnasse. Simone was laid to rest with Sartre. There are always fresh bouquets of flowers on their tomb.

19

King Edward VIII and Wallis Simpson

1930

*A*s with most girls raised on "Once upon a time," Bessie Warfield dreamed of one day marrying a handsome prince who would carry her off to the realm of happily-ever-after. In a twist on this tale, she did end up with the prince, albeit one who relinquished his kingdom for the sake of his true-life princess.

Bessie Warfield was born in Blue Ridge Summit, Pennsylvania, an inauspicious start for the woman who was to send shock waves of scandal throughout the British Empire. Her father died five months after his only child's birth, and to make ends meet, her mother took in boarders and depended on the largesse of a wealthy uncle, Solomon Warfield. Despite her straitened circumstances, Bessie was spoiled by her widowed parent, and her first words were "me me," as opposed to "mama." From a young age she had a desire for high society and named her dolls Mrs. Astor and Mrs. Vanderbilt. Believing the name Bessie was more suitable for a cow than an aspiring socialite, she adopted her more genteel middle name, Wallis. During an argument over her coming-out party, she fought with her uncle, who not only did not throw her a reception, he cut her out of his will.

Wallis's first foray into wedlock was with Earl Winfield Spencer, who passed himself off as the son of wealth. After the nuptials, she discovered that Spencer's background was a fabrication; in reality he was a U.S. navy pilot who was later stationed in the Far East. Wallis joined him there, and while visiting Peking she discovered ancient Asian sex secrets, which were later to stand her in good stead.

Her second marriage was to the British Ernest Aldrich Simpson, a shipping executive, who left his wife for her. In England, Wallis's youthful aspirations would soon come true beyond her wildest dreams.

Edward Albert Christian George Andrew Patrick David, of the House of Windsor, was baptized by the Archduke of Canterbury in England. As the eldest son of King George V and the great-grandson of Queen Victoria, he was born with the bluest of blood in his veins and the silverest of spoons in his mouth. Edward became the Prince of Wales on his sixteenth birthday, and from that time he was groomed to be king of Great Britain, Ireland, and the British Dominions beyond the Seas, and Emperor of India. His impeccable pedigree, good looks, charm, wealth, and prestige made him the most photographed celebrity of his era, as well as the world's most eligible bachelor. However, Edward's compulsive womanizing dismayed his protocol-conscious parents, and they were soon to discover just how loose a cannon the royal heir could be.

The first time Wallis met Edward was on January 10, when his mistress, Lady Thelma Furness, introduced them at her country home in Leicestershire, where the Simpsons had been invited as her houseguests. Wallis later recalled that she was taken with Edward's "slightly wind-rumpled hair, the turned-up nose, and a strange, wistful, almost sad look about the eyes when his expression was in repose." In his memoirs Edward writes that when he first met Wallis, she was suffering from a bad cold. He asked her if she missed American central heating, to which she replied, "I'm sorry, Sir, but you have disappointed me. Every American woman who comes to your country is always asked that same question. I had hoped for something more original from the Prince of Wales."

In 1934, Lady Furness needed to go to New York to support her sister in a custody battle over her daughter, Gloria Vanderbilt, and she asked Wallis, over a luncheon at the Ritz, for a favor in regard to her royal lover: "Look after the little man. See that he does not get into any mischief." Thelma viewed Wallis as unattractive and therefore not a threat, but soon after the lunch, Thelma discovered the naiveté of her beliefs.

Lady Simpson became the prince's ever-present shadow; a special branch of the police trailed them and reported "that the lady seemed to have POW [Prince of Wales] completely under her thumb." A besotted Edward said, "In character, Wallis was, and still remains, complex and elusive, and from the first I looked upon her as the most independent woman I had ever met. This refreshing trait I was inclined to put down as one of the happiest outcomes of 1776."

For Wallis's part, the prince proved the open sesame to a world she had always longed to enter. She said, "Yachts materialized; the best suites in the finest hotels were flung open; airplanes stood waiting . . . it was like being Wallis in Wonderland." Their love affair assumed critical mass with the death of King George when his son ascended the throne. Three months after his succession, he expressed his desire to marry Mrs. Simpson as soon as her divorce came through. The queen mother refused to accept his choice of bride and referred to Wallis as "that woman." Prime Minister Stanley Baldwin declared that the British people would never countenance a twice-divorced American woman as their queen; moreover, as the king was head of the Church of England, it would also be against its precepts for him to marry a divorcée. Edward's choice was clear: take a suitable bride or abdicate.

If Edward gave up the throne, it would mean renouncing his family, who would not forgive the royal scandal. He was informed that if he ever were to enter Britain without an invitation, his stipend would be terminated. Moreover, from age sixteen he had been trained for his royal role; he knew no other. The official motto of the Prince of Wales is the German motto *"Ich dien"* ("I serve"), and therefore his betrayal of his family extended to the betrayal of his countrymen. Despite these pressures, on December 11, 1936, Edward made his worldwide broadcast: "I have found it impossible to carry the heavy burden of responsibility and to discharge my duties as king as I would wish without the help and the support of the woman I love." Surprisingly, Wallis did not want the abdication, offering rather to assume the role of royal mistress. She explained, "How can a woman be a whole empire to a man?"

To commemorate Wallis's coup of having a royal abdicate on her behalf, *Time* named her "Woman of the Year," the first occasion the magazine had ever given its "Man of the Year" title to a woman. The man who would not be king, the newly titled Duke of Windsor, gave his fiancée an engagement ring with a massive 19.77-karat Mogul emerald with the inscription *WE are ours now*. (The *W* stood for Wallis, the *E* for Edward.) The couple married on June 3, 1937, at Chateau de Cande, France. The new king, George VI, forbade any members of the royal family to attend. The queen mother never changed her view of her despised daughter-in-law and forever maintained, "To give up all this for that." Proof of the spell their romance cast on the world: In 1998 Sotheby's sold, for $29,000, a slice of the couple's wedding cake in a box marked "A piece of our wedding cake WE WE 3-VI-37." Winston Churchill called their romance "one of the great loves of history."

For her part, the newly created Duchess of Windsor took as her maxim, "Never explain, never complain." Wallis later told writer Gore Vidal that the morning after her nuptials, she woke to find her husband "standing beside the bed, saying, 'And now what shall we do?'" For their honeymoon they spent time in Venice, where they attended a performance of *Romeo and Juliet*. As they entered, the audience rose to its feet and roared, *"Viva l'amore!"*

The duke and duchess did not have a common love story, nor was their world a common one. They lived in baronial splendor and assumed the role of social royalty who were invited to the grandest soirees of the world. Their own dinner parties were never-to-be-forgotten events; one fortunate guest stated, "An invitation from the Duchess was like a gift from God." They never had any children but were always surrounded by their adored pugs, who dined from silver bowls, were sprayed with Christian Dior perfume, and wore mink, diamond-studded collars, and gold Cartier leashes.

In the 1930s, as the Nazi storm clouds gathered over Europe, people welcomed the romance of the duke and his duchess, a true-life fairy tale in which a king relinquished his empire because it meant nothing without the woman he loved.

Postscript

→ Edward passed away in 1972 at his home in Paris. His body was returned from exile and he was laid in state in Windsor Castle. In attendance at the funeral were his niece, Queen Elizabeth II; the royal family, and his wife, the Duchess of Windsor. It concluded with a blessing given by the Archbishop of Canterbury. Eight soldiers from the Welsh Guard carried his coffin draped with the duke's personal standard. He was laid to rest in the Royal Mausoleum of Queen Victoria and Prince Albert at Frogmore.

➻ Wallis passed away fourteen years later in her Parisian home and was brought to London for the burial. One hundred guests, including Prime Minister Margaret Thatcher, Queen Elizabeth, and Prince Philip, as well as the entire royal family, were in attendance for the simple funeral service. Her tombstone bears the inscription "Wallis, Duchess of Windsor."

20

Clark Gable and Carole Lombard

1932

When the king of the silver screen fell for the queen of screwball comedy, their romance tugged at the collective strings of Hollywood's heart. Although their years together were few, their love story remains an iconic one from cinema's Golden Age.

Jane Alice Peters was born in Fort Wayne, Indiana, in 1908. After her parents divorced, her mother took Jane and her two brothers to Los Angeles. Protective of their younger sister, her siblings taught her to swear as a verbal shield to fend off unwelcome suitors. She made her film debut at age twelve after a director saw her playing baseball in the street. A natural ham, she dropped out of school at age fifteen to pursue an acting career. Two years later she was signed by Fox Studios; her main assets were her high cheekbones and figure, which she wore to perfection in her trademark clingy gowns. She borrowed the name Lombard from a family friend, as she thought it had more allure than her own. After a devastating car accident, she was dropped by Fox and began working for Mack Sennett, where the legendary director of slapstick helped Carole develop her superb comic timing. The Hoosier became known in Hollywood as "the profane angel" because of the juxtaposition of her flawless face and expert command of four-letter words.

Carole's destiny, William Clark Gable, was born in Ohio; his mother passed away when he was ten months old. He enjoyed hunting; however, he also enjoyed reciting Shakespeare. At age sixteen he was talked into traveling to Akron with a friend to work at a tire factory. It was in Ohio that Gable saw his first play and was hooked. He found work acting in a theatrical company until it folded. His net worth: twenty-six cents. Hopping freight trains, he piled logs, sold neckties, and became a telephone repairman. One of the last phones he fixed was at a theater, where he met Josephine Dillon, seventeen years his senior, a woman who was to be more of a mother figure than a wife. The two headed to Hollywood, where he hoped to break into movies.

While his marriage began to deteriorate, his career picked up momentum; he appeared in regional theater, in road shows, and as an extra in the movies. A 1930 Los Angeles stage production made the studios take notice, though many producers felt that Gable's ears would prove an impediment to success as a leading man. Two years later Clark had attained such heartthrob status that "Who do you think you are—Clark Gable?" became a standard put-down. One of his first reviews raved, "He's young, vigorous and brutally masculine." Gable's off-screen persona mirrored his on-screen persona, and his penchant for sleeping with any woman with a heartbeat led to the demise of his marriage to Josephine. A few days after his divorce came through, he married Texas socialite Ria Langham, a widow ten years his senior.

In 1932, Clark received a contract with MGM and starred in *Possessed* opposite Joan Crawford (then married to Douglas Fairbanks Jr.), in which they steamed up the room, both onscreen and off. Journalist Adela Rogers St. Johns deemed the relationship "the affair that nearly burned Hollywood down." However, it was Gable's unshaven lovemaking with braless Jean Harlow in *Red Dust* that put him on Hollywood's radar. Knowing he was box-office gold for those who possessed estrogen, he was cast as the lead in *It Happened One Night*. In one scene he took off his shirt to reveal his bare chest. This gesture touched off a crisis among undershirt manufacturers. It also earned him the title "King of Hollywood."

The first time Carole met Clark was when they were both hired to star in a Paramount production of *No Man of Her Own*. At the time, Lombard was married to actor William Powell, and though the marriage was rocky, she still entertained hopes of it lasting. Dorothy Mackaill, who portrayed Gable's onscreen discarded mistress, re-called a flare-up between Carole and Clark that ensued when Carole saw the leading man, on loan from MGM, under his studio's direc-tive, wearing a Hoover button. Lombard, objecting to his choice of candidate, ripped it off his lapel and told him he could "shove it up L. B. Mayer's ass." Clark, who felt that women should act like ladies, was not impressed. The feeling was mutual—at the final-day party, Lombard gave Gable a ten-pound smoked ham with his photograph pasted on the packaging. However, despite previous tensions, before they parted, they did so with a hug and farewell kiss.

Four years later Lombard (then divorced) organized the Mayfair Ball in Beverly Hills; for its theme she requested that the women dress in white gowns and the men in white tie and tails. When Norma Shearer entered, clad in crimson, Lombard wanted to de-mand her expulsion, but columnist Louella Parsons was able to dis-suade her.

William Randolph Hearst and Marion Davies brought along Gable (then estranged from Ria), and when he saw Carole, clad in a complimentary white gown, he approached her with words from *No Man of Her Own*: "I go for you, Ma." She responded, "I go for you too,

Pa." They began to dance, during which Gable held Carole so tightly he realized she was wearing nothing under her clinging silk dress. When Carole noticed his arousal she began to laugh, causing Gable to turn red. Lombard suggested they have a drink so he could calm down, but Gable proposed an alternative: a ride in his new $16,000 Duesenberg convertible. After his third circling of the Beverly Wiltshire Hotel, he asked if she'd like to see his room. Lombard, with her trademark sarcasm, responded, "Who do you think you are—Clark Gable?" It spoiled the moment and they returned to the ball.

Upon their arrival, actor Lyle Talbot made a comment about their absence, and Lombard had to restrain Gable from punching him. Then, spying the lady in red, Carole wanted to ask a waiter to dump a tray of dirty dishes on her. Clark had to restrain her. This led to an argument and his angry departure.

The next morning Gable awoke to a white dove perched on his chest and another on the chandelier. When he caught one, tied to its leg was the message, "How about it? Carole." She had bribed a hotel employee to plant the birdcage in his room while he slept. Later he received a note that a present would be arriving at nine p.m., which he assumed was from Carole. However, when he opened his door, standing at the other side in a long mink coat, carrying two bottles of champagne, was actress Merle Oberon. Not one to look a gift horse in the mouth (especially when the horse looked like Oberon), Gable embarked on an affair with her.

In February Oberon and Gable attended a party at J. H. Whitney's mansion to celebrate a friend's release from a psychiatric hospital. The festivity came to an abrupt halt when an ambulance pulled up and medics carried in a stretcher bearing Lombard. With a horrified crowd surrounding her, she suddenly sat up and began to laugh. Clark's face registered his disapproval of her gag, to which she muttered, "I always knew Gable was a stuffed shit—I mean shirt." Clark was about to storm off when she stood up, revealing her figure sheathed in a white gown. He informed her that she needed a psychiatrist, and she countered that he had lost his sense of humor married to a woman old enough to be his mother.

After the party, when Gable arrived at MGM he found Carole's belated Valentine Day mea culpa: an old white Model T with painted large red hearts. A note was attached to its steering wheel: "You're driving me crazy." In response, he invited her to dinner at the Café Trocadero. Though Carole may have anticipated Gable pulling up in the Duesenberg, the pair chugged along at ten miles an hour in the Valentine car.

During this time the actress became engrossed in the novel *Gone with the Wind* and envisioned Clark and herself playing Rhett and Scarlett. She sent it to Clark with the inscription, "Let's do it!" He immediately took it as a sexual invitation and phoned her that evening.

Carole had worried about succumbing to Clark's Casanova charms (when Gable left his hand and foot imprints on the Grauman's Chinese Theater forecourt, Lombard quipped that he should have imprinted his "cockprint" as well). However, realizing that his feelings for her were genuine, she allowed herself to lower her romantic resistances. And amazingly enough, the love that resulted was that Hollywood rarity: the real thing. Although Lombard didn't become Scarlett, when Clark's divorce came through, she ended up getting an equally coveted role: that of his wife.

Lombard was dreading a wedding that would resemble a "fucking circus," and during a few days' break on *Gone with the Wind*, they drove to a town hall in Arizona. On June 26, 1931, the clerk on duty stared in disbelief at the Hollywood legends; during the ceremony the bride cried nonstop. When they returned to their Bel Air estate, news of the nuptials between Hollywood's king and queen had leaked, and six MGM guards surrounded their estate. Carole told the press, "I'll let Pa be the star, and I'll stay home, darn the socks, and look after the kids."

Preferring life away from their glittering court, they purchased a ranch in Encino, whose gabled roof led to its moniker "the House of the Two Gables." Gable brought with them a host of pets, including the offspring of the two doves from the post–Mayfair Ball morning. Clark said of his wife, "You can trust that little screwball with your life or your hopes or your weaknesses, and she wouldn't even know how to think about letting you down." There they lovingly referred to each other as Ma and Pa; the only blight on their happiness was their lack of a baby.

In 1942, Clark received a request from Indiana for a star to promote war bonds, and he naturally offered the services of his Hoosier-born wife. He wanted to accompany her but could not because of his work on *Somewhere I'll Find You,* so Carole took her mother. Before she left, she gave her secretary sealed envelopes to be given to Clark each day of her absence. In their bed she placed a naked blond dummy with a tag tied around its neck: "So you won't be lonely." To even the score he obtained a male dummy, replete with a huge erect phallus, as a surprise gift for his wife's arrival home. Lombard was to return by train; however, eager to be reunited with Gable as soon as possible, she insisted on a plane, something her superstitious mother was against. They ended the impasse with a toss of a coin; Carole won.

In anticipation of "Ma's" return, Clark decorated their ranch with red, white, and blue balloons; however, he soon received the devastating news that Carole's plane had crashed near Las Vegas. Gable flew to the scene and had to be forcibly restrained from climbing the mountainside in an effort to rescue her. There were no survivors.

Distraught, Gable felt that as his wife had given her life for her country, he should do the same and he enlisted in the army. When he returned to the now-ironically named home, the House of the Two Gables, it echoed his loneliness, bereft of his profane angel.

Postscript

→ When Lombard died, in Hollywood every studio paused at noon for the playing of "Taps" and two minutes of silence in her honor. MGM placed full-page ads in which its trademark, Leo the Lion, dressed in mourning, stood with his head bowed; in his paw he held a large wreath.

→ Carole Lombard was interred in her white gown. The name on her crypt marker: Carole Lombard Gable.

→ When Clark Gable passed away in 1960 from a heart attack, all the Hollywood studios flew their flags at half staff. On his casket perched a crown made of miniature red roses. At the conclusion of his service, the Air Force Band played "Taps." He was laid to rest in the crypt next to Carole Lombard.

21

Desi Arnaz and Lucille Ball

1940

*I*n the 1950s, a favorite escape from the twin threats of communism and McCarthyism was to tune in to the antics of the country's zaniest housewife. However, while America loved Lucy, the
person behind the *I* of the show's name was the staff, support, and
soul mate of the iconic redhead.

The man who was to break television's color barrier, Desiderio
Alberto Arnaz y de Acha III, was born in Santiago, Cuba, the scion of
prestige. His maternal grandfather was a founder of Bacardi Rum; his
paternal grandfather was the doctor assigned to Teddy Roosevelt's
Rough Riders after their ride up San Juan Hill. But the privileged
life of his ancestors was not destined to be his. Desiderio's life was
derailed with Batista's revolution, and the family fled to Florida. To
save money, the family lived in a warehouse and subsisted on cans of
pork and beans; baseball bats warded off the rats.

Despite his fall down the social strata, Desiderio was a survivor
who quickly learned English and made American friends, including

his best buddy, Al Capone Jr. While still in high school, armed with a pawnshop guitar, Desiderio (known as "Desi") auditioned for a band with his piece "Babalu." He had practice with the instrument from serenading señoritas back in Cuba and was hired. Desi began his career for $39 a week at the Roney Plaza Hotel. In 1937 he started his own band in Miami Beach and helped launch the conga craze that swept over America. As acclaim spread, he was offered a role in *Too Many Girls* as the Latin lover.

The woman who became famous for making millions laugh was born into a Baptist family in Jamestown, New York. The great tragedy of Lucille's childhood was the death of her father when his wife was four months pregnant with their second child, Fred. Her grandfather, similarly named Fred, stepped in as her male role model, and as such took her to vaudeville shows and fostered her innate love of theater. When Lucille fell for the bad boy, a gangster's son, Johnny DeVita, her mother agreed to send the sixteen-year-old to the John Murray Anderson American Academy of Dramatic Art in Manhattan. Unlike Bette Davis, who was the school's shining star, Lucille left after a few weeks when her drama coaches informed her she "had no future at all as a performer." However, the word *no* was not part of Lucille's lexicon, and she eventually obtained work as a Goldwyn Girl in Hollywood. Her destiny would have remained that of a minor starlet except for an encounter that would make her one half of America's most beloved couple.

The first time Desi met Lucille was at RKO, one of the five big studios from Hollywood's Golden Age. She was dressed for a scene involving a catfight with Maureen O'Hara, which led to Desi's remark that she looked "like a two-dollar whore who had been badly beaten by her pimp." Later that afternoon Lucille happened to stroll by, sans costume, and Desi's first words to her were "Would you like me to teach you how to rumba? It may come in handy for your part in the picture." She accepted his invitation to join him at a Mexican restaurant, where they had dinner, danced, and drank. Lucille later recalled of their meeting, "It wasn't love at first sight. It took a full five minutes."

The following Sunday Desi and a date attended a Malibu party, where he decided to take a solitary stroll, on which he saw Lucille sitting alone on the beach. Desi later recalled, "I did not go back to the Hollywood Roosevelt. I went to Lucille's apartment, and that was our first night together." Six months later Desi and Lucy eloped to Connecticut, where they married on November 30, 1940. Lucy said of her nuptials, "My friends gave the marriage six months. I gave it six weeks." Because of the haste, they had to settle with a wedding ring purchased at the last minute from Woolworths; she wore it all through her marriage. The new wife did not change only her surname. In his autobiography, Arnaz explained, "I didn't like the name 'Lucille.' That name had been used by other men. 'Lucy' was mine alone."

Much to Lucille's unhappiness, holy matrimony did nothing to curtail Desi's amorous flings. The Arnazes had lived together for four years when Lucy, convinced of his serial infidelity, filed for divorce. However, they reconciled and returned to Desilu, their five-acre ranchito in California. In 1949 the couple renewed their vows, this time in a Catholic church to compensate for their earlier civil ceremony. They hoped this would help bring the children they both desperately wanted. However, an ongoing impediment was Desi's constant absences as he toured with his band. Lucy lamented about this situation, "You can't have a baby on the phone."

Eager to find a project that would keep her husband home, and faithful, Lucy became interested in CBS's offer of a television version of the radio show she was performing in, *My Favorite Husband*. However, the network vetoed her idea of Desi as her co-star. They thought of him as "just that bongo player." Moreover, executive Hubbell Robinson felt that American audiences would not be receptive to a show involving an interracial couple. The studio executives were concerned that an audience would not believe she was married to the man who, in actuality, she was married to. Once more, the word *no* would be Lucille's response to their rejection. Later Ball would remark, "How *I Love Lucy* was born? We decided that instead of divorce lawyers profiting from our mistakes, we'd profit from them."

The year 1951 was a golden one for the Arnazes. In July, one month before Lucy's fortieth birthday, after several miscarriages, Ball gave birth to Lucie Désirée Arnaz, and on October 15 *I Love Lucy* debuted. For his wife's twenty-ninth birthday Desi had given her a diamond-encrusted heart-shaped watch, which became the show's logo. Lucy's role of the zany housewife led to Desi's oft-repeated remark, "Lucy, you got some 'splainin' to do!" Often, in frustration, he would revert to Spanish, as if it took him two languages to deal with his wife. However, at the close of every episode, no matter what, Ricky still loved Lucy.

A year and a half later, Ball gave birth to Desiderio Alberto Arnaz IV, and his arrival was written into the script. This was groundbreaking news, as CBS had never before permitted a pregnant woman to even appear on TV. The event made the first cover of *TV Guide* in January 1953, and more people viewed the birth of "Little Ricky" than tuned in to the inauguration of President Eisenhower.

In 1953 Lucille found herself in a far more serious scrape than her fictitious counterpart ever did: She was subpoenaed by the House Un-American Activities Committee. Immediately before the filming of episode 68 of *I Love Lucy*, Desi informed the audience about the situation. He ended with a quip: "The only thing red about Lucy is her hair, and even that's not legitimate." When he presented his wife, the audience gave her a standing ovation. The Arnazes weathered the McCarthy storm; however, another one was brewing.

Desi's womanizing had not ended with marriage or parenthood. Tension between the two escalated when Desi's private indiscretions became public in the tabloid *Confidential*. Its headline blared, "Does Desi Really Love Lucy?" The article stated that Arnaz "proved himself an artist at philandering as well as acting." It also quoted an inebriated Desi stating, "A real man should have as many girls as he has hair on his head." The movie where they had first met, *Too Many Girls*, had taken on a symbolic overtone. After this scandal, it was Desi who had some "'splainin' to do."

Desi tried to fend off rumors of marital discord by remarking that when a redhead and a Cuban got together they were bound to argue, but eventually it got to the point where the couple could no longer deny their crumbling marriage. Just as the Ricardos said good-bye to television, Ball and Arnaz said good-bye to each other with a divorce. Lucy said, "I hate failure and that divorce was a Number One failure in my eyes. It was the worst period of my life. Neither Desi nor I have been the same since, physically or mentally."

Ball bought her ex-husband's share of their company Desilu for $3 million, which made her the first woman to single-handedly run a TV studio. Desi's comment on this was one of no regrets: "It ceased to be fun. I was happier chasing rats." As head of the world's largest production company, Lucille proved that she was not as ditzy as her character Lucy; she arranged the purchase of RKO Studios for $6.15 million and eventually sold it for $17 million.

Desi, pursued by his addictions to alcohol, gambling, and womanizing, retreated to a Del Mar, California, oceanfront estate, where he spent his days visiting the racetrack and smoking cigars. He also married his second wife, Edith Mack Hirsch, in 1963. As they prepared for their Palm Springs honeymoon, Lucy sent the couple roses in the shape of a horseshoe. The card read: "You Both Picked a Winner." In 1976, when Desi published his autobiography, its epilogue confirmed that his second wife had not supplanted his first: "I loved Lucy very much and, in my own and perhaps peculiar way, I will always love her."

After the divorce, Lucille Ball Arnaz was professionally secure, but she was emotionally distraught and lamented that she was in the horrific position of approaching fifty and being "lonely and loaded." She ended up marrying Gary Morton, who was referred to as "Mr. Ball," because she was the powerhouse; it was also because he was attempting to fill Desi's unfillable shoes.

In November 1986, on what would have been the Arnazes' forty-sixth wedding anniversary, Lucille called Desi, who was dying of lung cancer. When the phone rang, their daughter, Lucie, put the phone to her father's ear with the words, "It's the redhead." Lucie could hear her mother's pain-laden voice repeating over and over, "I love you. I love you, Desi, I love you." His last words to her were, "I love you, too, honey. Good luck with your show." Lucie said of her parents, "They had one of those historical marriages, like Napoleon and Josephine, Richard and Liz—destined to be trouble but destined for them to never find anyone as passionate or fabulous."

Five days later Lucille Ball was honored at the Kennedy Center. Robert Stack read a written statement that Desi had prepared just days before for the occasion. Desi's last words to his first love: "*I Love Lucy* was never just a title."

Postscript

➤ Lucille was among the hundreds of mourners who attended Desi's funeral at St. James Roman Catholic Church near San Diego. His eulogy was delivered by former Desilu actor Danny Thomas. He was cremated and his ashes were scattered in the Pacific Ocean, in front of his Del Mar home.

→ In 1989, Lucille died of cardiac arrest at Cedars-Sinai Medical Center. When the news broke, an easel bearing a memorial sign was erected over her Walk of Fame star on Hollywood Boulevard. A block-long condolence card bore the names of hundreds of fans. She was initially interred in Forest Lawn—Hollywood Hills Cemetery in Los Angeles. However, in 2002, her children moved her ashes to the family plot at Lake View Cemetery in Jamestown, New York.

22

Humphrey Bogart and Lauren Bacall

1943

*T*he word *whistle* carries different connotations for different people: To Disney aficionados, it is what seven dwarves do while they work; to those of an artistic bent, it is reminiscent of a painter's tribute to his mother; to those with wanderlust, it brings to mind the mournful sound of a train. However, to a legendary pair, the word symbolized their love.

The man who began his Hollywood career in the role of the noble thug, Humphrey DeForest Bogart, was born in New York, a child of wealth and private schools. He disappointed his parents when he followed the lure of the sea and enrolled in the navy instead of Yale. He later recalled, "At eighteen, war was great stuff. Paris! French girls! Hot damn!" He drifted into movies and became a star in *High Sierra*, in which he played a gangster with a soul; he got the audience to root for the bad guy. Bogart had his first romantic role in *Casablanca*, of which he was characteristically humble. Of his performance he stated, "When the camera moves in on that Bergman's face, and she's saying she loves you, it would make anybody look romantic." Although his role as the nightclub owner made him immortal, it was in an Ernest Hemingway adaptation where he first saw his Ilsa.

Humphrey's destiny, Betty Joan Perske, was a New York–born Jewish seventeen-year-old. To help support herself and her single mother, she began working as a model. Diana Vreeland, the legendary fashion editor of *Harper's Bazaar*, saw something in the unknown girl and placed her on a 1943 cover. When director Howard Hawks's wife saw her seductive beauty, she urged her husband to bring the teenager to Hollywood for a screen test. The erstwhile model would later remark of the *Harper's Bazaar* cover that it was "the twist of fate that changed my life forever."

Betty was chosen to star in the film *To Have and Have Not*, and Howard Hawk, in Svengali fashion, changed her name to Lauren Bacall.

The first time Bogart met Bacall was when Hawks introduced them on the set of the film *Passage to Marseilles*. A couple of weeks before *To Have and Have Not* began filming, as Lauren was walking out of the director's office her future co-star was about to walk in. When he encountered his leading lady, he said, "I just saw your test. We'll have a lot of fun together."

Just as life imitates art, so reel love often transforms to real love, as was the case with Bogie and Bacall. When the siren uttered, "You know how to whistle, don't you, Steve? You just put your lips together and blow," Bogie was bewitched. A short time into the filming of the picture, Humphrey came into Lauren's dressing room to say good night and suddenly leaned over, put his hand under her chin, and kissed her. He took a matchbook from his pocket and asked her to put her phone number on its back. She did so, though there were impediments to their romance: He was forty-five and she was nineteen, he was Christian and she was Jewish; and furthermore, he was married.

Humphrey's third wife, actress Mayo Methot, was an affable woman when sober, a virago when drunk. Bogart didn't believe in adultery, but Methot nevertheless was serially suspicious and threw objects, mostly plates, at what she assumed was her cheating spouse. In one rage, she stabbed him. Dorothy Parker said of their marriage that "their neighbors were lulled to sleep by the sounds of breaking china and crashing glass." The "Battling Bogarts" (as the press had dubbed them) kept a carpenter on call to repair the damage from their drunken fights. However, the chemistry between Bogart and Bacall was so magnetic that they eventually embarked on a clandestine affair, which soon became public.

Though Bogart's nickname for Bacall was "Baby," to the other people on the set she was nicknamed "the Cast"; this was because every time Bogie spent an evening with his girlfriend, he told his wife he was going out with the cast. News of the affair became public fodder when the gossip columnist Hedda Hopper came on the set; in an advance warning of her article she cautioned Lauren, "Better be careful. You might have a lamp dropped on you one day." Then Hedda followed her quip with a line in her paper: "You can have your B&B at lunch any day at Lakeside."

Howard Hawk warned Bacall to end the affair; he cautioned that she meant nothing to Bogart, and if she prolonged the scandal he would wash his hands of her and send her to Monogram (the studio that made the lowest pictures). Under his concern lay jealousy; although married, he too was smitten with Bacall. To distract his star, he fixed her up with Clark Gable; although the romantic icon kissed her under the moonlight, there were no sparks. Her mother, with whom she lived, was also aghast that her daughter consented every time Bogart called with his customary phone greeting, "Hello, Baby," to arrange for a tryst. However, Lauren was willing to bet her heart on her belief that Humphrey's love for her would triumph.

When *To Have and Have Not* wrapped, Bogart did not forget Lauren and sent her a love letter: "And now I know what was meant by 'to say good-bye is to die a little.'" He also gave her a gold ID bracelet; on one side was her name, and on the other were the words *the whistler*. However, he still was not willing to end his marriage. For her part, Mayo tried to stay on the wagon and change her behavior; she knew how enamored her husband was of the young and beautiful starlet.

At that juncture, Mary Chase's play *Harvey* was debuting in New York; it was the story of a man in love with a giant rabbit who was invisible. In deference to the fact that Humphrey was supposed to have ended the affair to placate his wife, Lauren bought Bogie a small bronze rabbit to signify that Harvey absent was Harvey still.

Finally, during their second film together, *The Big Sleep*, it became apparent to all members of the ménage à trois that Mayo had thrown her last plate. Rick Blaine in *Casablanca* was willing to let Ilsa get on the plane; Humphrey Bogart, however, could not let go of Bacall. Mayo, not able to admit otherwise, admitted defeat and agreed to a Reno divorce. As soon as the ink was dry, Bogie and Bacall were married in a quiet ceremony at the country home of Humphrey's close friend, Pulitzer Prize–winning author Louis Bromfield, at Malabar Farm in Ohio, on May 21, 1945. The head of Warner Brothers, Jack Warner, gave the couple the Buick from *The Big Sleep* (one of the four movies they were to star in together). Bogart joked that the "something old" was himself, and despite his tough-guy image, he cried as he watched "Baby" walking down the aisle.

Humphrey, the highest paid actor in Hollywood, purchased a white brick mansion in an exclusive neighborhood in Holmby Hills, replete with two Jaguars and three Boxers. One of their neighbors was close friend Judy Garland. A few years later their son, Stephen, was born, named after Humphrey's character in *To Have and Have Not*; this was followed by the birth of their daughter, Leslie, named after the British actor Leslie Howard, a friend of Bogart's who had been killed in World War II. Lauren kept her finger in acting, though she considered her greatest role that of Humphrey's wife. She was on location when he starred in *The African Queen*, as happy being a homemaker in the African jungle as on their Californian estate. It was a decision she never regretted. In her autobiography, *Lauren Bacall by Myself*, she wrote, "Whenever I hear the word happy now, I think of then."

The Bogie and Bacall marriage was an extremely happy one until an afternoon in 1956 when the Grim Reaper knocked at the Holmby Hills door. Bogie had come home and told his wife that he had run into Greer Garson, who advised him to see her doctor about his cough. Humphrey, who had always been a heavy smoker, had contracted cancer of the esophagus. An operation was undertaken, but it was too late to spread the halt of the disease. At age fifty-seven, Hollywood's once most romantic lead and resident tough guy was bedridden, his frame wasted away to eighty pounds.

In January 1957, Lauren was getting ready to pick up her children from Sunday school. Before departing, she asked Humphrey if he felt better after his terrible night, to which he replied, "It's always better in the daylight." She kissed him, and he said his last words to his first love, "Good-bye, kid. Hurry back." When Lauren and Humphrey had kissed in *The Big Sleep*, she had said, "I like that. I'd like more." Her words were prophetic of how she felt at the loss of her beloved husband after twelve years of bliss.

Postscript

→ Humphrey Bogart's funeral was accompanied to musical selections from Bach. On the altar was a model of the ship from

The African Queen. In accordance with his wishes, he was cremated. Warner Brothers Studios and 20th Century Fox held moments of silence.

➻ Urban legend relates that Bacall placed in his urn the small gold whistle he had given his wife before their marriage. It was inscribed with the words *If you want anything, just whistle.*

23

Ronald Reagan and Nancy Davis

1950

*F*irst Ladies have at times achieved renown apart from their famous husbands: Abigail Adams for promoting the rights of women, Eleanor Roosevelt for creating the March of Dimes, Jacqueline Kennedy for imbuing Camelot with elegance. Nancy Reagan's legacy, however, is the love affair she enacted against the backdrop of the White House, wherein she walked, hand in hand, with her life's leading man.

Anne Frances Robbins was born in New York, the daughter of an actress and a car salesman. When the marriage disintegrated, Edith Luckett, unable to care for her infant, whom she called Nancy, left her in the care of her sister. Six years later Edith married Loyal Davis, a prominent Chicago neurosurgeon, who formally adopted her daughter.

In her Smith College yearbook, Nancy wrote, "My greatest ambition is to have a successful, happy marriage"; however, still not having met Mr. Right, Nancy followed in her mother's footsteps and began her Hollywood career. She did not become a star; however, through serendipity, she became the North Star to a Hollywood leading man.

Nancy's destiny, Ronald Wilson Reagan, was born in Illinois and lived over the H. C. Pitney Variety Store. After attending Eureka College, because of his compelling voice he was hired as an announcer for the Chicago Cubs until a screen test led to Warner Brothers Studios. He spent the majority of his Hollywood years in B movies, where, he joked, the producers "didn't want them good, they wanted them Thursday." His career was derailed by his stint in the army; when he returned, he was elected president of the Screen Actors Guild. It was through this position that he was to meet his forever First Lady, to whom he would later say, "God must think a lot of me to have given me you." However, their first encounter had less to do with divine intervention than with Nancy's own machinations.

As a twenty-six-year-old starlet, Nancy was aghast to discover her name on a list of Communist sympathizers. MGM promptly placed an item in a gossip column noting that she was not *that* Nancy Davis; however, she saw opportunity in the mix-up. She had seen Ronald Reagan on the silver screen and she had liked what she saw. Deciding to kill two birds with the one stone, she cajoled her friend into persuading Reagan into inviting her to dinner, ostensibly to discuss her situation. Ronald agreed, but as protection from a bad blind date, warned her that it would have to be an early evening as he had a predawn call the next day. Nancy responded with a similar early-exit line.

The first time Nancy met Ronald was on November 15, when they had dinner at LaRue's, a glamorous restaurant on the Sunset Strip. After their meal, Ronald asked her to a Sophie Tucker performance, where they would take in the first act. They stayed for the second show, which ended at three a.m. The following evening they met once more at an Oceanside restaurant. Nancy later remarked,

"I don't know if it was exactly love at first sight. But it was pretty close."

From that first date Nancy knew she wanted Ronnie's ring to grace her finger; however, Reagan, having recently divorced actress Jane Wyman, was cautious. After two years of dating, Nancy once more decided to nudge fate; she told him she was going to leave for New York City to star in a play. Shortly afterward, while they were having dinner at their usual booth at the Beverly Hills Chasen's, he said, "I think we ought to get married." Nancy responded, "Let's." At the onset of their union, no one could have predicted that the two actors would one day play their greatest roles: he as the leader of the free world, and she as the woman who loved him.

Not wanting to turn their wedding into a paparazzi buffet, the couple decided to wed in a private ceremony on March 4, 1952, at the Little Brown Church in the Valley, with only William Holden and his wife as guests. Nancy recalled of her nuptials that she was so far into the stratosphere that the only words she was able to hear were "I now pronounce you man and wife." The bridal night was at the Old Mission Inn, where Ronald carried her over the threshold to a room that held red roses, followed by a Phoenix honeymoon to spend time with Nancy's ecstatic parents. Later Nancy would adoringly beam, "What can you say about a man, who on Mother's Day sends flowers to his mother-in-law, with a note thanking her for making him the happiest man on Earth?" Seven months later Patti was born; their second child was son Ron. Nancy was only too happy to trade in her career to be a full-time wife and mother. Later she wrote of her devotion, "My life began when I met Ronald Reagan."

During their first year of marriage, Ronald's career constantly took him on the road. Nancy's ritual for her husband's departure was to slip little notes and jelly beans into his suitcase and then drive him to the station, where she would remain until the very last minute. Then, depressed, she would go home and knit him socks. Ronald's ritual was to write her letters of longing on hotel stationery: "My Darling, I'm sitting here on the 6th floor beside a phony fireplace looking out at a gray wet sky and listening to a radio play music not intended for one person alone."

Ronald's next job was as a host for the television series *Death Valley Days* until his passion for politics led him to two terms as the California governor. When he embarked on the campaign trail for chief executive, after an exhausting day of events, Nancy, too wound up to sleep, ate apples in bed while she read. Worried that the noise from chewing would disturb her man, she switched to bananas.

When elected president, Reagan quipped that he was "living above the store again." Though life changed greatly, one constant was that President Reagan continued to write love letters, though this time on White House stationery. That year, one read, "Our wedding anniversary. 29 years of more happiness than any man could rightly deserve." And Nancy continued with "the gaze": a long, adoring look that came to her eyes when she looked upon her spouse.

One of the legacies of Reagan's administration was his campaign in the cold war, wherein he called Russia "the evil empire" and, in front of the Berlin Wall, demanded, "Mr. Gorbachev, tear down this wall!" His most moving speech was on the night of the explosion of the *Challenger*: "The future doesn't belong to the fainthearted; it belongs to the brave.... We will never forget them ... as they ... 'slipped the surly bonds of earth' to 'touch the face of God.'" For her part, as First Lady, Nancy Reagan embarked on many projects—such as her anti-drug campaign with its famous slogan, "Just Say No"—but first and foremost her job was as the fierce protector of her husband.

Unfortunately, even as the dragon at the gate she could not be a talisman against harm. Three months after Reagan's election, John Hinckley Jr., in an insane plot to impress actress Jodie Foster, attempted to assassinate Reagan. The bullet lodged an inch from his heart. In the operating room Reagan joked to the surgeons, "I hope you're all Republicans," to which one replied, "Today, Mr. President, we're all Republicans." When Nancy was allowed to see him, Ronald removed his oxygen mask and joked, "Honey, I forgot to duck," a reference to the defeated boxer Jack Dempsey's jest to his wife. Devastated, Nancy returned to the White House and slept on her husband's side of the bed, holding one of his shirts, where she was comforted by its scent. She wrote in her diary, "Nothing can happen to my Ronnie. My life would be over." The bullet was successfully removed and Ronald said he believed God had spared his life so that he might go on to fulfill a greater purpose—and remain at Nancy's side.

Although he made a full physical recovery, Nancy never made a full psychological one. In the fashion of Caesar's wife, to avoid any further ides of March, she began to consult astrologer Joan Quigley to assist in planning the president's schedule. When word of this leaked, it brought her a storm of criticism along with ire over her out-of-control spending. Her inaugural gown cost $10,000, and other designer gowns earned her the name Queen Nancy. In an attempt to deflect the criticism, she donned a bag lady costume for a 1982 dinner and sang "Second Hand Clothes," mimicking Streisand's "Second Hand Rose." Her detractors referred to her as "Mrs. President" and claimed that she ruled the Oval Office with a Gucci-clad fist.

After departing the White House, the Reagans were looking forward to constant togetherness in their Bel Air home. Reagan expressed this when he said that Nancy was his respite at the end of the day and could make him feel lonely just by leaving the room. Tragically, the golden years were anything but. In 1994 Reagan took pen to gold-embossed stationery: "I have recently been told that I am one of the millions of Americans who will be afflicted with Alzheimer's disease. . . . I only wish that there was some way I could spare Nancy from this painful experience." Nancy now had to heed her husband's words: "The future doesn't belong to the fainthearted;

it belongs to the brave." Nancy, who had centered her life on Ronald for the past forty years, became his fierce protector more than ever. At the same time she had to school herself for a life without her leading man.

In 2004, her gaze full of agony, Nancy said good-bye to her dear Ronnie, comforted in the belief that he had "slipped the surly bonds of earth" to "touch the face of God."

Postscript

→ When Ronald Reagan passed away, President George W. Bush declared June 11 a national day of mourning. Reagan lay in state in Washington, DC, where more than a hundred thousand people came to pay their respects. At his state funeral, President Bush said, "Ronald Reagan belongs to the ages now, but we preferred it when he belonged to us." The Reagan Library in California held a memorial service and interment, during which Mrs. Reagan lost her composure for the first time. After accepting the folded flag, Nancy kissed the casket and mouthed *I love you* before departing.

24

Richard Burton and Elizabeth Taylor

1952

*T*he Richard Burton–Elizabeth Taylor union was one of epic proportions, a two-decade odyssey as tumultuous as the twentieth century against which it was enacted. Their love affair called for the greatest roles the two larger-than-life actors had ever played and became a romance that shocked and mesmerized the world.

Richard Walter Jenkins's father was known as a "twelve-pints-a-day man" whose chief possessions were a shovel and a gift for words. When his wife died giving birth to their thirteenth child, Richard was sent to live with his sister. He started to smoke at age eight and began to drink regularly at age twelve. The stabilizing influence on him was his teacher, Philip H. Burton, who introduced him to theater; his first role was in his school's production *The Apple Cart*. In tribute to his mentor, Richard adopted his surname.

When he was eighteen Richard left for London's stage; he also married Sybil Williams, an actress who was also the daughter of a Welsh coal miner. They had two daughters with Shakespearean names: Kate and Jessica. His 1960 production of *Camelot* proved to be the turning point of his life. His performance as the king impressed 20th Century Fox, which signed him for the film that would make him a star and where he would encounter the woman who would cast him in the role of a lifetime.

Richard's destiny, Elizabeth Rosemond Taylor, was born to American parents residing in England. When she was twelve, her ethereal beauty landed her the role that made her a star—Velvet Brown in MGM's *National Velvet*. In 1960 Taylor attained superstardom when she was chosen to play the Queen of the Nile, Cleopatra, for which she commanded the unprecedented salary of $1 million.

The first time Richard met Elizabeth was when she and her husband, Michael Wilding, were invited to a Sunday brunch at the home of Jean Simmons. Elizabeth, who was sitting by the pool reading a book, saw her hostess's houseguest quoting Dylan Thomas. She felt that he was full of himself. She later recalled of the Welsh womanizer, "Ohhh, boy—I'm not gonna become a notch on his belt." She said she gave him "the cold fish eye." Burton recalled the event in his diary: "A girl sitting on the other side of the pool lowered her book, took off her sunglasses and looked at me. She was lavish. She was a dark, unyielding largesse. She was, in short, too bloody much, and not only that, she was ignoring me. Her breasts were apocalyptic, they would topple empires." It would be another nine years before their paths would cross once more.

Though Burton was still married to Sybil, his appetite for women was as insatiable as his alcoholic intake. Joan Collins told him she believed he would sleep with a snake if he had the chance, to which he replied, "Only if she were wearing a skirt, darling." He romanced co-stars Claire Bloom, Jean Simmons, and Susan Strasberg and was often seen in the company of a woman dubbed "the Copacabana Cutie." However, he always returned to Sybil, whom he considered his emotional rock, and their daughters.

Elizabeth's appetite for the opposite sex was as voracious as Burton's; however, she ended up wedding the men she bedded. Her relationship with her fourth husband, Eddie Fisher, had earned her the reputation of card-carrying home-wrecker when she lured him away from Debbie Reynolds.

In 1963, 20th Century Fox embarked on the epic film *Cleopatra*. When production continued in Rome, the replacement director was Joseph L. Mankiewicz, who had filmed the classic *All about Eve*, and the replacement for the doomed lover, Marc Antony, was Richard Burton. At first Burton dismissed his diva co-star as "Miss Tits"; she told her friends that Burton was a "duffer" who tried to flirt with her with the uninspired "Has anybody told you you're a very pretty girl?" Of this pickup line Taylor later recalled, "Oy gevalt, here's the great lover, the great wit, the great intellectual of Wales, and he comes out with a line like that."

One morning, Burton, in his first big scene with Taylor, appeared on the set with a hangover. Elizabeth, never particularly maternal, immediately became so and felt an urge to not only mother, but smother him with attention. She gazed into his intense green eyes and, as she recalled: "And that was it—I was another notch."

When it came time for the love scene between Antony and Cleopatra, Burton and Taylor were no longer playing a role. When Mankiewicz told them to cut after a passionate scene, his order went unheeded. The director recalled, "To be on the set was like being locked in a cage with two tigers."

Fisher tried to get his wife to stop, but that was akin to telling Niagara not to fall. When it appeared Richard was not going to leave his wife, Taylor took an overdose of pills. Perhaps touched at this display of love, Burton proposed to Taylor with a Bulgari pendant, platinum set with an 18.61-karat emerald surrounded by diamonds, designed so it could be detached and worn as a brooch. The diamonds he lavished on Liz would become as legendary as their romance. He later said of his destiny, "I cannot see life without Elizabeth. She is my everything—my breath, my blood, my mind, and my imagination."

Mankiewicz realized that although his earlier film had been all about Eve, *Cleopatra* was going to be all about Liz and Dick, as the international press, which was swarming the location, had dubbed them in tabloid shorthand. The fallout exceeded even the opulent production: The Vatican accused Taylor of "erotic vagrancy," tabloids preempted John Glenn's orbit of Earth, and the cold war tensions heating up were back-burnered. The rapidly aging director joined the media circus when a paper stated that he was the one dating Taylor and was using Burton as a decoy. Mankiewicz called a press conference and said, "It's time for the real story to be told. I am in love with Richard Burton and he is in love with me—and we are using Elizabeth Taylor, with her consent, as our cover-up." He ended by kissing Burton full on the mouth. Liz dubbed the period *"le scandale."*

During filming in Italy, six thousand extras had been hired to cheer Queen Cleopatra's entrance, a scene that Elizabeth felt might instead result in her impromptu stoning, a fear predicated on the Vatican's condemnation. Nevertheless, in the spirit of "the show must go on" and reassured by her co-star, she allowed herself to be hoisted atop the sphinx. Her fears were unfounded; the crowd instead burst into a wild chorus of "Leez! Leez!" During the screening of both the on-screen and off-screen epic, Darryl Zanuck remarked to Mankiewicz, in a tongue-in-cheek reference to its leading actors, "If any woman behaved toward me the way Cleopatra treated Antony, I would cut her balls off."

The Burton-Taylor marriage took place on March 15, 1964, in Montreal. The only jewelry the bride wore was the Bulgari pendant. When they stopped over at a hotel in Boston, a hysterical crowd clawed at the newlyweds. Burton's coat was ripped and Taylor's ear was bloodied when someone tried to steal one of her earrings. The age of Liz and Dick had begun.

As a token of his affection for Valentine's Day 1969, Burton presented his wife with the 50-karat La Peregrina Pearl, which had once belonged to Mary I of England. To showcase the gem, Richard also acquired a portrait of Queen Mary wearing the pearl.

However, Richard's gifts were not just material in nature. A lifelong wordsmith, he wrote countless letters to his lady love. In one he stated, "Well, first of all, you must realize that I worship you. Second of all, at the expense of seeming repetitive, I love you. Thirdly, and here I go again with my enormous command of language, I can't live without you."

Elizabeth also paid tribute: "Richard was magnificent in every sense of the word . . . and in everything he ever did. He was magnificent on the stage, he was magnificent in film, he was magnificent at making love . . . From those first moments in Rome we were always madly and powerfully in love. We had more time but not enough."

Unfortunately, their volatile tempers led to numerous fallings-out. At hotels they rented suites above and below their own so other guests wouldn't overhear their brawling. After one huge alcohol-fueled fight, Richard swore her off until he saw her in his favorite blue nightie, after which the door was slammed and they engaged in what he called "lovely love." In 1974, Taylor finally called off the marriage in a press release: "Maybe we loved each other too much."

However, the two remarried the very next year. Burton said of his remarriage, which followed on the heels of their divorce, "I found her irresistible, and in the end I found myself on one knee—literally— proposing to her. I'd actually stopped drinking by then, so I should have been sober enough to know what I was doing, but I didn't. So after she accepted, I got drunk . . . I knew it was over before it had begun." The second ceremony was in Botswana, officiated over by a commissioner of the Tswana tribe who asked if they "understood the consequences of marriage." Nevertheless, the couple each said, "I do." Richard vowed to stop drinking, but he binged on their honeymoon. Their second attempt at holy matrimony lasted less than a year. Elizabeth said of their second failed nuptials, "I love Richard Burton with every fiber of my soul but we can't be together."

The modern-day counterparts of Antony and Cleopatra, though divorced twice, always remained in touch and in each other's hearts. In 1984, in Switzerland, Richard died in his sleep of a brain hemorrhage. Upon hearing of his death, Elizabeth became so hysterical that her then-fiancé, Mexican lawyer Victor Luna, ended their engagement. When she returned to her Bel Air home after his memorial service, she found a last letter from Richard. In it he had written that he wanted to come home, and home was Elizabeth.

Postscript

➤ Sally Hay, Burton's widow, refused to allow Taylor to attend his funeral; he was interred in Switzerland. Richard was buried in a red suit, a tribute to his Welsh roots; also enclosed was a volume of Dylan Thomas's poems. Hay also barred Taylor from the memorial service in Wales. At a second memorial in London, Taylor likewise did not allow the last Mrs. Burton to attend, and Liz occupied the front pew with her beloved's relatives.

➤ Taylor is reputed to have made plans when she dies for her ashes to be scattered over Burton's Welsh hometown.

25

Joe DiMaggio and Marilyn Monroe

1952

*I*n front of a camera, Monroe was nonparalleled; on the baseball diamond, DiMaggio was peerless. However, their tragedy involved their ignorance of their emotional needs; only too late did the Blonde Bombshell and the Yankee Clipper understand that their path to salvation lay with one another.

Giuseppe Paolo DiMaggio was the son of Sicilian immigrants, and his father hoped his five sons would follow in his fisherman footsteps. When young Giuseppe explained that the smell of dead fish nauseated him, the elder DiMaggio pronounced his son lazy and good for nothing. At seventeen, Giuseppe started playing baseball with the San Francisco Seals, wherein he became a Bay Area celebrity. A year later the New York Yankees purchased his contract; when he appeared in the stadium for his debut game, twenty-five thousand cheering, flag-waving Italian-Americans showed up to welcome him. He Americanized his name, which led to his moniker

"Joltin' Joe" when he led his team to the World Series. Upon his retirement, the Yankees retired his number five in tribute.

Joe's destiny, Norma Jeane Mortenson (baptized Baker), was born in Los Angeles; her early years made her a poster girl for a Dickensian childhood. Because her father was AWOL and her paranoid schizophrenic mother was often a resident of Agnews State Hospital in San Jose, she was sent to a number of foster homes; in some of these she was sexually molested. At sixteen, as a means of escape, she married Jim Dougherty. When her husband was in the Marines, Norma Jeane worked in a munitions factory, where an army photographer spotted the young beauty and placed her picture in *Yank* magazine. After, on his recommendation, she approached the Blue Book Modeling Agency, who said they would accept her on the condition she lighten her hair. The new blonde became their top model, a fact her husband discovered when he saw his shipmate drooling over a sexy photo of her. Another who took notice was Ben Lyon, a 20th Century Fox executive, who, after giving her a screen test, remarked, "It's Jean Harlow all over again." He disliked her name and Norma Jeane became Marilyn Monroe.

A photograph led to the phenomenon of Marilyn Monroe, and another led to her falling in love with a fellow icon. DiMaggio spotted a picture of Marilyn clad in the shortest of shorts, wearing a baseball cap and high heels, playing baseball with two Chicago White Sox. Armed with his mythic status, he was able to contact her agent, who arranged a blind date. Marilyn was thrilled at the opportunity. She didn't know much about baseball, but as a yet-unknown actress and model she knew about publicity and was enthusiastic about appearing on the arm of an all-American hero.

The first time Joe met Marilyn was on March 15 in a booth in the Villa Nova restaurant on Hollywood's Sunset Boulevard. The time for the blind date was six thirty; Marilyn showed up two hours late. Her first comment was, "There's a blue polka dot exactly in the middle of your tie knot. Did it take you long to fix it just that way?" Marilyn was surprised when Joe turned out to be not the conceited sports figure; she was also taken aback that everyone, including Mickey Rooney, was awed by him. She said of this, "Sitting next to Mr. DiMaggio was like sitting next to a peacock with its tail spread.... No woman has ever put me so much in the shade." Joe commented that Marilyn was "like a good double-play combination." The next night a blue Cadillac with the license plate JOE D was parked outside Marilyn's apartment. Marilyn remarked of her beau, "I don't know if I'm in love with him yet but I know I like him more than any man I've ever met."

Joe proposed on Christmas, and they arranged for a private civil ceremony. The retired DiMaggio saw Marilyn as Norma Jeane, a grown-up orphan wanting to be a cherished wife and mother. The former New York Yankee was about to enter the toughest game of his life.

On January 14, 1954, Joltin' Joe (Marilyn's nickname for him was "Slugger") wedded Marilyn at San Francisco City Hall; Marilyn, who at this time, thanks to an appearance on Playboy's debut cover, packed a mean jolt herself, was dressed, uncharacteristically, non-provocatively. She sported an eternity band, and in her hands she carried three white orchids; when they began to wither, she asked Joe to place flowers on her grave every week after she died, as William Powell had done for Jean Harlow. DiMaggio sported the same polka-dot tie he had worn on their blind date. The bride and groom stated that they were very happy, as were the hordes of reporters who had converged outside the building. The "private" ceremony had attracted about five hundred people who had managed to hear about it in time to turn the corridor outside the judge's court into bedlam. Joe had planned the event with the secrecy of an atomic test; however, Marilyn had made the "mistake" of calling her studio, which "offhandedly" mentioned it to all the major news services. The private Joe was not thrilled with the public spectacle. As Cinderella and her Prince Charming made their escape, Marilyn called out that she had forgotten her coat, which she didn't return to retrieve. The judge remarked that Joe's oversight was even greater; he had forgotten to kiss the bride. The DiMaggios spent their first wedded night at the Clifton Motel in Paso Robles.

For a business/honeymoon trip, Joe took Marilyn to Japan; at the Tokyo airport the photographers were so frenzied that the couple had to escape through a baggage hatch. There was such Marilyn-mania that fans pushed each other into hotel pools and became jammed in revolving doors to see, as the Japanese newspapers wrote, "the Honorable Buttocks-Swinging Actress." At a cocktail party, a general asked Monroe to entertain the troops stationed in Korea. Marilyn was ecstatic at the opportunity; Joe was less enthusiastic. The star performed in front of thousands of soldiers, clad in a scanty dress despite the frigid temperature. She sang "Diamonds Are a Girl's Best Friend" and, in between songs, made wisecracks: "You fellas are always whistling at sweater girls. Well, take away the sweaters and what have you got?" The next morning, instead of saying *Sayonara* she said, *"Eleewah,"* Korean for "Come here," which triggered a mad stampede. She later quipped, "I'll never forget my honeymoon with the 45th division."

When she was reunited with her husband, she described the crowds: "Joe, you never heard such cheering," to which the famous player replied, "Yes, I have." Later Marilyn remarked of her need for adulation, "I knew I belonged to the public and to the world, not because I was talented or even beautiful, but because I had never belonged to anything or anyone else."

Upon her return home Marilyn told a reporter, "Marriage is my main career from now on," and the couple took up residence in San Francisco. However, unable to ignore the siren call of Hollywood,

Marilyn returned to her studio. When she left, DiMaggio became convinced she was seeing other men. One night Joe and his buddy Frank Sinatra broke down the door of an apartment where they believed Marilyn was having a sexual tryst. Instead they found a terrified middle-aged woman, alone in bed, hysterical at the sight of two Italians storming into her room. The lawsuit was settled for $7,500.

However, the affair came full circle when the romance, begun by a photograph, ended with one. Producer Billy Wilder, for a publicity shot for *The Seven Year Itch*, positioned Marilyn above a subway grate, legs akimbo, where the air from below raised her white dress to reveal what lay beneath. Although the scene was shot at two a.m., there was a crowd of a hundred reporters, thousands of cheering onlookers, and one irate husband who kept muttering, "What the hell." The iconic photograph was perfect for Marilyn Monroe, but not at all appropriate for Mrs. Joe DiMaggio. Wilder, who caught a glimpse of DiMaggio, remarked that his expression resembled a "look of death." That evening, in their St. Regis hotel room, a screaming match ensued and divorce followed. The slugger never lost his love for the star and never remarried. One of his friends said of his enduring love, "He carried a torch bigger than the Statue of Liberty."

Monroe had once remarked to a reporter, "To know that Joe is there is like having a life guard," and after the separation, she needed him more than ever. During the 1961 filming of *The Misfits* she was locked away in a psychiatric ward, a fate that had been her mother's own. She finally admitted the hollowness of fame that Joe had warned her about: "Hollywood's a place where they'll pay you $50,000 for a kiss and fifty cents for your soul. I know because I turned down the first offer and held out for the fifty cents." DiMaggio secured her release, and there were rumors of a remarriage.

The couple never got their second chance; in 1962, Marilyn died of an apparent drug overdose. DiMaggio claimed Marilyn's body from the morgue and made the funeral arrangements, in which he barred the Hollywood elite who "had only hurt Marilyn." He arranged for her to be clothed in her favorite green Pucci dress. DiMaggio spent the entire night beside her casket in the chapel.

The funeral took place on the same day rumored to have been the remarriage of Joe and Marilyn. Strains of "Over the Rainbow," one of Marilyn's favorite songs, echoed through the mortuary. DiMaggio stooped over her casket, overcome with emotion, kissed her, placed three roses in her coffin, and whispered, "I love you. I love you." For the next twenty years he had roses placed in the urn next to her crypt three times a week.

When Joe DiMaggio passed away, his last words were, "I'll finally get to see Marilyn."

Postscript

➼ Lee Strasberg delivered Marilyn's eulogy. In 2009 the crypt above Marilyn's was auctioned on eBay: "Spend eternity directly above Marilyn Monroe." The winning bidder, who paid $4.6 million, was identified only by his initials, O. S.

➼ In 1999, Joltin' Joe passed away from lung cancer in Florida; his private funeral was held in San Francisco. In tribute, the New York Yankees wore his number five pinned to their left sleeves for the 1999 season. Flags in San Francisco flew at half staff; radio stations around the country played the lyrics from "Mrs. Robinson" as an anthem for the baseball great.

26

Prince Rainier and Grace Kelly

1955

*A*s Grace Kelly she had caught the heart of Hollywood; as Grace Grimaldi she had caught the heart of a prince. What followed was a modern-day fairy tale, complete with a pink palace overlooking the Mediterranean.

Grace Patricia Kelly was born in Philadelphia, one of four children. She was named after an aunt who had died young, as well for the day of her birth: "Tuesday's child is full of grace." Her father, Jack, was the son of Irish immigrants and the scion of a brick empire—his family lived in a seventeen-room mansion, replete with tennis court. Much to Grace's parents' chagrin, despite their wealth, they were denied blue-blood status by their city's WASP upper crust because they were Roman Catholics and their money was not of the old variety.

Grace's personal pain came from the fact that her father (who had won three Olympic gold medals in rowing) preferred her more outgoing, athletic siblings. Grace chose to go her own route, and rather than settle for being a Philadelphia princess, at age eighteen, she determined to follow her first love: acting.

Armed with prodigious talent and ethereal beauty, Grace starred in MGM's *Mogambo*, filmed in Nairobi. There she embarked on what was later to be called in the press "L'Affaire Gable." This cat was let out of its bag when a member of the cast accidentally wandered into Clark Gable's tent and found Clark and Grace sharing the same sleeping bag; he reported that they were "both of them starkers." Her response: "What else is there to do if you're alone in a tent in Africa with Clark Gable?" This began Grace's pattern of bedding Hollywood's leading stars, many of them older and sporting wedding bands.

The apogee of Kelly's career occurred when she won an Academy Award for *The Country Girl*; at the Oscar ceremony she wore an aquamarine gown that showcased her willowy figure and the color of her eyes. Bob Hope as emcee declared, "I just wanna say, they should give a special award for bravery to the producer who produced a movie *without* Grace Kelly."

After the Oscars, *Life* magazine decided to put her on its next cover. The public Grace was glowing; the private one less so. She recounted that in her suite in the Bel Air Hotel, it was "just the two of us, Oscar and I. It was the loneliest moment of my life." However, she wouldn't be lonely for long.

Grace's destiny, Rainier Louis Henri Maxence Bertrand Grimaldi, was the descendant of Europe's longest-ruling family, the Grimaldis. His home was a two-hundred-room pink palace situated on a bluff overlooking the sea. When he was six, his parents divorced, and he was packed off to school in England, where he was called "Fat Little Monaco." In 1949, at age twenty-six, he found his life's vocation: as the ruling prince of his beloved country.

It was partly in deference to his principality that he was desperately seeking a wife; under the terms of a 1918 treaty, Monaco would revert to France if Rainier died without an heir. If that contingency were to take place, the prince's people, who were exempt from taxes and military conscription, would no longer enjoy these benefits. Not surprisingly, his twenty thousand subjects doubled as desperate matchmakers. Although he was Europe's most eligible bachelor, it was difficult to find a princess; she had to be Roman Catholic, able to procreate, wealthy (there was a requisite dowry of $2 million), and able to touch the prince's isolated heart. Of his situation he stated, "I told my people that I was keenly sensitive to the political implications of my bachelorhood—but I told them not to overlook the human factor, the duty of a man to fulfill himself as a human being by taking a wife he loves. I will not marry except for love. I will not agree to a loveless marriage of convenience." Rainier was to meet his vision in the flesh, through, appropriately, a magazine named *Match*.

The Cannes Film Festival had invited Grace to come to France; she acquiesced only when she renewed her affair with French actor Jean-Pierre Aumont, who asked her to rendezvous there. When she agreed, the editors of *Paris Match* decided to set up a meeting for a cover story that would launch an avalanche of sales: "Hollywood Movie Queen Meets Real-Life Prince."

The first time Grace met Rainier was on April 6 in his storybook palace. They strolled in his magnificent gardens and visited his private zoo; one of his animals was a baby Asian tiger, a gift from Emperor Bao Dai of Vietnam. When Grace went to take her farewell, the prince kissed her hand. On the way back to Cannes, Grace remarked to Jean-Pierre that the prince was "Charming. Very charming."

When Grace returned home, she and Rainier began an epistolary courtship; in December the prince went to the States for a second meeting and had Christmas dinner with the Kellys in their Philadelphia home. At Cartier in New York, Rainier purchased a

10.47-karat diamond engagement ring, and on December 27 Grace accepted his proposal. The woman who had been searching for a prince of a man had fallen for a man who was a prince.

The press was ecstatic with the news of the wedding of the century, and so was Grace's father, Jack Kelly, who could finally lord it over Philadelphia's WASP upper crust. Alfred Hitchcock was not pleased with losing his star and termed her "*dis*-Grace" for trading her talent for a tiara. However, he later softened: "I am glad Grace has found the best role of her life." Bing Crosby almost blew the nuptials when the prince asked who had been the greatest star he had ever bedded. Bing replied, "That's easy, Grace, er, Gracie Fields." Rainier had assumed that Grace was as chaste as her appearance led one to believe.

Another person who had misgivings over the wedding of the century was the bride, who called her nuptials the carnival of the century. On board the SS *Constitution* en route to Monaco, she recalled, "When I left New York our ship was surrounded in fog. What sort of world was awaiting me on the other side of that fog?" Grace was leaving her family, friends, and career for a world where she did not speak the language, protocol ruled, and the only person she knew was a man she had met less than a year before. In addition, the marriage clause stated that in the contingency of divorce, custody of any children would be granted to the father. Whatever scenario was to follow, Grace would do what she had always done: play her part to perfection.

The church ceremony was conducted on April 19, 1956, at Saint Nicholas Cathedral; the bride wore an $8,000 wedding dress, designed by MGM. The six hundred guests included European blue bloods, the international jet set, and American movie stars. The die was cast when the couple stated, *"Oui, je veux."* The service was viewed by an estimated 30 million television viewers. The prince and princess honeymooned on Rainier's yacht, *Deo Juvante II*. Before boarding, the bride told her groom, "Thank you, darling, for such a sweet, intimate wedding."

As events unfolded, Princess Grace remarked, "The idea of my life as a fairy tale is itself a fairy tale." One of the things that caused her pain was abandoning the profession she loved. For comfort she would repeat to herself a quotation from her favorite poet, Kahlil Gibran: "When love beckons to you follow him . . . though his voice may shatter your dreams." The energy she had once given to her career was soon channeled into the royal offspring. Nine months and four days after their wedding, their first child, Princess Caroline, was born. Monaco, ecstatic that its municipality was now secure from French rule, rejoiced. Twenty-one guns heralded the event, a national holiday was declared, gambling ceased, and champagne flowed. A year later, 101 guns saluted the arrival of the male heir, Prince Albert. Their last born was Princess Stephanie.

The family lived together for a quarter of a century in storybook splendor. But in September 1982, Grace and her seventeen-year-old daughter Stephanie were returning home from Roc Angel, their French estate. Grace had refused the services of her chauffeur; while driving, she suffered a minor stroke, which caused her car to crash down the mountainside. Stephanie survived; Grace never regained consciousness.

Rainier went into the hospital room to bid his wife a final farewell; when he departed he walked slowly down the corridor, supported on one side by his son, Prince Albert, and on the other by his daughter, Princess Caroline. He kept repeating, "This can't be true. Please, dear God. This can't be true."

A few years after the tragic accident, biographer Jeffrey Robinson asked Rainier, once more Europe's reigning bachelor, about remarrying. The response? "How could I? Everywhere I go, I see Grace." With the passing of the princess, the fairy tale had lost its enchantment.

Postscript

↣ An estimated worldwide television audience of 100 million watched as Grace Grimaldi was buried in the dynasty's crypt. The four hundred guests in attendance were American movie stars and the crowned heads of Europe; Diana, Princess of Wales, represented the British royal family.

↣ Rainier passed away in 2005 after suffering a host of health problems. His service was attended by dignitaries from sixty countries; the service was private. During the Mass, "Adagio for Strings" echoed through a nineteenth-century cathedral that overlooks the sea. He was buried beside Princess Grace.

27

Johnny Cash and June Carter

1956

*F*ire is a two-edged sword; it can both burn and warm. In the case of a man with a preference for black and a woman with a preference for blue, it brought first damnation and then, through the force of love, redemption.

Valerie June Carter was born in Virginia into a dynasty of music royalty. Her family became the first vocal group to become country stars, and their repertoire became Nashville's bedrock with classics such as "Will the Circle Be Unbroken." A natural beauty who possessed a razor-sharp wit, she achieved popularity by spicing up live performances with comedy routines and monologues.

Life on the road for a teenage girl in a group was difficult. "The old circuits sometimes called for five shows a day. While everyone else was dating, I was busy riding everywhere in our old Cadillac, setting up the PA system, and taking money at the door. My body ached. Then I stopped a show with a routine, and I was hooked. There would be no turning back now. I would not go to college, would not marry Freddie Fugate back home and raise children, cook three meals a day and be an average American housewife."

At age twenty-three she married her first husband, honky-tonk singer Carl Smith, and had a daughter, Rebecca, before separating later in the decade. In 1961 the Carters were invited to perform at the Grand Ole Opry, where June would meet her man in black.

June's destiny, J. R. Cash (he was so christened because his parents could not agree on a name), was born in Arkansas, one of seven children of Southern Baptist sharecroppers. By age five he toiled in the cotton fields, where his mother led the children in singing gospel songs to lighten their Depression-era existence. Music also helped him survive the tragic death of his brother in an accident with a power saw as well as an acrimonious relationship with his father. To chase away the blues he listened to his uncle's radio, especially the recordings of the Carter family. On a class trip to the Grand Ole Opry, he saw his idols in person and determined that one day he would obtain June's autograph.

After high school he enlisted and in Germany bought his first guitar, on which he composed "Folsom Prison Blues." When he returned he married Vivian Liberto and held a number of dead-end jobs to support his growing family. His segue to fame began when he obtained a recording contract with Sam Phillips's Sun label, which had clients Jerry Lee Lewis, Roy Orbison, and Elvis Presley. His first hit was "Cry, Cry, Cry." His signature color led to his nickname, "the Man in Black," which was in contrast to the rhinestones sported by other country stars, and he began each of his concerts with, "Hello. I'm Johnny Cash." When "I Walk the Line" began storming up the charts, the Man in Black decided it was time to knock on the door of the mecca of country music.

June was performing as an opening act for Presley when she saw

Elvis on his knee, grasping his guitar and strumming the words, "Everyone knows where you go when the sun goes down. Ah-ummm." When she asked him what was going on, he replied he was trying to tune his "blame guitar" and attempting to sing like Johnny Cash. When she said she didn't know Cash, Elvis replied that she would, that the whole world would. Later, on tour throughout the South, while June tried to protect Elvis from women, Presley would endlessly play Cash songs on all the jukeboxes. She recalled hearing the mournful words "You're gonna cry, cry, cry and you'll cry alone," and that Cash's mournful voice penetrated her heart and spoke to her own loneliness.

The first time June met Johnny was backstage at the Grand Ole Opry in 1956. She was tuning her guitar and humming "Ah-umm," when she heard the same voice that had emanated from the jukeboxes; however, this time it said, "Hello. My name is Johnny Cash. I've always wanted to meet you." She was able to compose herself and replied, "I feel like I know you already. Elvis plays you on the jukebox all the time and he can't tune his guitar without humming 'Cry, Cry, Cry.' Now he's got me doing it." Before they separated he told her, "I'm going to marry you someday." She laughed and said, "Well, good. I can't wait." Her answer was flippant because at the time, he was a married man with four daughters. June said that his eyes looked like black agates and that she was afraid to do more than glance at him for fear that she would be drawn into his soul, unable to walk away. Before they parted, she requested some of his records, which he gave her the next Saturday night; in return she gave him her picture, with its long-awaited autograph.

The years that followed were punches to Johnny's soul, despite the wealth and gold records. The competing demands of fame and family, and his ever-present feelings of alienation, made him sing the "Cocaine Blues"; he also was addicted to alcohol and prescription drugs. Under the influence of his demons, he trashed hotel rooms, totaled cars, failed to show up for gigs, and committed random acts of adultery. On one memorable occasion, he became enraged when he fumbled with his microphone, and then he used it as a weapon to smash sixty footlights on the stage of the Grand Ole Opry. For the price of their ticket, those in the front row were showered with glass. Restless, he was happy to always be on the move, and it would come as a relief to hear his band members ask, "Hey, John, how soon do you think you can leave?"

In the early 1960s, June started touring with her mother and sisters as the Carter Family, and shortly afterward Cash began accompanying them; this led to June and Johnny performing duets such as "If I Were a Carpenter." Soon the only thing rivaling their onstage chemistry was their offstage one. This caused a great deal of consternation for June, who was then remarried to Nashville police officer Rip Nix, with whom she had a daughter, Rosie. She was also against adultery, on both a moral and religious level. However, in 1965, in Las Vegas, at the Mint, Johnny and June gave in to their passion. June had fallen for the Man in Black, a complex soul, equal parts saint and sinner.

In an emotional tsunami, June found herself afterward driving her car as fast as she could at four in the morning. When she asked herself what she was doing, her answer was that she was "falling in love with someone she had no right to fall in love with." Not only were they both married and parents, but she was alarmed with becoming involved with a man whose lifestyle had ended the life of her friend Hank Williams. She likened her dilemma to a ring of fire, a metaphor born from her fundamentalist Christian faith. This phrase later became one of her most famous lyrics.

June's response to Johnny's begging her to be with him was that until he was free from his chemical dependencies, their one-night stand would remain just that. Cash was unable to shake his drug habit or his love for June. However, ultimately for her he was able to "walk the line" of sobriety, at least as much as he was able. Cash wrote of the woman who had saved his life both physically and spiritually, "What June did for me was post signs along the way, lift me up when I was weak, encourage me when I was discouraged, and love me when I felt alone and unlovable. She's the greatest woman I have ever known. Nobody else, except my mother, comes close."

In one of the most romantic of all proposals, while performing live at a concert in London, Ontario, Johnny Cash asked June Carter to marry him. Her answer was to just get on with the show. However, when the crowd of seven thousand roared for her to say yes—she did. After eighteen years, multiple music awards, drug addiction, and three failed marriages between them, Johnny and June were married one week later on March 1, 1968, in Kentucky. The bride's dress and the flowers in her hair were in her favorite color of light blue. A nonalcoholic reception followed at their lakeside estate in Tennessee, which they had christened Camelot. Their nuptials produced another Carter/Cash classic, "Jackson."

In 1970, June gave birth to their son, John Cash Carter, whom they idolized and took on stages throughout the world, even before he could walk. Of their marriage, which lasted for thirty-five years, Cash said he could not envision life without her. She was equally laudatory: "God puts his hand on some people and says, 'You can be Johnny Cash.'"

Unfortunately, Camelot had its dark side. Johnny at times lapsed into drug abuse (he once overdosed on pills he had smuggled into his hospital room), but for the most part, with June's help, he was able to apply the brakes to his self-destructive behavior.

The circle was broken when June passed away, holding Johnny's hand. Through their unconditional devotion they had transformed the ring of fire from one of damnation to one of redemption.

Postscript

➤ June was buried in a light blue coffin in Tennessee. At her funeral, her stepdaughter Rosanne Cash stated, "If being a wife were a corporation, June would have been a CEO. It was her most treasured role." Singers Emmylou Harris, Sheryl Crow, and others sang at her funeral.

➤ Cash succumbed to diabetes, and grief, four months later. The mourners sang "Will the Circle Be Unbroken."

28

Aristotle Onassis and Maria Callas

1957

The Olympians went into creative overdrive when meting out punishment: Prometheus, for daring to steal fire from the gods, was chained to a rock; every night a vulture would feast on his liver, only to have the organ grow back the following day. In similar fashion, when Onassis betrayed Callas, for his sin of hubris, the tycoon and the diva were cast as leading players in a twentieth-century tragedy.

Sophia Cecelia Kalogeropoulos (who would achieve fame as Maria Callas), whose life emulated a Greek drama both on and off stage, was raised in Queens. As an adolescent she was overweight, with bad skin and thick glasses, which was especially painful in comparison with her attractive sister. However, for compensation she had a gift from the gods: an ethereal voice.

In 1937, Maria's parents divorced, and her mother, Evangelia, relocated her two children to Athens, where she hoped to launch Maria's singing career. Two years later the swastika was flying over the Acropolis, and the Kalos family suffered severe starvation and terror. After the war Maria left Greece and the mother with whom she clashed. When she next stepped foot in Greece, it was as La Divina; it was also when she would fall in love with the man who would dominate her life.

Maria's destiny, Aristotle Sokratis Onassis, was born in Turkey; however, when the country turned on its ethnic population, members of his family were killed and he fled to Greece. In 1923 he left for Buenos Aires with $250 and limitless ambition. He started a tobacco import business with Turkey, and his road to his first million was helped along through smuggling and other illegal activities. His business ethics can be gleaned from his remark that he would never trust a person who did not accept a bribe. When he returned to Greece, it was as a self-made millionaire with an ego equivalent to his fortune. He married Athina Livanos, daughter of a shipping magnate, whose old money lent respectability to his new money. His son, Alexander, to whom he referred as his alpha and omega, was followed by daughter Christina. Onassis's happiness and hubris were at their height.

The first time Maria met Aristotle was on the evening of September 3, at an international jet-set ball held in the Hotel Danieli, overlooking a Venetian canal. The event, hosted by the grande dame of the gossip column, Elsa Maxwell, was in Maria's honor to celebrate her opera performance in *Anna Bolena*. The hostess arranged Maria's introduction to Aristotle, feeling that two of Greece's most famous citizens (Callas had been on the cover of *Time* magazine in 1956) should make each other's acquaintance. By this time, Maria, who had undergone a metamorphosis by shedding sixty-five pounds, was a beauty with the world of opera at her feet. There was an immediate rapport between the diva and the tycoon, and they began to converse in animated Greek. Soon they discovered they had far more in common than language: Hellenistic heritage, survival of the war, and self-made success. Moreover, there was a magnetic physical rapport.

Onassis repeatedly invited Maria and her Italian manager husband, Giovanni Battista Meneghini, to his floating pleasure dome, *The Christina*; however, as they were focused solely on her career, they repeatedly declined. A year and a half later, Callas performed *Medea* in London, and her not-very-secret admirer flew in for the event, though he had little appreciation of opera, saying, "It sounds like a lot of Italian chefs shouting risotto recipes at each other." Afterward he staged an elaborate reception for her at the Dorchester Hotel, decorating it with thousands of red roses and inviting world-renowned guests.

A month later the Meneghinis finally agreed to a cruise, little imagining that the getaway would alter all of their destinies. Onassis gave a tour of the splendors of his ship; amid the opulence were bar stool cushions covered with the foreskins of whales killed by his whaling fleet. This permitted Aristotle to deliver his bon mot: "Madame, you are sitting on the largest penis in the world." Maria enjoyed Aristotle's ribald humor; one can assume it was not for the ears of his other high-profile guests, Sir Winston and Lady Churchill, or their beloved green parakeet, Toby, who had accompanied them. On one evening Maria found her host so charming that she stayed up long after her husband had retired. After that, every night was a late one for Maria and Aristo, as she called him. She began to sense the possibility of freedom, both personal and sexual, that her marriage to her husband, thirty years her senior, had denied her. Before the fateful cruise ended, there was an evening when she never returned to her cabin; she had met her life's grand passion. For his part, Aristotle did not resist his siren.

Maria informed her husband that their marriage was over: "Aristo and I have been caught up in this twist of fate and we are unable to combat it." Meneghini was never to recover, and for the rest of his life he mourned the loss of his wife. In their Italian villa he kept everything as she had left it, as her shrine. Onassis, however, was not willing to break up his family and empire and wanted to keep Maria as his mistress. Callas, madly in love, was willing to settle for this; she had never experienced love before. As she said, "It is wonderful to be happy and to know it right at the time you are." However, with the gossip-friendly litany of money, celebrity, and adultery, the scandal became international gossip, and Athina (although she had her own lover) filed for divorce. Maria was jubilant, hoping the mistress could now become the wife, especially when, at age forty-two, she discovered she was pregnant.

Callas retreated to Switzerland to await the birth while Onassis split his time between visiting her and his life in Greece. When she was in her eighth month, ill and swollen, and not wanting her lover to return to her while she was in that condition, she urged her doctor to deliver her baby by an early cesarean. The result was a premature son, Omeros, who survived for two hours. Maria, who had longed all her life for a child, was beside herself with grief. Onassis flew to the hospital to comfort her; Maria was to spend the rest of her days in the painful realm of "what could have been."

In 1963, Onassis purchased the island of Skorpios, where one could see Ithaca; Maria's dream was to spend her life with her Aristo in their Aegean retreat. Perhaps had their son lived, that scenario would have come to pass.

Nine years into their affair, Maria found herself caught in the horrific role of the pursuer rather than the pursued. With mounting alarm, Callas read of the romance of the Greek billionaire and the most famous widow in the world: Jacqueline Kennedy. Aristotle acted as if it were all rumors and continued his relationship with Maria even as huge bouquets of flowers bearing four letters—JILY (Jackie, I Love You)—arrived for Jackie. The Greek billionaire wed the former Mrs. Kennedy in a ceremony on Skorpios. The international press dubbed the new Mrs. Onassis "Jackie O"; Callas would have used a different epithet.

Aboard the *Christina*, Aristotle celebrated the acquisition of his ultimate trophy wife while Jacqueline celebrated the acquisition of her trophy ring—with a price tag of $1.25 million. However, not all were pleased. Alexander, who viewed Jackie's attention to his father as one of the purse rather than the heart, said of his new stepmother's nuptials, "It's a perfect match. My father loves names and Jackie loves money."

Another person who was not pleased was Maria, and the paparazzi awaited her volcanic meltdown. Callas prepared for the performance of her life. With her heart shattered, she dressed in diamonds and gown and attended the seventy-fifth-anniversary party for Maxim's, the famous French eatery. Her dazzling presence eclipsed even that of fellow attendee Elizabeth Taylor. When the press questioned her about the wedding, she replied, "Mrs. Kennedy did well to give a grandfather to her children. Onassis is as beautiful as Croesus." After the party she went into seclusion in her Parisian apartment. Reviewing her life, she stated, "First I lost weight, then I lost my voice, and then I lost Onassis."

A week after his wedding to Jackie, Aristotle was whistling outside Maria's apartment, begging to be let in. When she relented, he told her she was the only woman he had ever loved, to which she replied that he had a very original way of showing it. He was grateful for her forgiveness, especially when Alexander was killed while piloting his plane. Maria took him into her arms, understanding all too well the bottomless grief of losing a son.

Onassis was planning a divorce when he was taken ill and opted to enter a Paris hospital to be in the same city as the woman he loved. The only possession he took with him was his red Hermes blanket, Callas's last gift. On her final visit to him, he told her, "I loved you, not always well, but as much and as best as I was capable of. I tried." Before the Grim Reaper came for him, he clutched the red blanket.

The gods, to punish Prometheus, attacked his liver, the price he had to pay for his theft. The gods, to punish Onassis, attacked his heart, the price he had to pay for his hubris.

Postscript

➤ Aristotle Onassis passed away in France in 1975 and was interred in the same crypt as Alexander on the island of Skorpios.

➤ Maria Callas died in 1977; her ashes were interred in Pere-Lachaise Cemetery. After they were stolen and later recovered, they were scattered over the Aegean Sea.

29

Elvis Presley and Priscilla Beaulieu

1959

*I*t is ironic that the King of Rock and Roll, who sang some of the most achingly romantic songs in the history of music, was doomed to lose the woman whom he wanted to love him true till the end of time. However, although they went their separate ways, in the words of the King, she remained always on his mind.

Priscilla Beaulieu grew up on army bases throughout the United States; her father, Captain Paul Beaulieu, was an Air Force officer. Priscilla received a staggering emotional shock when she stumbled upon a family skeleton in a closet. Rummaging through a box, she found a photograph of a man who bore a striking resemblance to her. When she confronted her mother, Ann, she discovered that her biological father had been killed in a plane crash and her birth surname had been Wagner. Once the secret was out, Ann gave her daughter a gold locket her first husband had given her; Priscilla wore it for years, believing that her departed dad was her guardian angel.

A second emotional storm erupted when Paul received a transfer from Texas to West Germany. Priscilla, who had just been crowned queen of her junior high, felt her world crashing down. Little could she have envisioned that an unimaginable meeting in Europe would lead her to a crown far greater, and far heavier, than the one bequeathed by her Austin classmates.

Priscilla's destiny, Elvis Aaron Presley, was born in Tupelo, Mississippi, in a two-room house built by his father, Vernon. The tragedy of his birth was that his twin was stillborn, an event that traumatized his mother, Gladys Love. When Elvis was three, Vernon was sent to jail for writing a bad check, and his now-homeless wife and son moved in with relatives. With her husband in prison, with no money, Gladys turned all her attention on her only son; it was a bond that would make him a poster boy for the Oedipal complex. The family later relocated to Memphis; at school he was teased by his classmates as the trashy mama's boy who played hillbilly music.

Upon graduation Presley became a truck driver and wore his hair in a pompadour, the current truck driver style, along with long sideburns. However, his greatest wish was to become a famous entertainer, and it was granted in 1956 when RCA recorded his song "Heartbreak Hotel," which became a number one hit. With his devastating good looks of bedroom blue eyes, thick black hair, pouty mouth, and slim physique, coupled with his angelic voice and overtly sexual presence, female fans literally wanted to kiss his blue suede shoes. He took to performing in elaborate jumpsuits; he eschewed jeans because they were all he could afford in his hardscrabble youth.

With his newfound wealth, he purchased a pink Cadillac for his mother and bought an eighteen-room Memphis mansion, Graceland, where he promptly installed Gladys and Vernon. Adoring fans lined the estate at all hours, desperate to catch a glimpse of their idol. With his film debut in the film *Love Me Tender* and his appearance on *The Ed Sullivan Show*, where he was filmed only from the waist up because of his gyrating hips (hence his nickname "Elvis the Pelvis"), he was crowned the King of Rock and Roll.

Throughout his life, only two groups adored Elvis uncon-ditionally—his mother and his fans—and both became hysterical when Presley was drafted into the army in 1958. While Elvis was in training, Gladys passed away from a heart attack, an emotional blow that knocked Elvis's world from its axis. A few months later he was stationed in Germany, where he was to meet the girl who would one day share his throne.

In Germany Priscilla was once again, as a military brat, alien-ated and isolated. To compound the situation, she was living in a country where she did not speak the language, and because of the scarce and expensive housing, the Beaulieus were forced to rent an apartment in a brothel. She was thrilled when she discovered the Eagles Club, a place where Americans could socialize. She would go there after school, listen to the jukebox, and write depressed letters to friends back in Austin. In the club she made the acquaintance of Currie Grant, an American recruit, who told her he knew Elvis and could arrange an introduction. When she learned he really could make it happen, Germany, rather than being the far corner of the earth, became its center.

The first time Priscilla met Elvis was on September 13, when the fourteen-year-old, clad in a blue-and-white sailor dress, walked into his living room at his off-base home in Bad Nauheim, Germany. Elvis was wearing a red sweater and tan slacks, and sitting in an armchair, a cigar dangling from his lips. When Presley saw Priscilla, he jumped up as if he had been sitting on a hot plate. Her cameo face was a powerful draw to the old-fashioned Southern boy, much more so than the half-clad Bridgette Bardot picture displayed on one of the walls. Moreover, she struck a chord of resemblance to Gladys when she had been young. A few moments later he walked to his piano and played for Priscilla (whom he called "Cilla") "Are You Lonesome Tonight?" Afterward they went to the kitchen where his grandmother, Minnie Mae Presley, made them some bacon sandwiches.

Later Priscilla recalled that he was lonely; he missed Memphis and most of all he missed his mother. He later told her that from the night he met her, he knew she was his "twin soul," his destiny. As her car sped home along the Autobahn, a feeling of unreality hung over the evening. A few days later she was summoned back; however, this evening ended in Elvis's bedroom, as would all her subsequent visits during Elvis's five remaining months in Germany. Considering she was only fourteen and the news spread of their relationship, it is surprising that he did not compose "Jailhouse Rock" from firsthand experience. However, he would not have full intercourse with Priscilla, though she wanted to, as he told her that special moment had to be reserved for their wedding night; virginity was something Gladys would have required of Elvis's bride. When Elvis returned to the States, Priscilla was devastated; all she prayed for was becoming the beloved of Elvis. They found separation painful; he burned up the long-distance wires and she sent love letters in pink envelopes.

Despite the headlines that Presley was having affairs with the most sought-after stars of the era, when Priscilla was sixteen he persuaded her parents to allow her to move with him to Graceland, promising them she would attend a Catholic girls' school. He arranged for her auburn hair to be dyed to match his black pompadour, and her makeup was heavy on Cleopatra-style eyeliner.

Over the years Priscilla and Elvis's love ever deepened. However, though she was envied by Elvis fans worldwide, she once more felt the pain of being the army brat; with Elvis's constant performances and movies, she was often alone and alienated once more. And when he was home, he was always surrounded by the "Memphis Mafia," a group composed of his flunkies. To compound her situation, after she graduated from high school Elvis did not allow her to pursue a career. He claimed he always needed her to be around when he wanted her. Equally painful, he engaged in numerous affairs; Priscilla was far from pleased when she discovered a letter from a woman who signed herself "Lizard Tongue." To add to Priscilla's problems, Elvis's behavior had become increasingly erratic with his escalating drug and food abuse. He also fired shots at his innumerable televisions when he did not like their programs. Priscilla was in dire need of her guardian angel.

Nevertheless, in 1966, still madly in love, Priscilla accepted his proposal, which was accompanied by a 3.5-karat diamond ring, and they were married in the Aladdin Hotel in Las Vegas on May 6, 1967. They were flown to their Palm Springs honeymoon on Frank Sinatra's Learjet, the *Christina*, and Elvis carried his bride over the threshold singing "The Hawaiian Wedding Song." Priscilla was overjoyed that the love of her life was now her husband and she would now have the respect due Mrs. Presley, something she was always denied when the press dubbed her "Elvis's Live-In Lolita."

Nine months later Lisa Marie Presley was born. Although her birth brought them together, it also helped contribute to the demise of their marriage. Elvis had a Madonna complex; he no longer sexually desired the woman who had given birth to his child. By 1976, Priscilla had washed the makeup from her eyes; Cilla could no longer exist. No longer able to live happily in the world of Graceland, Priscilla made the most difficult decision of her life—she began an affair with her karate teacher and moved out of the mansion that had become her prison. Although she would forever love Elvis, she could not live with him. To do so would have meant her emotional demise. She knew she could not save the King; all she could do was save herself. Overcome by his misery, Elvis sat down in a Las Vegas suite and wrote a prayer asking God to forgive him for anything he might have done to hurt Priscilla and his little girl. Sequined and stoned on stage,

Elvis serenaded his audience, though the songs were for the woman he had lost: "Hurt," "Separate Ways," "Always on My Mind."

While a single Priscilla blossomed, Elvis's life spiraled ever further out of control. With the loss of the trinity of the only women he had ever loved, Graceland became his Heartbreak Hotel.

Postscript

➤ Elvis Presley passed away in 1977 in Memphis from ailments exacerbated by drug use; he had fourteen different drugs (both legal and illegal) in his system. His funeral was held at Graceland. Outside the gates, a car plowed into a group of fans, killing two women and critically injuring a third. Approximately one hundred thousand people, despite the stifling heat, lined the processional route to Forest Hill Cemetery. More than a hundred vans were needed to transport the floral tributes from his fans. A motorcade of fourteen white Cadillacs and a hearse made its way to the plot where Presley was interred next to Gladys Love Presley. It was a fitting send-off for a king. An attempt was made to steal his body; afterward the remains of both Elvis and his mother were reburied in Graceland's Meditation Garden.

30

John Lennon and Yoko Ono

1966

John Lennon, whose 1960s mantra was to give peace a chance, was gunned down by a random act of madness. The world mourned his passing, but none more than the woman with whom he had helped define an era.

John Winston Lennon was born in 1940 on a night when the sky rained death from the Luftwaffe attack on England. When his sailor father returned and found his wife pregnant by another man, he took off, and custody of John was ultimately regulated to his Aunt Mimi. However, John stayed close to his mother, Julia, and was devastated when she was killed in a car accident when he was seventeen. He met his wife Cynthia when both were enrolled in the Liverpool College of Art. Eventually his group, the Beatles, afforded him superstardom, though happiness remained elusive.

John's destiny, Yoko Ono, was born in Japan to a wealthy banking family with imperial ties. She survived the bombing of Tokyo when her family sheltered in a special bunker. After a failed first marriage she wed Anthony Cox, who tracked her down to a Japanese mental institution, where her family had placed her after a suicide attempt. Their union disintegrated and the couple threatened one another with kitchen knives; however, they stayed together for the sake of their careers and their daughter, Kyoko.

The first time John met Yoko was on November 9 when Lennon went to the London-based Indica Gallery to view an avant-garde exhibit. When John entered, the Japanese artist who was in charge of the show, Yoko Ono, passed him a card that bore one word: *Breathe.* One exhibit was a white board with a sign that invited visitors to hammer an illusory nail in its surface. Yoko told John Lennon that he could hammer in a nail for five shillings. John then responded with his first words to the woman who would become his last love, "I'll give you an imaginary five shillings if you let me hammer in an imaginary nail." Their connection was instantaneous.

One of the main impediments with John and Yoko having a relationship was their respective spouses and children. Nevertheless, John felt, from the onset, that their love was preordained, that Yoko was both his soul mate and muse. In 1980, in an interview with *Playboy* magazine, he explained that when he wrote "Lucy in the Sky with Diamonds," his mind harbored "the image of the female who would someday come save me—a 'girl with kaleidoscope eyes.' It turned out to be Yoko, though I hadn't met Yoko yet." At one point, John and Yoko decided to be together, despite all marriages.

In May 1968, John treated his wife Cynthia to a vacation in Greece. On the night before her return he invited Yoko to his country home in Weybridge. They talked for hours and made an experimental recording that would later be released under the title *Unfinished Music No. 1: Two Virgins.* It was thus christened because they considered themselves virgins emotionally and physically, until they had met one another. Its cover depicted the couple, sans clothes, from the back. At dawn they consummated their union. When Cynthia returned home, she found her husband and Yoko sitting together in robes (Yoko was wearing Cynthia's), drinking tea, and sharing an undeniable aura of intimacy.

Cynthia later said of her reaction to the tableau, "I was absolutely shattered . . . I felt I had to get out of there immediately," which she did. After a brief reconciliation, the couple divorced in May; Cynthia received custody of five-year-old Julian. Paul McCartney penned "Hey Jude" for their son to help soften the pain of his father's departure. In future years Cynthia stated, "John is neither a saint or a sinner. He was just human, like the rest of us." In the same interview, when asked about her relationship with Yoko, she responded, "A freezing day in Moscow, before the cold war ended."

Lennon moved to a London flat owned by Beatle drummer Ringo Starr. He later said of this "summer of love," "It was a strange cocktail of love, sex and forgetfulness. When we weren't in the studio we were in bed."

It was in the studio where, partially because of John's consuming relationship with Yoko, problems arose between him and the other Beatles. Not willing to be apart from the woman he loved, John began to bring Yoko to recording sessions; at the time the Beatles were working on the White Album. Ono, never one to keep her strong opinions to herself, wasn't shy about offering musical suggestions, which exacerbated tensions that were already simmering. Lennon felt that his bandmates and others at Apple Studio disliked Yoko because she was strong willed and Japanese; he said they judged her "like a fucking book." Ono said of the situation, "I sort of went to bed with this guy that I liked, and suddenly the next morning I see these three in-laws standing there."

In October, more trouble followed when John was arrested for possession of an illegal drug. Although it did not seem significant at the time, it was to later pose grave problems. By 1970 the in-laws had gone their own ways and John embarked on a solo career. In 1973 he penned his immortal "Imagine," his vision of a utopian world.

On March 20, 1969, John Lennon and Yoko Ono were married at the British consulate on the Rock of Gibraltar in a ten-minute ceremony. In deference to Yoko, the adoring husband legally changed his name to John Winston Ono Lennon. The couple decided to use their notoriety to promote the issues they believed in. The Lennons' unconventional honeymoon became an integral part of the Beatles mythology. Though it is not unusual for newlyweds to spend an inordinate amount of time in bed, the Lennons spent seven days in theirs. They booked room 902, the presidential suite in the Amsterdam Hilton, in what they termed a "bed-in." The press excitedly pursued them, assuming that the famous nudists would provide a provocative peep show. Instead, the pajama-clad newlyweds spoke out for international peace. It was the honeymoon as performance art: its theme a protest against the Vietnam War.

In May they staged a second weeklong bed-in in Montreal, at the stately Queen Elizabeth Hotel, where they recorded their famous pacifist anthem. John and Yoko, along with Dr. Timothy Leary, Montreal Rabbi Abraham Feinberg, Petula Clark, and members of the Canadian Radha Krishna Temple sang the chorus for "Give Peace a Chance." While the hippies embraced the song, Lennon did the same with his dearly beloved: "When I fell in love with Yoko, I knew, my GOD, this is different from anything I've ever known . . . This is more than a hit record, more than gold, more than anything."

Unfortunately, even a honeymoon that consisted of a bed-in has an expiration date. The fabric of their relationship began to tear when John was threatened with deportation from the States because of his earlier drug arrest, and Yoko could not move to Britain because she was sharing parenting of Kyoko in New York City. Then, in 1971, Cox kidnapped their eight-year-old daughter and disappeared into a cult: the Church of the Living Word. He changed his daughter's name to Rosemary.

As a refuge from their troubles, John began to find solace in alcohol, and by 1973 the couple's relationship went the way of the Beatles. John moved to Los Angeles, where he started living with Yoko's former assistant, May Pang. It soon became apparent that he was miserable without Yoko. He later told *Playboy* that without Yoko, "I was on a raft alone in the middle of the universe . . . It was the lost weekend that lasted 18 months. I've never drunk so much in my life. I tried to drown myself in the bottle."

He begged his wife for another chance; she relented and he moved back to their New York City home in the Dakota. Realizing that Yoko was central to his life, he penned "God," in which he wrote he didn't believe in any "ism." All he believed in was "Yoko and me."

In 1975, after several miscarriages, at age forty-two, Yoko became pregnant. John, who had not been very involved in his son Julian's life, and Yoko, who had lost Kyoko, decided that their baby would be the focus of their lives. Yoko offered John a deal that he readily accepted: "I am carrying the baby nine months, and that is enough. You take care of it afterward." Sean Taro Ono Lennon was born on his father's thirty-fifth birthday; John was only too happy to be a stay-at-home dad. He retired from performing and Yoko managed their $200 million portfolio as if it were her new art form. John was able to make the transition because it was only his music he had taken seriously, never himself. An oft-repeated comment was, "I'm just a rocker."

After years in seclusion, John decided to make a musical comeback. In December 1980, he and Yoko spent an evening recording "Walking on Thin Ice"; they were elated that John's latest album had gone gold that day. To celebrate, Yoko suggested they go out for dinner; John refused with what were to be his last words: "No. Let's go home because I want to see Sean before he goes to sleep." When their limo pulled up to the curb, deranged fan Mark David Chapman, who a few hours earlier had received Lennon's autograph, was waiting in the shadows. Within seconds of John's arrival, Chapman fired five shots; one shattered a window in the Dakota, and the other four inflicted fatal injuries. Ono, in utter shock, kept sobbing, "Oh no, no, no, no . . . tell me it's not true."

The following day, before Yoko went into an extended period of seclusion, she issued the following message: "There is no funeral for John. John loved and prayed for the human race. Please pray the same for him." The love story that had begun on an imaginative note had ended on a tragic one.

Postscript

➤ Lennon's ashes were kept by his grieving widow. Yoko's ex-husband, Anthony Cox, as well as seventeen-year-old Kyoto sent a message of condolence, though they remained in hiding.

➤ Thousands gathered in Central Park; his songs were played. One grieving fan held up a sign with John's photograph, the peace sign, and the single word *WHY?*

➤ On December 14, millions of people around the world responded to Yoko's request to pause for ten minutes of silence to remember John. Thirty thousand gathered in Liverpool; a hundred thousand converged in Central Park, close to the scene of the shooting.

31

Paul McCartney and Linda Eastman

1967

*T*he troubadour of romance, Paul McCartney, ironically trod a long and winding road until he met the one he would immortalize in his song "Lovely Linda." He met her at a club called the Bag O'Nails. There, the man who could have any woman he wanted found the one he needed; she was to become his soul mate. His term of endearment for her: *lovely*.

Linda Louise Eastman was born and raised in Scarsdale, New York. Her father, the son of Jewish-Russian immigrants, changed his name from Leopold Vail Epstein to Lee Eastman; he became a Harvard-educated entertainment lawyer. Her mother, Louise Linder, was the status-conscious heiress of a department store fortune. Their multimillion-dollar home was lined with works by de Kooning and other eminent painters. Linda, however, did not relish the role of Scarsdale society; her favorite fashion statement was to wear one red argyle sock and one green one. While her peers rode in sports cars, she was happiest on horseback and her room was lined with blue ribbons.

Linda was devastated when her mother died in a plane crash, and she sought solace with fellow classmate from the University of Arizona, Joseph Melvin See Jr. They married in 1962 and six months later their daughter, Heather, was born. When he asked Linda to move with him to Africa, she refused, realizing that her marriage had just been undertaken in the wake of grief. They divorced in 1965; he committed suicide in 2000. After graduation Linda and Heather moved to New York City, where she became a receptionist at *Town & Country* magazine, written for the rich and those intrigued by the rich (Linda did not fall into either category, as she was self-supporting). Yet through this job, she was to receive an invitation which would lead her down a road as fascinating as Dorothy's yellow brick one.

Linda's destiny, James Paul McCartney, was born into a working-class family in Liverpool, England, where he enjoyed a happy, uneventful childhood, along with younger brother Michael. Paul's life was shattered when his mother, Mary, died suddenly from breast cancer when he was fourteen years old. To help him cope with his devastating loss, he turned to music and songwriting; at age sixteen he composed "When I'm Sixty-Four." A short time later he was performing at a local church party when, in the music industry's greatest instance of serendipity, he met John Lennon, who invited him to join his band, the Quarrymen. Later, in a nod to Buddy Holly's band the Crickets, they changed the group's name to the Beatles. The rest, as the saying goes, was history.

After their release of "Please Please Me," Beatlemania exploded. There were any number of girls who wanted to hold the hand of the "cute" Beatle, Paul, whose face was emblazoned on reams of posters. A string of one-night stands led Lennon to dub McCartney a "sex gladiator." However, soon he was to meet the one who made him wish "to dance with no other."

Through her magazine, Linda received an invitation to attend a Rolling Stones party on the yacht, the SS *Sea Panther*, which was docked in the Hudson River. During the event, photographers snapped the Rolling Stones' portraits, but the results were stilted; however, photos taken by Linda captured the boys in all their youthful vitality. Her work became so in demand that she became the visual chronicler of the sixties. In the process she also bedded some of her portraits' subjects: Mick Jagger, Jim Morrison, Neil Young, and Jimi Hendrix. Linda was elated when she left her job at *Town & Country* to become *Rolling Stone*'s magazine photographer, and in that capacity she was sent to swinging London to capture the images that were making it swing.

The first time Linda met Paul was on May 15 at the Bag O'Nails. Paul saw Linda across a crowded room and was mesmerized by her smile; he later recalled of that magic moment, "Across a crowded room, as they say, our eyes met and the violins started playing . . . There was an immediate attraction between us. As she was leaving—she was with the group The Animals, whom she'd been photographing—I saw an obvious opportunity. I said: 'My name's Paul. What's yours?' I think she probably recognized me. It was so corny, but I told the kids later, had it not been for that moment, none of them would be here."

He invited her and The Animals, as well as the British singer Lulu, to another club, the Speak Easy. There they heard, for the first time, "A Whiter Shade of Pale," which was to become Linda and Paul's personal song. The group ended up in McCartney's home, where Linda was impressed with his Magritte paintings and Paul was impressed with her knowledge of them. Four days later, their paths crossed once more at the home of the Beatles' producer, Brian Epstein, at a party thrown to celebrate the release of *Sergeant Pep-*

per's Lonely Hearts Club Band. The celebration was an A-list event, but Linda secured her entry by trading a portrait of Brian Jones for a coveted invitation. Linda was able to snap pictures of the Beatles, as well as to have a further conversation with Paul, and it was on that evening that their first picture together was taken. After the party, Linda returned to New York City, sans her heart. She was in love with the man with whom she had to compete with every other female on both sides of the Atlantic.

In June 1968, Paul flew to Los Angeles to promote his new Apple label, and two days later he phoned Linda in New York to ask her to join him at the Beverly Hills Hotel. The sexual chemistry was such that before Paul could ask if she had a good flight, they were discovering that their physical connection matched their emotional one. Two months after this rendezvous, he called Linda to ask her to live with him. Shortly afterward, with Heather calling Paul "Daddy" and with Linda's pregnancy, Paul proposed. He said her ring was symbolic of his bride-to-be: simple and gold.

The couple wanted a quiet wedding with Heather as the bridesmaid. On March 12, 1969, they said their "I do's" in a seven-minute civil ceremony in the Marylebone registry office; the bride was clad in yellow. When they emerged, they were greeted by hundreds of hysterical girls, and the news, which made headlines in the international press, resulted in females around the world donning black. Heather had to be rescued from the crush of the crowd by a policeman. Linda told the *Daily Mail*, "Just write that the bride wore a big smile." The civil ceremony was followed by a religious one at St. John's Wood church; the reception was held at the Ritz Hotel in Piccadilly. Their honeymoon, which included Heather, whom Paul adopted, was to the States to visit Linda's family. Because the Beatles were in the midst of disbanding, his former bandmates were not in attendance.

Although the world harbored the view that contentment had come for the cute, promiscuous young rock star, the reality did not mirror that illusion. In 1971, the McCartneys were living on their Scottish farm, with Heather and their first child together, Mary, while the Beatles disintegrated. Paul was distraught and felt that without John he would not be able to write. However, Linda's belief that he could led to his belief in himself. He credited her as the woman who gave him "the strength and courage to work again." That same year Linda was in the hospital giving birth to their daughter Stella; complications set in and the lives of both mother and child were in jeopardy. Paul recounts that as he was in the hospital, feverishly praying, the vision of wings came into his mind. With their recovery, he decided to start his own group, and named it Wings after the image that had come to him in prayer.

Linda performed backup vocals in the band, as they wanted to spend as much time together as possible. The fans who had initially resented Linda for snagging the cute musical demigod soon came to embrace her as the good Beatle wife, the anti-Yoko who kept the home fires, and her man, stoked. McCartney wrote a number of love songs, all for his wife.

Paul and Linda, who had a fourth child, James, shared such a close bond that the only nights they spent apart were the ten when Paul was in a Japanese jail for marijuana possession. This event was overshadowed when Paul received a knighthood and they became Sir Paul and Lady Linda. Another bond they shared was their aversion to eating meat, and they became staunch supporters of PETA. Asked about the secret of their marriage's success, Paul replied, "I guess it's because we just adore each other."

The long, winding, and joyous road came to its end when Linda was diagnosed with the same killer that had taken Paul's mother. The hair that was once adorned with flowers was shorn when it began falling out in clumps from chemotherapy.

Knowing the inevitable was coming, Paul took Linda and the children to their ranch in Arizona; she rode her horse up to two days before her passing. In 1998, Paul said his last words to his first love: "You're up on your beautiful Appaloosa stallion. It's a fine spring day. We're riding through the woods. The bluebells are all out, and the sky is clear blue." Lovely Linda was gone, though her memory never would be. Of his loss of the woman he called his best friend, Paul said, "People say time heals, but what it's doing is not healing, it is making you forget. In some ways that's a bad thing. I don't want to forget her." The greatest tribute to Linda's memory—Paul's "Maybe I'm Amazed."

Postscript

➤ Linda McCartney was cremated at her Tucson ranch; her ashes were scattered there as well as on the family farm in Scotland. A memorial service was held at St. Martin-in-the-Fields in London, which was attended by the remaining Beatles George Harrison and Ringo Starr. Paul asked that in lieu of flowers, donations be made to cancer research and animal welfare charities. Then he added that if people really wanted to pay tribute to his wife, "Go veggie."

32

Patrick Swayze and Lisa Niemi

1971

*P*atrick Swayze, seriously sexy in his prime, danced his way into American hearts in his role as Johnny Castle in the ultimate chick-flick romance *Dirty Dancing*. Audiences swooned along with "Baby" Houseman (Jennifer Grey) as she found the heat of first passion in his powerful arms. What was not apparent, however, was Patrick's love affair with his noncelluloid leading lady, the woman he immortalized in his song "She's Like the Wind."

Patrick Wayne Swayze, born in Houston in 1952, was one of five children. His aspiration to a football scholarship ended with a high school knee injury. During his convalescence he heard his mother, Patsy, sobbing in the next room, "His life is over." However, he traded his dream for another: to become an Olympic gymnast. He worked out at the Swayze Dance Studio (later merged with another), run by Patsy. Patrick said of his mother's studio, "All these girls were studying with my mum and I used to go and check them out in their leotards. It was like being in a candy store."

Patrick's destiny, Lisa Anne Haapaniemi, was born in Houston, the only daughter of six children to parents of Finnish descent. At age fifteen she encountered the two passions that were to dominate her life: dance and her "till death do they part."

The first time Patrick met Lisa was in the Houston Ballet Dance Company, when he was immediately drawn to the lithe fifteen-year-old with the long blond hair. However, unlike other girls, she stared at twenty-year-old Patrick with indifference. To get her attention, he pinched her on the rear and said, "Hey there, cutie!" The ploy did not earn the desired response. Lisa wasn't interested because she was turned off by his Casanova reputation and ego the size of Texas. In addition, Lisa was focused not on romance, but on dance, which she wanted to parlay into an exit from a home punctuated by her parents' contentious relationship.

Despite her apathy, Patrick continued to be captivated by the quiet girl who was so unlike other seventies Texan teens who sported big hair and were no strangers to makeup. However, the magic moment came when they rehearsed a dance: At one point Patrick had to ease Lisa onto the floor and lie on top of her. This had quite a heady effect on the twenty-year-old male. Patrick could not wait for the next rehearsal. He also asked her out.

On the date, the only part of the evening Patrick was not looking forward to was the scrutiny of her five tall, Nordic-looking brothers. During the evening, however, Lisa and Patrick's mutual shyness made Patrick run his mouth, and the conversation mainly revolved around Patrick's narcissism. The dinner was not the romantic encounter that Patrick had hoped it would be.

At age twenty, after completing two years of college, Swayze left Houston when he joined Disney on Parade Ice Follies in the role of Prince Charming. As most of the cast were women and few of the men were straight, Casanova held court once more. Despite new conquests, Swayze still carried the torch for his Texas Cinderella.

While Patrick was skating, Lisa was still in Houston, skating on thin ice. Because of her home-life she began to suffer from depression; desperate, she approached Patsy and asked if she could move into the Swayze home. When Patrick returned to Houston, he was thrilled to see the girl of his dreams living with his family, and the two began making out on every possible occasion. As it turned out, Lisa had actually been interested in Patrick all along, but had just camouflaged her feelings as a shield against getting hurt and to mask her shyness.

Patrick received a scholarship to study dance in New York City, and for his final Houston evening, he picked up Lisa (once more staying with her family) and took her for dinner, where she gave him a fifty-cent coin for luck. He gave her a broken Mickey Mouse watch from Disney on Parade. He also presented her with a card expressing his love, one that she would keep forever. It ended, "Work hard on your dancing and I'll do the same, and maybe, someday . . . ! My heart be united with yours, Buddy." Unfortunately, the night ended on a low note. After he had dropped Lisa off, he was arrested for a traffic violation, and the fine forced him to part with his lucky coin.

Two years later, in 1974, Lisa received the same ballet scholarship and joined him in his New York City apartment as a roommate. However, when their platonic relationship evolved into a physical one, Patrick insisted that they get married, and they were wed in Houston on June 12, 1975, two months after getting engaged. The ceremony took place in her family's backyard, and the reception was held in the dance studio where they had met. Lisa sewed both her wedding gown and her groom's three-piece suit. For their honeymoon the newlyweds borrowed a motorcycle and rode to Lake Travis, 180 miles outside Houston. Patrick wrote of the low-cost getaway, "We had the time of our lives."

In the tradition of "Go west, young man, go west," Patrick and Lisa decided that opportunity beckoned in Hollywood; armed with

$2,000 in savings, they said farewell to New York City. Upon arrival they stayed in a hotel that rented by the hour.

Swayze landed on Hollywood's radar when Francis Ford Coppola hired him as well as other unknown young men (all of whom would achieve star status) to play the Greasers in *The Outsiders*, the 1983 adaptation of S. E. Hinton's teen-angst novel. However, immortality truly knocked when he played the role of a Catskills dance instructor in *Dirty Dancing*. Swayze and Grey danced as if they had been going cheek to cheek and pelvis to pelvis all their lives, and females fantasized about being Baby to Patrick, who was profiled in 1991 as *People* magazine's Sexiest Man Alive. The film seared the catchphrase "Nobody puts Baby in a corner" into the lingo of every female who saw it, and the blockbuster became one of the most reliable date movies ever.

However, although having attained sex symbol status, Patrick only had eyes for Lisa, with whom he had practiced all his dance moves. In fact, one of the film's main songs, "She's Like the Wind," was written by Patrick for Lisa.

Patrick had the armor of love, fame, and fortune; depression, nevertheless, still slipped through the chinks. This was brought on by a series of slings and arrows: the death of his father, the suicide of his sister, Lisa's miscarriage, and the passing of a beloved dog. For consolation, Patrick began drinking, which led to tensions in his marriage. Lisa had been there during the lean years and several death-defying injuries (her husband said he was an adrenaline junkie), but her husband's alcoholism was something she could not tolerate, and she moved out of their ranch. Patrick went cold turkey, and through the assistance of a psychic the couple reconciled, much to their mutual relief. Lisa said, "Love is supposed to start with bells ringing and go downhill from there. But it was the opposite for me. There's an intense connection between us, and as we stayed together, the bells rang louder."

In Aspen, as Lisa and Patrick toasted the New Year in 2008, Patrick felt ill; the diagnosis was stage four pancreatic cancer. He battled his disease with a cowboy's grit and a dancer's grace. In the summer of 2008, the couple decided to have a second wedding ceremony to commemorate their union. In front of a few guests, Patrick rode to his beloved bride on a white stallion and recited his last vows to his first love, "You are my woman, my lover, my mate, and my lady. I've loved you forever, I love you now, and I will love you forever more." Ironically, the lyric that Patrick had composed became a metaphor for himself; like the wind Lisa would never see Patrick, but his presence would forever be felt.

Postscript

➤ On September 14, 2009, Patrick passed away; he was cremated and his ashes were scattered over his New Mexico ranch.

33

Prince Charles and Camilla Shand

1971

F. Scott Fitzgerald wrote, "There are no second acts in American lives." However, at least in one instance, this did not hold true in Britain, where Prince Charles was able to find in middle age the love that had eluded him in his youth. He was able to obtain that rarest of gifts: a second chance.

Camilla Rosemary Shand was born in Sussex, the oldest child of Major Bruce Shand, a wine merchant, and Rosalind Cubitt. As the daughter of wealth, Camilla was educated in Paris and Switzerland; she graduated with an ability to fence and a £500,000 inheritance from the Cubitt family, who had developed much of Belgravia. When she returned to England she became part of the moneyed horse set of London, where she pursued her passion for all things equestrian, including fox hunting. Her only connection with royalty was that she was a descendant of Alice Keppel, who was King Edward VII's mistress. Camilla's station groomed her for a place in society as the wife of a wealthy aristocrat. However, the Fates had far too fertile an imagination for such a mundane scenario.

Camilla's destiny, Charles Philip Arthur George, was born in Buckingham Palace and baptized with water from the River Jordan by the Archbishop of Canterbury. At age four, when his mother, Princess Elizabeth, became queen, his titles exceeded even the length of his name. He was raised by a nanny until he was sent to school in Scotland, of which dreadful experience he said, "Colditz in kilts."

As the Prince of Wales, heir to the powerful, prestigious, and fabulous fortune that went along with his role as the man who would be king, his every romantic gesture was a matter of public speculation, and a bevy of beauties were willing to fall into his royal arms. Nevertheless, irrespective of the truth of rumors, the hurdles of marriage for the heir were high ones; his wife had to meet certain exact standards as she had to produce future monarchs, and, because of a 1772 Act, he was legally obliged to obtain his mother's approval of spouse as a condition of ascending the throne. For his first marriage, approval was granted with alacrity; for the second, he was to have to wait three decades.

The first time Camilla met Charles was in June at the Guards Polo Club in Windsor when she approached him with her British variation of chutzpah: "My great-grandmother was the mistress of your great-great-grandfather, so how about it?" With such an opening gambit, what man could resist? The icebreaker proved refreshing to a man treated only with the utmost politically correct obsequiousness. Prince Charles was immediately captivated by the "breath of fresh air," as he later described Camilla. And so commenced a courtship cemented by time-honored relationship glues: a shared sense of humor; a love of dogs, horses, polo, gardening, and the countryside; as well as a passion for blood sports. They became inseparable and were the high-profile couple seen in London's hottest spots.

Alas, the course of true love, even for him who would wield the scepter, did not run smooth. Had the prince then proposed, tabloid journalism would have lost its crown jewel of scandal. Instead, unable to navigate his heart, Prince Charles went to serve his stint of eight months in the Caribbean with the Royal Navy, only to find, upon his return, that Camilla was engaged to cavalry officer Andrew Parker Bowles, with whom she was to have two children. The price of prevarication was to lose the one woman with whom he could have found happiness. This left the bereft prince to troll the aristocracy, dating the kind of girls who would make a fitting consort for a king. Heartbroken, Charles wrote to his great-uncle Lord Mountbatten (who was later killed in an IRA terrorist attack), "I suppose the feeling of emptiness will pass eventually."

Prince Charles married Lady Diana Spencer in 1981 at St. Paul's Cathedral in a ceremony referred to as "a fairy tale wedding," one in which she rode to the church in a glass carriage and white gown with a twenty-five-foot train. The television audience numbered 750 million and the occasion was a national holiday in the United Kingdom. Unfortunately, the coach soon turned into a pumpkin. Although Diana quickly became the people's princess, emotionally there was no connection between the royal couple. Diana may have been a godsend for the House of Windsor's gene pool and for the tabloid press, but she was a complete mismatch for her spouse. She was twelve years his junior with a life experience of absolutely nothing beyond some light work as a kindergarten teacher. Diana's interests were a passion for fashion, celebrities, and, later on, humanitarian causes; Charles's interests are architecture, horses, the environment, and philosophy.

Marital tensions began even before the tying of the Windsor knot when Diana chanced upon a bracelet Charles had bought for Camilla, engraved with the letters "GF" for Gladys and Fred, nicknames the childhood sweethearts had conferred on one another from Charles's beloved *Goon Show*. Similarly, a few days after the honeymoon, Charles appeared at an official dinner for President Sadat of Egypt on board the royal yacht *Britannia* wearing new gold cuff links—a present from the other woman in the form of two interlinked *C*s. However, as her face was already on the tea towels of the souvenir shops and too timid to break it off, Diana plunged ahead, naively believing that love was to follow marriage, rather than the other way around.

A few years later, their only commonalities were their two sons, as well as a mutual dislike of one another. Diana was angry at being one side of a royal triangle, with the other two being Charles and Camilla. Diana's name for Camilla was "the Rottweiler"; Camilla called Diana "that ridiculous creature." The media chronicled Diana's misery through reports of bulimia, crying jags, and suicide attempts.

One pro-Diana source, in an attempt to deflect the negative spotlight onto her philandering husband, created a scandal known as Camillagate, one of the least proud moments in the history of the British monarchy. The individual taped a mobile telephone call in which Camilla told Charles, "I'd suffer anything for you. That's love." Charles replied, a tad less lyrically, that he hoped to be reincarnated as her tampon. Queen Elizabeth's private reaction to the public tidbit is not known, but suffice it to say that the servants must have ducked for cover.

The tape's leak served to turn the Windsors' marital tribulations into the most publicized in history, and life at Kensington Palace became an international soap opera. People were sharply divided into who was more the sinner or who was the more sinned against, but in one area they were united: How could the prince prefer the other woman to the princess? In an effort at damage control, the prince agreed to appear on BBC television, and though he did not mention Camilla by name, he did admit he had committed adultery, though only after his marriage had irretrievably broken down. This public mea culpa signaled the death knell of the Parker Bowles marriage, and they amicably divorced. Diana went on to state in her own television interview, "There were three of us in this marriage, so it was a bit crowded." Charles and Diana acrimoniously divorced, thus ending the War of the Windsors. One year later she was dead as a result of a Parisian car crash. A backlash of anger was turned on Camilla. However, with time, and with a carefully orchestrated campaign of public appearances and Valentino gowns, the British populace grudgingly came around. After all, Charles was their prince and had a right to his happiness.

In 2005, Prince Charles, wearing his most expensive Savile Row suit, knelt to ask for something that, for years, Camilla had always extended—her hand. On her finger he placed an engagement ring that had once belonged to the Queen Mother. Charles's mistake was to get his weddings out of order; he married his true love second and his trophy wife first.

The April 9 wedding (which had been postponed for a day so Charles could attend the pope's funeral) did not possess the pomp and circumstance of his first, and Camilla was not the stereotypical princess bride, but this time the groom's feeling of emptiness had finally passed. In the sense that love can endure over time, this too was a fairy-tale wedding, one in which we can only hope the erstwhile star-crossed lovers will, at long last, live happily ever after.

34

René Angélil and Céline Dion

1980

*F*rench Canada's most famous face, Céline Dion, made her American debut in *Beauty and the Beast* with her song "Tale as Old as Time"; she earned the moniker "the voice of the century" in *Titanic* with her song "My Heart Will Go On." However, Celine had the wisdom to understand that the acclaim of the many was nothing compared to her relationship with René, the man whom she described as "the color of love."

René Angélil was born in Montreal in 1942, a French-Canadian of Catholic Syrian-Lebanese ancestry. As a teenager, he developed two passions: playing cards and performing pop music. He, along with three friends, formed the group the Baronets (named after a hockey team) which catered to the short-lived Quebec market for translations of English-language pop hits from Britain and the United States. At age twenty-four he married Denyse Duquette, with whom he had one child, Patrick, in 1968; the marriage ended in 1973. After the dissolution of his group, he became a managing artist for singer Ginette Reno. However, a future client would introduce him to the international spotlight and a romance that is the stuff that dreams are made of.

René's destiny, Céline Marie Claudette Dion, was born in Charlemagne, Quebec, in 1968, to a mother who already felt overwhelmed with thirteen children. She received her name because of the Hugues Aufray song "Céline," which was a huge success in her province. From a young age, Céline would perform on the kitchen table, a fork as her microphone. Her first public appearance was in her parents' small piano bar, where the family performed in a French-Canadian version of the Austrian von Trapps. Word spread that the little girl possessed a voice that would make even the angels weep.

When Céline was twelve, her mother decided that her daughter needed an original song to break into show business; the result was *"Ce n'était qu'un rêve"* ("It Was Only a Dream"). Her mother Thérèse and brother Jacques composed the lyrics, and Céline supplied the vocals. It then fell upon her brother Michel to find the agent, whom he discovered on a Ginette Reno album. The demo was sent off in a brown paper bag, tied with a red ribbon. After two weeks, when the desperately desired call never came, Michel contacted the agent and asked why he had not listened to his sister's tape. When the man asked him how he knew he hadn't, Michel replied that if he had done so, he would have called. An audition was arranged that very afternoon.

The first time René met Céline was when she and her mother entered René's office, where he asked her to sing. When she said she needed a mike, he handed her a pen. During the rendition, René had tears in his eyes.

René was so convinced that the girl was Canada's Judy Garland that he mortgaged the home he shared with his second wife, singer Manon Kirouac, and their two children, Jean-Pierre and Anne-Marie, to produce Céline's first album, *La Voix du bon Dieu* (*The*

Voice of God). On the cover of the album she refused to smile because two of her teeth gave her a vampire look, which had made her classmates dub her "Dracula." With her first paycheck she indulged in her first high-heeled black shoes.

At age eighteen she told René she wanted to be a star like Michael Jackson, which meant breaking into the American market. René arranged for her to disappear from the spotlight while she underwent dental work and learned English. She also used her hiatus to work on her sex appeal; the girl who always sang about the power of love had fallen hopelessly in love—with her manager. During her break she set herself a goal: "I was going to train myself in the art of seduction, like a top athlete, and snag René Angélil once and for all."

When she returned and he got his first glimpse of his protégée, she noted with elation that "she could see him reeling." She recalled, "For the first time, I felt him looking at me the way a man who desires a woman looks at her, not just looking at me the way an impresario looks at his artist." Céline knew one day they would be intimate, and, in the words of her song, their love would go on.

When René's wife asked for a divorce, Céline saw a glimmer of hope, which her mother did not share. Thérèse wrote a furious letter to Angélil accusing him of betraying her trust and that she wanted a prince for her princess, not a twice-divorced man, the father of three, who was two and a half times her daughter's age.

In Dublin, on April 30, 1988, after Céline won the Eurovision Song Contest, René accompanied her back to her room, as he had after each performance since he had become her manager. While he was talking about her success, she was pleased to be alone in a hotel room (her mother was ill and had not accompanied her) with the man she loved. Picking up on her intent, René inched to the door and was about to exit when she kissed him on the lips. He fled. Céline immediately called him and said if he didn't return immediately she would go to his room. He stammered that he needed time. René called several minutes later from the lobby and said, "If you really want to, I'll be the first." Her answer, "You'll be the first. And the only."

René insisted on secrecy of their affair, fearing that fans would think of her as his Lolita, as they had met when he was thirty-eight and she was twelve. Although Céline wanted to sing of their love from the rooftops, she reluctantly agreed, until she no longer could. At the Academy Awards, on Céline's twenty-fourth birthday, she performed "Tale as Old as Time" from Disney's *Beauty and the Beast*, for which she had won an Oscar. That evening, even though she sang for an audience of a billion, she also sang for one man. René had tears in his eyes as he listened to his protégée, the woman he loved.

When René gave Celine an engagement ring, she knew she could finally break her vow of secrecy. On her album *The Color of My Love*, she wrote, "René, you're the color of my love."

Celine and René were married on December 17, 1994, at Notre Dame Cathedral in Montreal. Thousands of fans were massed along the bridal route in homage to French Canada's royal wedding. The bride walked down the aisle on her father's arm with her eight sisters carrying her twenty-foot train; during the procession the instrumental was "The Color of Love." The royal wedding ceremony was broadcast live on Canadian television.

In 2003 Céline Dion signed a contract to perform at Caesar's Palace in Las Vegas for a staggering sum: $100 million. She was a resounding sensation, though René found himself under unwelcome scrutiny. Angélil was accused of sexual assault. He eventually paid the woman $2 million to settle the case; he claimed the money was not an admission of wrongdoing, but rather to avoid negative publicity that might upset his wife. Another unwelcome spotlight was directed on him when the London-based newspaper *The Observer* wrote, "Céline Dion's husband is a big gambler. He probably gambles $1 million a week, but he can afford to." Yet despite her fame and his infamy, the couple always maintained a united, and devoted, front.

At the end of 1999, Dion bid a farewell to the spotlight in Caesar's Palace in Las Vegas, where she planned on a hiatus, although she was a self-confessed stress junkie. She needed to concentrate on looking after the man who had spent his life looking after her: René had been diagnosed with neck cancer. His prayer was *"In Allah Rad"* ("By the grace of God"). Her final concert, dedicated to her husband, closed with her mother's song, "It Was Only a Dream." At the stroke of midnight, René came onstage and the two kissed for a very long time.

Five days later, Caesar's Palace was transformed into Céline's Palace when the couple renewed their marriage vows in an over-the-top gala, whose Arabian-inspired theme (replete with camels) was in tribute to René. In her autobiography, *My Story, My Dream*, she wrote, "René was a resounding success in the role of Grand Vizier; I was Scheherazade." Five months later, they received news that René's cancer was in remission and Céline was pregnant. René Charles, the baby for whom they had long prayed, was born in 2001. (Nine years and six fertility attempts later, Celine became pregnant with twins.)

Looking back at her Cinderella story, Celine must sometimes think *"Ce n'était qu'un rêve"* ("It Was Only a Dream").

BIBLIOGRAPHY

1. JACOB AND RACHEL

Coleman, Angela. "The Greatest Real Life Love Stories in History." Associated Content. www .associatedcontent.com/article/119352/the_greatest_real_life_love_stories.html?cat=37 (accessed March 24, 2010).

Cross Faith Ministry. "The Story of Rachel." http://crossfaithministry.org/rachel.html (accessed March 24, 2010).

Fletcher, Elizabeth. "Rachel: Love at First Sight." www.bible-people.info/Rachel.htm (accessed March 24, 2010).

Fletcher, Elizabeth. "Rachel: Love Conquers All." http://womeninthebible.net/1.4.Rachel.htm (accessed March 24, 2010).

Strauss, Richard L. "Never Satisfied!—The Story of Jacob and Rachel." Bible.org. http://bible .org/seriespage/never-satisfied-story-jacob-and-rachel (accessed March 24, 2010).

Wikipedia. "Jacob." http://en.wikipedia.org/wiki/Jacob (accessed March 24, 2010).

Wikipedia. "Rachel." http://en.wikipedia.org/wiki/Rachel (accessed March 24, 2010).

2. ABELARD AND HÉLOISE

Absolute Astronomy. "Héloise (student of Abelard)." www.absoluteastronomy.com/topics/He loise_(student_of_Abelard) (accessed June 20, 2009).

BBC. "The Love Story of Abelard and Héloise." www.bbc.co.uk/dna/h2g2/A36163938 (accessed June 20, 2009).

Bennett, Steve. "Héloise and Abelard: A Legendary Love." Review of *Love: A Suspect Form*, by Judith Infante. *San Antonio News*, December 7, 2008. www.mysanantonio.com/entertainment/ Heloise_and_Abelard_A_legendary_love.html (accessed June 20, 2009).

Bramwell, Sarah M. "Lusting after Wisdom." Review of *Heloise & Abelard: A New Biography*, by James Burge. Claremont Institute, August 22, 2005. www.claremont.org/publications/crb/id.1087/article_detail.asp (accessed June 20, 2009).

Crabtree, Samantha. "The Love Story of Peter Abelard and Héloise: The Tutor Falls in Love with the Pupil." Associated Content. March 18, 2009. www.associatedcontent.com/article/1495334/the_love_story_of_peter_abelard_and.html?cat=37 (accessed June 20, 2009).

"Héloise and Abelard: A New Musical. The Story." www.abelardandheloise.com/Story.html (accessed June 20, 2009).

"Héloise to Abelard." www.gyford.com/archive/2009/04/28/www.geocities.com/Paris/Parc/9893/heloise2.html (accessed March 28, 2010).

Jain, Priya. "Lust, Revenge and the Religious Right in 12th Century Paris." Review of *Heloise & Abelard: A New Biography*, by James Burge. *Salon*. http://dir.salon.com/story/books/review/2004/12/18/heloise/index.html (accessed June 20, 2009).

James, Caryn. "Review/Film: Doomed Passion of Abelard and Héloise." Review of the film *Stealing Heaven*. *New York Times*, April 28, 1989. http://movies.nytimes.com/movie/review?res=950DE1D8143FF93BA15757C0A96F948260 (accessed June 20, 2009).

Joseph, Leslie. "Ageless Love." Review of *Heloise & Abelard: A New Biography*, by James Burge. PopMatters.com, February 22, 2005. www.popmatters.com/books/reviews/h/heloise-and-abelard.shtml (accessed June 20, 2009).

Lombardi, Esther. "Abelard and Héloise: The Love Affair and the Letters." About.com: Classic Literature. http://classiclit.about.com/cs/articles/a/aa_abelard.htm (accessed June 20, 2009).

Love Letters Blog. "A Sad Tale of Love." April 29, 2007. http://ladybythewater.wordpress.com/2007/04/29/a-sad-tale-of-love/ (accessed June 20, 2009).

Medieval Life and Times. "Peter Abelard." www.medieval-life-and-times.info/medieval-religion/peter-abelard.htm.

Middle Ages. "Héloise." www.middle-ages.org.uk/heloise.htm.

Middle Ages. "Peter Abelard." www.middle-ages.org.uk/peter-abelard.htm.

O'Brien, Murrough. "Héloise and Abelard: A 12th-Century Love Story." Review of *Heloise & Abelard: A New Biography*, by James Burge. *Independent*, November 16, 2003. www.independent.co.uk/arts-entertainment/books/reviews/heloise-and-abelard-a-12thcentury-love-story-by-james-burge-736182.html (accessed June 20, 2009).

Scandalous Women Blog. "Scandalous Lovers: Abelard and Héloise." October 3, 2007. http://scandalouswoman.blogspot.com/2007/10/scandalous-lovers-abelard-and-heloise.html (accessed June 20, 2009).

Wikipedia. "Héloïse (abbess)." http://en.wikipedia.org/wiki/Héloise_(abbess) (accessed June 20, 2009).

Wikipedia. "Peter Abelard." http://en.wikipedia.org/wiki/Peter_abelard (accessed June 20, 2009).

Winner, Lauren F. "Love Story: New Light on Héloise and Abelard." Review of *Heloise & Abelard: A New Biography*, by James Burge. Christianity Today Library, January 1, 2005. www.ctlibrary.com/bc/2005/janfeb/2.15.html.

3. ANTONY AND CLEOPATRA

"Cleopatra: The Last Greek (Macedon) Queen of Egypt." http://macedonians.multiply.com/journal/item/49 (accessed March 28, 2010).

Cochrane-McIvor, Mary. "Dangerous, Alluring and Legendary: 'Antony and Cleopatra' at PA Shakespeare Festival." *Philadelphia Performing Arts Examiner*, July 22, 2009. www.examiner

.com/x-13327-Philadelphia-Performing-Arts-Examiner~y2009m7d22-Dangerous-allur
ing-and-legendary-Antony-and-Cleopatra-at-PA-Shakespeare-Festival (accessed March
27, 2010).

Crawford, Amy. "Who Was Cleopatra? Mythology, Propaganda, Liz Taylor and the Real Queen
of the Nile." *Smithsonian Magazine*, April 1, 2007. www.smithsonianmag.com/history
-archaeology/biography/cleopatra.html (accessed March 28, 2010).

EyeWitness to History. "Cleopatra Seduces Antony, 41 BC." http://eyewitnesstohistory.com/
pfcleopatra.htm (accessed March 28, 2010).

Old and Sold. "The Story of Antony and Cleopatra." www.oldandsold.com/articles23/famous
-people-1.shtml (accessed March 27, 2010).

Peel, Janette. "Love Can Be a Battlefield." Associated Content. February 27, 2009. www.associ
atedcontent.com/article/1518344/love_can_be_a_battlefield.html?cat=7 (accessed March
28, 2010).

Scandalous Women Blog. "Cleopatra Last Pharoah [sic] of Ancient Egypt." November 19, 2007.
http://scandalouswoman.blogspot.com/2007/11/cleopatra-last-pharoah-of-ancient
-egypt.html (accessed March 28, 2010).

Seabrook, Kim. "Cleopatra: The Last Pharaoh." February 27, 2010. http://quazen.com/reference/
biography/cleopatra-the-last-pharaoh/ (accessed March 28, 2010).

Stritof, Sheri, and Bob Stritof. "Marc Antony and Cleopatra Marriage Profile." About.com: Marriage. http://marriage.about.com/od/ancientegyptian/a/cleopatra.htm (accessed February 9, 2010).

Travel Egypt. "Cleopatra." www.travelegypt.com/peopleinfo/cleopatra.htm (accessed March
27, 2010).

Wikipedia. "Cleopatra VII." http://en.wikipedia.org/wiki/Cleopatra (accessed March 28, 2010).

Wikipedia. "Mark Antony." http://en.wikipedia.org/wiki/Mark_Antony (accessed March 28,
2010).

4. PRINCE KHURRAM AND MUMTAZ MAHAL

Adventure South Asia Tours & Travel, Ltd. "Taj Mahal Tour." www.adventurenepaltravel.com/
tajmahal.htm (accessed May 5, 2008).

BookRags. "Shah Jahan Biography." *Encyclopedia of World Biography.* www.bookrags.com/
biography/shah-jahan/ (accessed May 7, 2008).

Camarillo Dunn, Jerry, Jr. "The Taj Mahal." HowStuffWorks. http://travel.howstuffworks.com/
taj-mahal-landmark.htm (accessed May 7, 2008).

Envocare. "An Historical Account of the Taj Mahal." www.envocare.co.uk/taj_mahal_history
.htm (accessed May 8, 2008).

Exotic India. "The Taj Mahal—Architecture of a Love Story." www.exoticindiaart.com/tajmahal
.htm (accessed May 6, 2008).

Grill, Mindy. "The Life of Shah Jahan: Emperor, Brutal Conqueror, and Builder." EncycloMedia
.com. www.encyclomedia.com/shah_jahan.html (accessed May 7, 2008).

Harish Hebbar, Neria. "King of the World: Shah Jahan (1592–1666)." Boloji.com, June 12, 2002.
www.boloji.com/history/013.htm (accessed May 7, 2008).

Haryana Online. "Taj Mahal." www.haryana-online.com/taj_mahal.htm (accessed May 8, 2008).

"Historical Introduction, Part Five: Shah Jahan." www.columbia.edu/itc/mealac/pritchett/
00artlinks/agra_havell/05shahjahan.html (accessed May 5, 2008).

Hubpages. "Mumtaz Mahal—Symbol of Love." www.hubpages.com/hub/taj_wonderoftheworld
(accessed May 7, 2008).

iMahal.com. "The Taj Mahal." http://imahal.com/about/taj_mahal.htm (accessed May 7, 2008).

Islamic Arts and Architecture Organization. "The Taj Mahal." www.islamicart.com/library/empires/india/taj_mahal.html (accessed May 6, 2008).

JCS Group, Inc. "Taj Mahal." www.jcs-group.com/outstanding/1652taj.html (accessed May 5, 2008).

Johnson, David. "Shah Jahan and Mumtaz Mahal: Grieving Emperor Who Built the Taj Mahal for His Late Wife." Infoplease. www.infoplease.com/spot/love3.html (accessed May 7, 2008).

Lal, Vinay. "Shah Jahan." www.sscnet.ucla.edu/southasia/History/Mughals/Shahjahan.html (accessed May 6, 2008).

Maps of World. "Taj Mahal." www.mapsofworld.com/travel-destinations/taj-mahal.html (accessed May 7, 2008).

Panse, Sonal. "The Story of the Taj Mahal." www.buzzle.com/articles/story-taj-mahal-mughal-emperor-shah-jahan-empress-mumtaz.html (accessed May 8, 2008).

PBS. "Taj Mahal: Memorial to Love." www.pbs.org/treasuresoftheworld/taj_mahal/tmain.html (accessed May 6, 2008).

Riley, Sarah. "The Taj Mahal—The Monument of Love." www.ccds.charlotte.nc.us/History/India/02/riley/riley.htm (accessed May 8, 2008).

Sethi, Atul. "How Agra Got the Taj." *Times of India*, April 6, 2008. http://timesofindia.indiatimes.com/How_Agra_got_the_Taj/articleshow/2929624.cms (accessed May 8, 2008).

"Taj Mahal Agra: Mumtaz Mahal." www.magic.indiatourism.com/taj-mahal-agra/mumtaz-mahal.html (accessed May 7, 2008).

"Tajmahal—A Tribute to Beauty." www.angelfire.com/in/myindia/tajmahal.html (accessed May 6, 2008).

"The Taj Mahal India and Shah Jahan." http://thetajmahalindia.com (accessed May 7, 2008).

Taj Mahal India Travel. "Mumtaz Mahal." www.taj-mahal-india-travel.com/mumtaz-mahal-agra-india.html (accessed May 7, 2008).

"Taj Mahal: Memorial to a Favorite Wife." www.judypat.com/india/tajmahal.htm (accessed May 7, 2008).

"Tajmahal—The Making." www.mytajmahal.net/my-tajmahal-articles/tajmahal-the-making.html (accessed May 5, 2008).

TutorGig Encyclopedia. "Mumtaz Mahal." www.tutorgig.com/ed/Mumtaz_Mahal (accessed May 7, 2008).

Wikipedia. "Mumtaz Mahal." http://en.wikipedia.org/wiki/Mumtaz_Mahal (accessed May 7, 2008).

Wikipedia. "Shah Jahan." http://en.wikipedia.org/wiki/Shah_Jahan (accessed May 6, 2008).

Wikipedia. "Taj Mahal." http://en.wikipedia.org/wiki/Taj_Mahal (accessed May 6, 2008).

Wilson, Pip. "Mumtaz and Jahan: The Love Affair That Created the Taj Mahal." Wilson's Almanac. www.wilsonsalmanac.com/mumtaz.html (accessed May 7, 2008).

5. NAPOLEON BONAPARTE AND JOSEPHINE BEAUHARNAIS

Academic Dictionaries and Encyclopedias. "Joséphine de Beauharnais." http://en.academic.ru/dic.nsf/enwiki/39630 (accessed April 17, 2009).

Biography.com. "Napoleon I Biography." www.biography.com/articles/Napoleon-I-9420291 (accessed April 18, 2009).

Charles Hobson: Word & Image. "Parisian Encounters: Napoleon and Josephine." www .charleshobson.com/paris/napoleon.html (accessed December 6, 2009).

Dummies.com. "Napoleon's Josephine: A Rose by Any Other Name." www.dummies.com/ how-to/content/napoleons-josephine-a-rose-by-any-other-name.html (accessed April 17, 2009).

Encyclopedia of World Biography. "Napoleon Bonaparte." www.notablebiographies.com/ Mo-Ni/Napoleon-Bonaparte.html (accessed April 18, 2009).

Gulland, Sandra. "Historical Notes: Was Josephine the Key to Napoleon's Power?" *Independent*, January 26, 1999. www.independent.co.uk/arts-entertainment/historical-notes-was-jose phine-the-key-to-napoleons-power-1076337.html (accessed April 17, 2009).

Gulland, Sandra. "Josephine before Napoleon: Fact and Fiction." From a speech given to the Napoleonic Society of America. www.sandragulland.com/articles/by_3.html (accessed April 17, 2009).

"Napoleon to Josephine." www.geocities.com/Paris/Parc/9893/napoleon2.html (accessed April 17, 2009).

PBS. "Napoleon and Josephine." www.pbs.org/empires/napoleon/n_josephine/courtship/ page_1.html (accessed April 24, 2009).

"Review of *Napoleon & Josephine: The Sword & the Hummingbird* by Gerald and Loretta Hausman." http://blc.edu/cs/blogs/library/archive/2007/08/30/napoleon-josephine-the-sword -the-hummingbird.aspx (accessed April 24, 2009).

Schneider, John. "Napoleon and Josephine." The Napoleon Series. http://napoleon-series.org/ research/napoleon/c_napjos.html (accessed April 17, 2009).

Wikipedia. "Joséphine de Beauharnais." http://en.wikipedia.org/wiki/Joséphine_de_Beauhar nais (accessed April 16, 2009).

Wikipedia. "Napoleon I." http://en.wikipedia.org/wiki/Napoleon_I_of_France (accessed April 18, 2009).

6. PRINCE ALBERT AND QUEEN VICTORIA

Advice Diva. "Queen Victoria and Prince Albert Love Story." http://advicediva.com/ad/ famouslovestories/queenvictoriaprincealbertlovestory.asp (accessed June 27, 2009).

Answers.com. "Queen Victoria." www.answers.com/topic/queen-victoria (accessed June 27, 2009).

BBC. "Berkshire's Greatest Royal Love Story." www.bbc.co.uk/berkshire/content/articles/ 2009/02/09/queen_victoria_albert_windsor_feature.shtml (accessed June 27, 2009).

Dobbin, Muriel. "Book Review: Albert 'Fell into Step behind' Victoria." Review of *Victoria and Albert: Rulers, Partners, Rivals*, by Gillian Gill. *Washington Times*, June 10, 2009. www .washingtontimes.com/news/2009/jun/10/he-fell-into-step-behind-her/ (accessed June 30, 2009).

Female Ancestors. "Queen Victoria." http://female-ancestors.com/daughters/victoria.htm (accessed June 27, 2009).

Incredible People. "Biography of Queen Victoria." http://profiles.incredible-people.com/queen -victoria/ (accessed June 29, 2009).

MacMillan, Alissa. "Queen of Hearts." Review of *Victoria & Albert* (A&E). *New York Daily News*, October 11, 2001. www.nydailynews.com/archives/entertainment/2001/10/21/2001-10 -21_queen_of_hearts.html (accessed June 30, 2009).

Maddocks, Melvin. "Books: Beautiful Warts Prince Albert." *Time*, January 21, 1985. www.time .com/time/magazine/article/0,9171,956297,00.html (accessed June 30, 2009).

Mitchell, Erik. "Prince Albert: The Real Monarch of Modern Britain." Associated Content. October 6, 2008. www.associatedcontent.com/article/1064380/prince_albert_the_real_ monarch_of_modern.html?cat=37 (accessed June 30, 2009).

NineteenTeen Blog: Being a Teen in the Nineteenth Century. "Queen Victoria, Part VIII: Love at Last." December 9, 2008. http://nineteenteen.blogspot.com/2008/12/queen-victoria -part-viii-love-at-last.html.

Schneider, Jessica. "Queen Victoria's Marriage." Monsters and Critics, June 22, 2009. Review of *Victoria and Albert: Rulers, Partners, Rivals*, by Gillian Gill. www.monstersandcritics.com/ books/news/article_1484946.php/Queen_Victoria_s_marriage (accessed June 27, 2009).

Spark Notes. "Queen Victoria: Life with Prince Albert." www.sparknotes.com/biography/victo ria/section3.rhtml (accessed June 29, 2009).

Spartacus Educational. "Queen Victoria: Biography." www.spartacus.schoolnet.co.uk/PRvicto ria.htm (accessed June 27, 2009).

Sydney, Grace. "Legendary Lovers: Queen Victoria & Prince Albert." Lovetripper. www.lovetrip per.com/issues/issue-33/victoria-albert.html (accessed June 27, 2009).

Tytler, Carolyn. "Albert, Prince Consort of Queen Victoria." Associated Content. www.associ atedcontent.com/article/1607181/albert_prince_consort_of_queen_victoria.html?cat=37 (accessed June 29, 2009).

Wikipedia. "Albert, Prince Consort." http://en.wikipedia.org/wiki/Albert,_Prince_Consort (accessed June 28, 2009).

Wikipedia. "Victoria of the United Kingdom." http://en.wikipedia.org/wiki/Victoria_of_the_ United_Kingdom (accessed June 27, 2009).

Williams, Kate. "Queen Victoria: The Original People's Princess." *Telegraph*, September 14, 2008. www.telegraph.co.uk/culture/donotmigrate/3560626/Queen-Victoria-the-original -peoples-princess.html (accessed June 29, 2009).

7. ROBERT BROWNING AND ELIZABETH BARRETT BROWNING

Basic Famous People. "Elizabeth Barrett Browning Biography." www.basicfamouspeople.com/ index.php?aid=450 (accessed July 15, 2009).

Cope, Dorian. "The First Meeting of Elizabeth Barrett and Robert Browning." EzineArticles.com. http://ezinearticles.com/?The-First-Meeting-of-Elizabeth-Barrett-and-Robert-Browning &id=2510315 (accessed July 15, 2009).

"Elizabeth Barrett Moulton-Barrett Browning." www.cwrl.utexas.edu/~ulrich/RHE309/vicfem bios/ebb.htm (accessed July 15, 2009).

Encyclopedia of World Biography. "Elizabeth Barrett Browning." www.notablebiographies.com/ Br-Ca/Browning-Elizabeth-Barrett.html (accessed July 15, 2009).

Everett, Glenn, and Jason B. Isaacs. "The Life of Elizabeth Barrett Browning." The Victorian Web. http://victorianweb.org/authors/ebb/ebbio.html (accessed July 16, 2009).

Female Ancestors. "Elizabeth Barrett Browning." http://female-ancestors.com/daughters/brown ing.htm (accessed July 15, 2009).

Hampson, Thomas. "I Hear America Singing: Robert Browning (1812–1889) Elizabeth Barrett Browning (1806–1861)." www.pbs.org/wnet/ihas/poet/browning.html (accessed July 15, 2009).

Huntington Fletcher, Robert. "Elizabeth Barrett Browning and Robert Browning." From Chapter XI, Period IX, The Victorian Period, about 1830 to 1901, in *A History of English Literature*. 1918.

http://classiclit.about.com/library/bl-etexts/rfletcher/bl-rfletcher-history-11-browning .htm (accessed July 15, 2009).

Incompetech Creative Industries. "Elizabeth 'Ba' Barrett Browning." http://incompetech.com/ authors/ebrowning/ (accessed July 15, 2009).

Literature Network. "Elizabeth Barrett Browning." www.online-literature.com/elizabeth -browning/ (accessed July 15, 2009).

Liukkonen, Petri. "Elizabeth Barrett Browning (1806–1861)—Née Barrett." www.kirjasto.sci.fi/ ebrownin.htm (accessed July 15, 2009).

Lombardi, Esther. "Love and the Brownings: Robert Browning and Elizabeth Barrett Browning." About.com: Classic Literature. http://classiclit.about.com/od/loveliterature/a/aa_ browning.htm (accessed July 15, 2009).

Notable Names Database. "Elizabeth Barrett Browning." www.nndb.com/people/036/ 000031940/ (accessed July 15, 2009).

Wikipedia. "Elizabeth Barrett Browning." http://en.wikipedia.org/wiki/Elizabeth_Barrett_ Browning (accessed July 15, 2009).

Wikipedia. "Robert Browning." http://en.wikipedia.org/wiki/Robert_Browning (accessed July 15, 2009).

8. SIR RICHARD BURTON AND ISABEL ARUNDELL

Answers.com. "Biography: Sir Richard Francis Burton." www.answers.com/topic/richard -francis-burton.

"Books: Victorian Eccentrics." Review of *Sir Richard Burton's Wife*, by Jean Burton. *Time*, June 23, 1941. www.time.com/time/magazine/article/0,9171,851202,00.html (accessed August 2, 2009).

Brendon, J. A. "True Love-Stories of Famous People. No. 19. Sir Richard and Lady Burton." *Every Woman's Encyclopaedia*. www.chest-of-books.com/food/household/Woman-Encyclopae dia-3/True-Love-Stories-Of-Famous-People-No-19-Sir-Richard-And-Lady-Burton.html.

Brendon, J. A. "True Love-Stories of Famous People. No. 19. Sir Richard and Lady Burton. Part 2." *Every Woman's Encyclopaedia*. http://chestofbooks.com/food/household/Woman -Encyclopaedia-3/True-Love-Stories-Of-Famous-People-No-19-Sir-Richard-And-Lady -Burton-Part-2.html (accessed August 1, 2009).

Burtoniana.org. "Isabel Burton: 1831–1896." http://burtoniana.org/isabel/ (accessed August 2, 2009).

Burton, Isabel. "Chapter IV: Boulogne: I Meet My Destiny (1850–1852)." *The Romance of Lady Isabel Burton*. http://ebooks.adelaide.edu.au/b/burton/isabel/romance/chapter4.html.

Encyclopedia.com. "Sir Richard Francis Burton." www.encyclopedia.com/doc/1G2-3404701021. html (accessed August 1, 2009).

Hubpages. "Sir Richard Burton: Knight of the Orient." http://hubpages.com/hub/Sir-Richard -Burton-Knight-of-the-Orient (accessed August 1, 2009).

London Borough of Richmond upon Thames. "Richard Burton meets Isabel Arundell." www.richmond.gov.uk/home/leisure_and_culture/local_history_and_heritage/local _studies_collection/local_history_notes/sir_richard_and_lady_isabel_burton/richard _burton_meets_isabel_arundell.htm (accessed August 1, 2009).

Lovell, Mary S. "A Rage to Live." www.lovellbiographies.com/aragetolive/aragetolive.html (ac cessed August 1, 2009).

Ondaatje, Christopher. "The Fierce Couple: Richard and Isabel." Review of *A Rage to Live: A Biography of Richard and Isabel Burton*, by Mary S. Lovell. *Spectator*, October 10, 1998.

http://findarticles.com/p/articles/mi_qa3724/is_199810/ai_n8815125/ (accessed August 2, 2009).

Philosopedia. "Richard F. Burton." http://philosopedia.org/index.php?title=Richard_F._Burton (accessed August 2, 2009).

Reader, John. "Two for the Road." Review of *A Rage to Live: A Biography of Richard and Isabel Burton*, by Mary S. Lovell. *National Review*, December 7, 1998.

St. Mary Magdalen's Roman Catholic Church. "The Tomb of Sir Richard Burton." www.stmarymags.org.uk/church/burton_tomb.html (accessed August 1, 2009).

Trivia Library. "Famous Marriages Richard Burton and Isabel Arundell Part 1." www.trivia-library.com/b/famous-marriages-richard-burton-and-isabel-arundell-part-1.htm (accessed August 1, 2009).

Wikipedia. "Isabel Burton." http://en.wikipedia.org/wiki/Isabel_Burton (accessed August 1, 2009).

Wikipedia. "Richard Francis Burton." http://en.wikipedia.org/wiki/Richard_Francis_Burton (accessed August 1, 2009).

Wright, Thomas. "Chapter V: 1849 to 3rd April, 1853 Chiefly Boulogne." *The Life of Sir Richard Burton*. http://ebooks.adelaide.edu.au/b/burton/richard/b97zw/chapter5.html (accessed August 1, 2009).

9. CHARLES PARNELL AND KATHARINE O'SHEA

Answers.com. "Biography: Charles Stewart Parnell." www.answers.com/topic/charles-stewart-parnell (accessed November 1, 2009).

Clare County Library. "Charles Stewart Parnell." www.clarelibrary.ie/eolas/coclare/people/parnell.htm (accessed November 1, 2009).

Clarke, Norma. "Kitty O'Shea to the Irish, Katie to her friends." Review of *Ireland's Misfortune: The Turbulent Life of Kitty O'Shea*, by Elisabeth Kehoe. *Times Literary Supplement*, June 17, 2008.

Corrigan, Rebekah. "The Life of Katherine O'Shea." www.angelfire.com/pe/riversdale/Rebcorr.htm (accessed November 1, 2009).

Essortment Articles. "Who Was Charles Stewart Parnell?" www.essortment.com/all/whowas charles_rlhl.htm (accessed November 10, 2009).

"Ireland's Misfortune: The Turbulent Life of Kitty O'Shea." Review of *Ireland's Misfortune: The Turbulent Life of Kitty O'Shea*, by Elisabeth Kehoe. *Times Higher Education*, September 4, 2008. www.timeshighereducation.co.uk/story.asp?storyCode=403388&sectioncode=26 (accessed November 1, 2009).

"'Kitty' O'Shea: Katherine Parnell 1845–1921." www.womenofbrighton.co.uk/katieoshea.htm (accessed November 1, 2009).

Lynch, Andrew. "Revisiting the Greatest Scandal in Irish History." Review of *The Captain and the King: William O'Shea, Parnell and Late Victorian Ireland*, by Myles Dungan. *Sunday Business Post Online*, April 12, 2009. http://archives.tcm.ie/businesspost/2009/04/12/story40871.asp (accessed November 1, 2009).

Maddocks, Melvin. "Books: The Magic Bucket." Review of *The Uncrowned Queen of Ireland*, by Joyce Marlow. *Time*, July 28, 1975. www.time.com/time/magazine/article/0,9171,913359,00.html (accessed November 1, 2009).

McCarthy, Mary. "Book Review: *Kitty O'Shea: An Irish Affair* by Jane Jordan." RTE Ten, The Entertainment Network. www.rte.ie/ten/2006/0404/jordanj.html (accessed November 1, 2009).

McCullough, Joseph Allen. "Charles Stewart Parnell (1846–91): The Fight for Home Rule of Ireland." Suite101, June 29, 2009. http://ukirishhistory.suite101.com/article.cfm/charles_stewart_parnell_184691 (accessed November 1, 2009).

McNamara, Robert. "Charles Stewart Parnell, Irish Politician Called 'Ireland's Uncrowned King.'" About.com: 19th Century History. http://history1800s.about.com/od/irelandinthe1800s/p/Parnell01.htm (accessed November 10, 2009).

O'Connor, John J. "Love, Politics and Disaster in 19th-Century Ireland." Review of *Parnell and the Englishwoman* (Masterpiece Theater). *New York Times*, December 27, 1991. www.nytimes.com/1991/12/27/news/love-politics-and-disaster-in-19th-century-ireland.html (accessed November 1, 2009).

"Parnell and the Parnell's." www.glendalough.connect.ie/pages/articles/history/pages/Parnell.html (accessed November 1, 2009).

Reid, Lorna. "Kitty & Parnell Scandalised." Review of *Kitty O'Shea: An Irish Affair*, by Jane Jordan Sutton. *Irish Independent*, October 15, 2005. www.independent.ie/opinion/analysis/kitty-amp-parnell-scandalised-235770.html (accessed November 1, 2009).

Sieff, Martin. "The Laurel and the Ivy: The Story of Charles Stewart Parnell and Irish Nationalism." Review of *The Laurel and the Ivy: The Story of Charles Stewart Parnell and Irish Nationalism*, by Robert Kee. *Insight on the News*, February 13, 1995. http://findarticles.com/p/articles/mi_m1571/is_n7_v11/ai_16679982/ (accessed November 1, 2009).

Welmer Blog. "A National Affair: A Man Ruined, a Cause Abandoned, a Nation Torn in Two." www.welmer.org/2009/07/02/a-national-affair-a-man-ruined-a-cause-abandoned-a-nation-torn-in-two/ (accessed November 1, 2009).

Wikipedia. "Charles Stewart Parnell." http://en.wikipedia.org/wiki/Charles_Stewart_Parnell (accessed November 1, 2009).

Wikipedia. "Katharine O'Shea." http://en.wikipedia.org/wiki/Katharine_O'Shea (accessed November 10, 2009).

10. NICHOLAS ROMANOV AND PRINCESS ALIX

Baiker, Marian. "Nicky & Alix: The Love of the Century." www.russianroyalty.com/love.htm (accessed February 22, 2010).

Emmet Labs. "Nicholas II of Russia & Alexandra Romanov." www.emmetlabs.com/pair/Nicholas-Romanov_267/Alexandra-Romanov_268 (accessed February 22, 2010).

Find a Grave. "Alexandra Romanov." www.findagrave.com/cgi-bin/fg.cgi?page=gr&GRid=8391065 (accessed February 22, 2010).

Gray, Francine du Plessix. "Nicholas and Alexandra: The Sequels." Review. *New York Times*, October 29, 1995. www.nytimes.com/books/97/08/03/nnp/18621.html (accessed February 22, 2010).

Massie, Robert K. *Nicholas and Alexandra*. New York: Ballantine Books, 2000.

Wikipedia. "Alexandra Feodorovna (Alix of Hesse)." http://en.wikipedia.org/wiki/Alexandra_Fedorovna_of_Hesse (accessed February 22, 2010).

Wikipedia. "Nicholas II of Russia." http://en.wikipedia.org/wiki/Nicholas_II_of_Russia (accessed February 22, 2010).

11. FRANZ FERDINAND AND SOPHIE CHOTEK

Absolute Astronomy. "Sophie, Duchess of Hohenberg." www.absoluteastronomy.com/topics/Sophie,_Duchess_of_Hohenberg (accessed July 23, 2009).

AllExperts Encyclopedia. "Archduke Franz Ferdinand of Austria." www.associatepublisher.com/e/a/ar/archduke_franz_ferdinand_of_austria.htm.

AllExperts Encyclopedia. "Sophie, Duchess of Hohenberg." www.associatepublisher.com/e/s/so/sophie,_duchess_of_hohenberg.htm.

Cambridge Encyclopedia, Vol. 28. "Gavrilo Princip—Early Life, Assassination, Trivia." http://encyclopedia.stateuniversity.com/pages/8259/Gavrilo-Princip.html (accessed July 24, 2009).

Everything2 Database. "Archduke Franz Ferdinand Karl Ludwig Joseph Maria von Habsburg-d'Este." http://everything2.org/node/1400011 (accessed July 24, 2009).

Find a Grave. "Sophie Maria Josephine Albina Chotek, Duchess of Hohenburg." www.findagrave.com/cgi-bin/fg.cgi?GRid=9506914&page=gr (accessed July 24, 2009).

Firstworldwar.com. "Who's Who—Archduke Franz Ferdinand." www.firstworldwar.com/bio/ferdinand.htm (accessed July 24, 2009).

"Franz Ferdinand & Sophie Chotek." www.btinternet.com/~J.Pasteur/Sophie.html (accessed July 24, 2009).

"Franz Ferdinand & the Family." www.btinternet.com/~J.Pasteur/Family.html (accessed July 24, 2009).

Geller, Jordan. "The Assassination of Archduke Franz Ferdinand: Prequel to 'The War to End All Wars.'" Associated Content. February 9, 2007. www.associatedcontent.com/article/137906/the_assassination_of_archduke_franz.html?cat=37 (accessed July 24, 2009).

"Sophie Duchess von Hohenberg (1868–1914)." www.camo.ch/sophie.htm (accessed July 24, 2009).

Spartacus Educational. "Archduke Franz Ferdinand: Biography." www.spartacus.schoolnet.co.uk/FWWarchduke.htm.

Spartacus Educational. "Sophie von Chotkova." www.spartacus.schoolnet.co.uk/FWWsophie.htm.

Tattersall, Kerry R. J. "A Bohemian Love Story and a Tragic End." http://edpaha.com/livingthedream/bohemianlovestory.htm (accessed July 23, 2009).

Trivia Library. "World War I and Archduke Franz Ferdinand Part 2." www.trivia-library.com/a/world-war-i-and-archduke-franz-ferdinand-part-2.htm (accessed July 24, 2009).

Wijesiri, Lionel. "Famous Trials That Shook the World: Assassination of Franz Ferdinand." *Sunday Observer*, August 7, 2005. www.sundayobserver.lk/2005/08/07/fea17.html (accessed July 24, 2009).

Wikipedia. "Archduke Franz Ferdinand of Austria." http://en.wikipedia.org/wiki/Archduke_Franz_Ferdinand_of_Austria (accessed July 23, 2009).

Wikipedia. "Sophie, Duchess of Hohenberg." http://en.wikipedia.org/wiki/Sophie,_Duchess_of_Hohenberg (accessed July 23, 2009).

12. LEONARD WOOLF AND VIRGINIA STEPHEN

"Cocktail Party Cheat Sheets: Virginia Woolf." *Mental Floss*. www.mentalfloss.com/cheatsheets/virginia-woolf/ (accessed November 23, 2009).

Gross, John. "Mr. Virginia Woolf." *Commentary Magazine*, November 2006. www.commentarymagazine.com/viewarticle.cfm/-mr--virginia-woolf--10801 (accessed November 22, 2009).

History.com. "This Day in History. Aug. 10, 1912: Virginia and Leonard Woolf Marry." www.history.com/this-day-in-history/virginia-and-leonard-woolf-marry (accessed November 23, 2009).

Literature Network. "Virginia Woolf." www.online-literature.com/virginia_woolf/ (accessed November 22, 2009).

Liukkonen, Petri. "Virginia Woolf (1882–1941)—In Full Adeline Virginia Woolf, Original Surname Stephen." www.kirjasto.sci.fi/vwoolf.htm (accessed November 22, 2009).

Macdonald, Moira. "The Man in the Shadow of Virginia Woolf." Review of *Leonard Woolf: A Biography*, by Victoria Glendinning. *Seattle Times*, November 24, 2006. http://seattletimes .nwsource.com/html/books/2003443642_woolf26.html (accessed November 23, 2009).

Mantex Information Design. "Leonard Woolf—A Biographical Sketch." www.mantex.co.uk/ou/ a319/1-woolf.htm (accessed November 23, 2009).

Sittenfeld, Curtis. "Yes, Virginia." Review of *Virginia Woolf: An Inner Life*, by Julia Briggs. *New York Times*, November 20, 2005. www.nytimes.com/2005/11/20/books/review/20sittenfeld. html (accessed November 22, 2009).

Wikipedia. "Leonard Woolf." http://en.wikipedia.org/wiki/Leonard_Woolf (accessed November 22, 2009).

Wikipedia. "Virginia Woolf." http://en.wikipedia.org/wiki/Virginia_Woolf (accessed November 22, 2009).

Wineapple, Brenda. "A Life of His Own." Review of *Leonard Woolf: A Biography*, by Victoria Glendinning. *Nation*, November 20, 2006. www.thenation.com/doc/20061211/wineapple/print (accessed November 24, 2009).

13. GERTRUDE STEIN AND ALICE B. TOKLAS

Biography.com. "Gertrude Stein Biography." www.biography.com/articles/Gertrude-Stein-9493261 (accessed July 17, 2009).

"Books: A Salute to Gertrude Stein." A Review of *What Is Remembered*, by Alice B. Toklas. *Time*, March 21, 1963. www.time.com/time/magazine/article/0,9171,896704,00.html (accessed July 17, 2009).

"Books: Stein's Way." *Time*, September 11, 1933. www.time.com/time/magazine/article/0,9171, 746058,00.html (accessed July 18, 2009).

Boykin, Sam. "Great Love Affairs in History." CNN. www.cnn.com/2007/LIVING/personal/12/03/ great.love.affairs/index.html (accessed December 20, 2009).

Encyclopedia of World Biography. "Gertrude Stein." www.notablebiographies.com/Sc-St/Stein -Gertrude.html (accessed July 17, 2009).

"Gertrude Stein." *Fyne Times Gay and Lesbian Magazine*. www.fyne.co.uk/index.php?item=516 (accessed July 18, 2009).

"Gertrude Stein & Alice B. Toklas: For Four Decades, the Imperious Writer and Her Diminutive Companion Ruled the Avant-Garde of Paris—and Each Other's Hearts—with Surprising Propriety." *People*, February 12, 1996. www.people.com/people/archive/article/0,2010 2772,00.html (accessed July 17, 2009).

Hurwitt, Sam. "A Match Made in Paris." *San Francisco Chronicle*, June 17, 2007. http://articles. sfgate.com/2007-06-17/entertainment/17250924_1_stein-and-toklas-stein-s-death -gertrude-stein (accessed July 17, 2009).

Jewell, Brian. "Two Lives: Gertrude and Alice." Review of *Two Lives: Gertrude and Alice*, by Janet

Malcolm. *Edge* (Boston), January 5, 2008. www.edgeboston.com/index.php?ch=entertain ment&sc=books&sc2=reviews&sc3=&id=54339 (accessed July 17, 2009).

Johnson Lewis, Jone. "Gertrude Stein (1874–1946)." About.com: Women's History. http://wom enshistory.about.com/od/gertrudestein/a/gertrude_stein.htm (accessed July 17, 2009).

Liukkonen, Petri. "Alice B. Toklas (1877–1967)." www.kirjasto.sci.fi/toklas.htm (accessed July 17, 2009).

Mason, Janet. "Gertrude Stein and Alice B. Toklas: Love Notes." www.amusejanetmason.com/ Getrude_Stein.htm (accessed July 17, 2009).

McGuigan, Cathleen. "They'll Always Have Paris: Janet Malcolm's new book refuses to let Gertrude Stein and Alice B." Review of *Two Lives: Gertrude and Alice*, by Janet Malcolm. *Newsweek*, November 5, 2007. www.newsweek.com/2007/10/27/they-ll-always-have-paris.html (accessed July 17, 2009).

O'Connor, John J. "2 Works on Gertrude Stein and Alice B. Toklas." Review of *Waiting for the Moon* and *Gertrude Stein and a Companion*. *New York Times*, June 15, 1987. www.nytimes .com/1987/06/15/arts/2-works-on-gertrude-stein-and-alice-b-toklas.html (accessed July 17, 2009).

Peschel, Bill. "Alice B. Toklas and Gertrude Stein Meet Cute (1907)." www.planetpeschel.com/ index?/site/comments/alice_b_toklas_and_gertrude_stein_meet_cute_1907/ (accessed December 20, 2009).

Roiphe, Katie. "Portrait of a Marriage." Review of *Two Lives: Gertrude and Alice*, by Janet Malcolm. *New York Times*, September 23, 2007. www.nytimes.com/2007/09/23/books/review/Roiphe-t .html (accessed July 17, 2009).

Salih, Zak M. "The Moderns: Re-Examining the Relationship between Gertrude Stein and Alice B. Toklas." Review of *Two Lives: Gertrude and Alice*, by Janet Malcolm. *Baltimore City Paper*, December 5, 2007. www.citypaper.com/arts/story.asp?id=14932 (accessed July 17, 2009).

Simon, Linda. "Alice Babette Toklas." Jewish Women's Archive. http://jwa.org/encyclopedia/ article/toklas-alice-babette (accessed December 20, 2009).

Simon, Linda. "Gertrude Stein." Jewish Women's Archive. http://jwa.org/encyclopedia/article/ stein-gertrude (accessed July 17, 2009).

Wikipedia. "Alice B. Toklas." http://en.wikipedia.org/wiki/Alice_B._Toklas (accessed December 21, 2009).

Wikipedia. "Gertrude Stein." http://en.wikipedia.org/wiki/Gertrude_Stein (accessed December 21, 2009).

Wilson, Frances. "Gertrude Stein, Fearless and Flushed." Review of *Two Lives: Gertrude and Alice*, by Janet Malcolm. *Telegraph*, November 8, 2007. www.telegraph.co.uk/culture/ books/non_fictionreviews/3669116/Gertrude-Stein-fearless-and-flushed.html (accessed July 17, 2009).

"World: Together Again." *Time*, March 17, 1967. www.time.com/time/magazine/article/0,9171, 836808,00.html (accessed July 17, 2009).

14. WILLIAM RANDOLPH HEARST AND MARION DAVIES

Answers.com. "Marion Davies." www.answers.com/topic/marion-davies (accessed March 4, 2010).

Biography Base. "Marion Davies Biography." http://biographybase.com/biography/Davies_ Marion.html (accessed March 4, 2010).

Bowen, Jerry. "Return to Xanadu: Revisiting the Hearst Castle." CBS News, August 25, 2002. www.cbsnews.com/stories/2001/05/04/sunday/main289579.shtml (accessed March 4, 2010).

Chirone, Brooke. "Ocean House: A Captivating Love Story." Examiner.com. www.examiner .com/x-11973-Santa-Monica-Community-Examiner~y2009m10d30-Ocean-House-a-cap tivating-love-story (accessed March 4, 2010).

Davies, Marion. *The Times We Had: Life with William Randolph Hearst.* New York: Ballantine Books, 1977.

Encyclopedia of World Biography. "William Randolph Hearst." www.notablebiographies.com/ Gi-He/Hearst-William-Randolph.html (accessed March 4, 2010).

Find a Grave. "Marion Davies." www.findagrave.com/cgi-bin/fg.cgi?page=gr&GRid=257 (ac cessed March 4, 2010).

Kastner, Victoria. "William Randolph Hearst: King of the Castles." *Telegraph*, April 19, 2009. www.telegraph.co.uk/culture/5159002/William-Randolph-Hearst-King-of-the-Castles .html (accessed March 4, 2010).

King, Susan. "Hearst-Davies an Ill-Fated Duo." *Los Angeles Times*, November 21, 2008. http:// articles.latimes.com/2008/nov/21/entertainment/et-davies21 (accessed March 4, 2010).

Nasaw, David. *The Chief: The Life of William Randolph Hearst.* Boston: Houghton Mifflin, 2000.

San Francisco History Index. "William Randolph Hearst." www.zpub.com/sf/history/willh .html (accessed March 4, 2010).

Wikipedia. "Marion Davies." http://en.wikipedia.org/wiki/Marion_Davies (accessed March 4, 2010).

Wikipedia. "William Randolph Hearst." http://en.wikipedia.org/wiki/William_Randolph_Hearst (accessed March 4, 2010).

"William Randolph Hearst & Marion Davies: The Man Who Inspired Citizen Kane Found His Equal in a Fun-Loving Chorus Girl." *People*, February 12, 1996. www.people.com/people/ archive/article/0,20102777,00.html (accessed March 4, 2010).

Wood, Gaby. "Who Made Marion? There Was More to William Randolph Hearst And Marion Davies Than Citizen Kane Suggested, as Biographies from David Nasaw and Louis Pizzitola Show." Review of *The Chief: The Life of William Randolph Hearst*, by David Nasaw, and *Hearst over Hollywood: Power, Passion and Propaganda in the Movies*, by Louis Pizzitola. *Observer*, May 19, 2002. www.guardian.co.uk/books/2002/may/19/biography.highereducation (ac cessed March 4, 2010).

15. F. SCOTT FITZGERALD AND ZELDA SAYRE

Beautiful and Damned. "The Fitzgeralds: The Romantic Egoists." www.beautifulanddamned .com/fitzgeralds/index.asp (accessed February 27, 2010).

"Books: The Muse behind Gatsby." Review of *Sometimes Madness Is Wisdom: Zelda and Scott Fitzgerald, a Marriage*, by Kendall Taylor. *Scotsman*, August 24, 2002. http://living.scots man.com/features/Books-The-muse-behind-Gatsby.2355398.jp (accessed February 28, 2010).

Definitive Touch. "F. Scott Fitzgerald: An American Icon." http://definitivetouch.com/features/ scott-fitzgerald-american-icon/ (accessed February 28, 2010).

"F. Scott Fitzgerald & Zelda Sayre: Beautiful, Gifted and Reckless, These Free-Spirited Ex patriates Defined the Dazzle and the Decadence of the Jazz Age." *People*, February 12,

1996. www.people.com/people/archive/article/0,20102783,00.html (accessed February 27, 2010).

Jarvis, Gail. "Southern Belles." LewRockwell.com. www.lewrockwell.com/jarvis/jarvis45.html (accessed February 28, 2010).

Keats, Jonathon. "For the Love of Literature." *Salon*, August 25, 2001. http://dir.salon.com/sex/feature/2001/08/25/fitzgerald/index.html (accessed February 28, 2010).

Lanahan, Eleanor. "Scott and Zelda: Their Style Lives." *New York Times*, September 1, 1996. www.nytimes.com/books/00/12/24/specials/fitzgerald-lanahan.html (accessed February 27, 2010).

Moore, Lucy. "The Long Twilight." Review of *Sometimes Madness Is Wisdom: Zelda and Scott Fitzgerald, a Marriage*, by Kendall Taylor. *New Statesman*, September 23, 2002. www.newstatesman.com/200209230040 (accessed February 27, 2010).

Planet Papers. "F. Scott Fitzgerald: His Beautiful and Damned World." http://planetpapers.com/Assets/3324.php (accessed February 27, 2010).

Wikipedia. "F. Scott Fitzgerald." http://en.wikipedia.org/wiki/F._Scott_Fitzgerald (accessed February 27, 2010).

Wikipedia. "Zelda Fitzgerald." http://en.wikipedia.org/wiki/Zelda_Fitzgerald (accessed February 27, 2010).

Yahoo! Lifestyle. "Zelda Fitzgerald: American Beauty." http://au.lifestyle.yahoo.com/marie-claire/features/life-stories/article/-/5880734/zelda-fitzgerald-american-beauty/ (accessed February 28, 2010).

16. DIEGO RIVERA AND FRIDA KAHLO

Botis, Betty. "Frida Kahlo and Diego Rivera. Love or Lust?" Diego Rivera Prints. www.diego-rivera.org/article2-frida-kahlo-and-diego-rivera.html (accessed February 16, 2010).

Frida Kahlo Fans. "Frida Kahlo Complete Biography." www.fridakahlofans.com/biocomplete.html (accessed February 16, 2010).

Herrera, Hayden. *Frida: A Biography of Frida Kahlo.* New York: HarperPerennial, 2002.

Malkin, Elisabeth. "Beyond the Myth, Art Endures." *New York Times*, July 7, 2007. www.nytimes.com/2007/07/07/arts/design/07frid.html (accessed February 17, 2010).

Mark Harden's Artchive. "Frida Kahlo (1907–1954)." www.artchive.com/artchive/K/kahlo.html (accessed February 16, 2010).

Tuchman, Phyllis. "Frida Kahlo: The Mexican Artist's Myriad Faces, Stranger-Than-Fiction Biography and Powerful Paintings Come to Vivid Life in a New Film." Review of the film *Frida. Smithsonian Magazine*, November 2002. www.smithsonianmag.com/arts-culture/frida.html (accessed February 16, 2010).

Wikipedia. "Diego Rivera." http://en.wikipedia.org/wiki/Diego_Rivera (accessed February 16, 2010).

Wikipedia. "Frida Kahlo." http://en.wikipedia.org/wiki/Frida_Kahlo (accessed February 16, 2010).

17. GEORGE BURNS AND GRACIE ALLEN

Answers.com. "Biography: George Burns." www.answers.com/topic/george-burns.

Burns, George. *Gracie: A Love Story.* New York: Signet, 1991.

"Business & Finance: Nat & Googie." *Time*, January 30, 1933. www.time.com/time/magazine/article/0,9171,745048,00.html (accessed December 25, 2009).

Find a Grave. "George Burns." www.findagrave.com/cgi-bin/fg.cgi?page=gr&GRid=150 (accessed December 25, 2009).

Find a Grave. "Gracie Allen." www.findagrave.com/cgi-bin/fg.cgi?page=gr&GRid=22 (accessed December 25, 2009).

"George Burns & Gracie Allen: A Love Story." *Beach Browser*, February 14, 2003. www.beachbrowser .com/Archives/eVoid/Febuary-2003/George-Burns-Gracie-Allen-A-Love-Story.htm (accessed December 25, 2009).

"George Burns and Gracie Allen: A Love Story." February 2, 2004. www.tommcmahon .net/2004/02/george_burns_an.html (accessed December 25, 2009).

Hubbard, Kim, and Dirk Mathison. "George Burns Writes a Final Loving Tribute to Gracie Allen." *People*, October 31, 1988. www.people.com/people/archive/article/0,20100336,00 .html (accessed December 25, 2009).

Internet Movie Database. "Biography for Gracie Allen." www.imdb.com/name/nm0020555/bio.

Krebs, Albin. "George Burns, Straight Man and Ageless Wit, Dies at 100." *New York Times*, March 1996. www.nytimes.com/1996/03/10/nyregion/george-burns-straight-man-and-ageless -wit-dies-at-100.html (accessed December 25, 2009).

Marx, Arthur. "The Ultimate Cigar Aficionado: Ninety-Eight-Year-Old George Burns Shares Memories of His Life." *Cigar Aficionado*. www.cigaraficionado.com/Cigar/CA_Profiles/ People_Profile/0,2540,3,00.html (accessed December 25, 2009).

Murray, Sue. "George Burns and Gracie Allen." *St. James Encyclopedia of Pop Culture*, January 29, 2002. http://findarticles.com/p/articles/mi_g1epc/is_bio/ai_2419200155/ (accessed December 25, 2009).

"Television: Burns without Allen." *Time*, March 3, 1958. www.time.com/time/magazine/arti cle/0,9171,893874,00.html (accessed December 25, 2009).

Wikipedia. "George Burns." http://en.wikipedia.org/wiki/George_Burns (accessed December 25, 2009).

Wikipedia. "Gracie Allen." http://en.wikipedia.org/wiki/Gracie_Allen (accessed December 25, 2009).

Zecher, Henry. "Goodnight, George! The World's Best-Loved Cigar Smoker Takes His Final Bow." *Pipe Smoker's Ephemeris*, 1996. www.henryzecher.com/georgeburns.htm (accessed December 25, 2009).

18. JEAN-PAUL SARTRE AND SIMONE DE BEAUVOIR

Biography.com. "Jean-Paul Sartre Biography." www.biography.com/articles/Nean-Paul-Sartre -9472219 (accessed October 21, 2009).

Buss, Robin. "Writing, Whisky, Cigarettes and Sex." Review of *Tête-à-Tête: The Tumultuous Lives and Loves of Simone de Beauvoir and Jean-Paul Sartre*, by Hazel Rowley. *Independent*, January 8, 2006.

de la Durantaye, Leland. "Swinging and Nothingness. Leave It to Beaver: For Jean-Paul Sartre Centenary, Think of Pascal's Spiked Girdle." Review of *Tête-à-Tête: The Tumultuous Lives and Loves of Simone de Beauvoir and Jean-Paul Sartre*, by Hazel Rowley. *Village Voice*, December 20, 2005. www.villagevoice.com/2005-12-20/books/swinging-and-nothingness/ (accessed October 22, 2009).

Encyclopedia of World Biography. "Simone de Beauvoir." www.notablebiographies.com/Ba-Be/ Beauvoir-Simone-de.html (accessed October 23, 2009).

Flaherty, Tarraugh. "Simone de Beauvoir." www.webster.edu/~woolflm/beauvoir.html (accessed October 21, 2009).

Grimes, William. "Tête-à-Tête: Simone de Beauvoir and Jean-Paul Sartre." Review of *Tête-à-Tête: The Tumultuous Lives and Loves of Simone de Beauvoir and Jean-Paul Sartre*, by Hazel Row-

ley. *New York Times*, October 7, 2005. www.nytimes.com/2005/10/06/arts/06iht-bookven
.html (accessed June 2, 2010).

Grimes, William. "The Value and Complexities of an Existential Love Affair." Review of *Tête-à-Tête: The Tumultuous Lives and Loves of Simone de Beauvoir and Jean-Paul Sartre*, by Hazel Rowley. *New York Times*, October 5, 2005. www.nytimes.com/2005/10/05/books/05grim
.html (accessed October 28, 2009).

"The Heart of Simone de Beauvoir." Review of *Simone de Beauvoir*, by Lisa Appignanesi. *Open Democracy*, January 8, 2008. www.opendemocracy.net/arts-Literature/feminist_2670.jsp (accessed October 23, 2009).

"Jean-Paul Sarte [sic] Overwhelmed by Beauvoir's Sex Drive." Review of *A Dangerous Liaison*, by Carole Seymour-Jones. *New York Post*, July 19, 2009. www.nypost.com/p/pagesix/item_
b0BvyhOlHH5q2ftzi3XL0I (accessed October 21, 2009).

Johnson, Diane. "The Life She Chose." Review of *Simone de Beauvoir: A Biography*, by Deirdre Bair. *New York Times*, October 22, 2009. www.nytimes.com/1990/04/15/books/the-life
-she-chose.html (accessed October 22, 2009).

Joris, Pierre. "Simone de Beauvoir at 100." January 24, 2008. http://pjoris.blogspot.com/2008/01/
simone-de-beauvoir-at-100.html (accessed October 21, 2009).

Laciofano, Carol. "The Disturbing Exploits of a Renowned Romance." Review of *Tête-à-Tête: The Tumultuous Lives and Loves of Simone de Beauvoir and Jean-Paul Sartre*, by Hazel Rowley. *Boston Globe*, November 16, 2005.

Liukkonen, Petri. "Jean-Paul Sartre (1905–1980)." www.kirjasto.sci.fi/sartre.htm (accessed October 21, 2009).

Liukkonen, Petri. "Simone de Beauvoir (1908–1986)—In Full Simone Lucie-Ernestine-Marie-Bertrand de Beauvoir." www.kirjasto.sci.fi/beauvoir.htm (accessed October 21, 2009).

Martin, Tim. "Simone de Beauvoir? Meet Jean-Paul Sartre." Review of *A Dangerous Liaison*, by Carole Seymour-Jones. *Telegraph*, April 12, 2008. www.telegraph.co.uk/culture/books/
non_fictionreviews/3672534/Simone-de-Beauvoir-Meet-Jean-Paul-Sartre.html (accessed October 21, 2009).

Menand, Louis. "Stand by Your Man: The Strange Liaison of Sartre and Beauvoir." Review of *Tête-à-Tête: The Tumultuous Lives and Loves of Simone de Beauvoir and Jean-Paul Sartre*, by Hazel Rowley. *New Yorker*, September 26, 2005. www.newyorker.com/archive/2005/09/
26/050926crbo_books (accessed October 21, 2009).

Miller, Jim. "Book Review: Simone de Beauvoir." Review of *Simone de Beauvoir: A Biography*, by Deirdre Bair. *Entertainment Weekly*, April 13, 1990. www.ew.com/ew/article/0,317151,00
.html (accessed October 23, 2009).

"'Our Relationship Was the Greatest Achievement of My Life.' But Did Simone de Beauvoir's Scandalous Open 'Marriage' to Sartre Make Her Happy, Asks Lisa Appignanesi." Review of *Simone de Beauvoir*, by Lisa Appignanesi. *Guardian*, June 10, 2005. www.guard
ian.co.uk/world/2005/jun/10/gender.politicsphilosophyandsociety (accessed October 21, 2009).

Robb, Graham. "A Dangerous Liaison by Carole Seymour-Jones Reviewed by Graham Robb." *Times Online*, April 6, 2008. http://entertainment.timesonline.co.uk/tol/arts_and_enter
tainment/books/non-fiction/article3674580.ece.

Roberts, Glenys. "Dangerous Liaisons and Sex with Teens: The Story of Sartre and de Beauvoir as Never Told Before." Review of *A Dangerous Liaison*, by Carole Seymour-Jones. *Mail On-line*, April 12, 2008. www.dailymail.co.uk/femail/article-559137/Dangerous-liaisons-sex
-teens-The-story-Sartre-Beauvoir-told-before.html (accessed October 22, 2009).

Rowley, Hazel. *Tête-à-Tête: The Tumultuous Lives and Loves of Simone de Beauvoir and Jean-Paul Sartre.* New York: HarperPerennial, 2006.

Salem Press. "Simone de Beauvoir." Sample text from *Magill's Survey of World Literature.* http://salempress.com/store/samples/survey_world_lit/survey_world_lit_beauvoir.htm (accessed October 23, 2009).

Seymour-Jones, Carole. *A Dangerous Liaison: A Revolutionary New Biography of Simone de Beauvoir and Jean-Paul Sartre.* New York: Overlook Press, 2008.

Thurman, Judith. "Introduction to Simone de Beauvoir's 'The Second Sex.'" Excerpted from *The Second Sex,* by Simone de Beauvoir. *New York Times,* May 27, 2010. www.nytimes.com/2010/05/30/books/excerpt-introduction-second-sex.html (accessed June 6, 2010).

Wikipedia. "Jean-Paul Sartre." http://en.wikipedia.org/wiki/Jean-Paul_Sartre (accessed October 21, 2009).

Wikipedia. "Simone de Beauvoir." http://en.wikipedia.org/wiki/Simone-de-Beauvoir (accessed October 21, 2009).

19. PRINCE EDWARD VIII AND WALLIS SIMPSON

Find a Grave. "Edward VIII." www.findagrave.com/cgi-bin/fg.cgi?page=gr&GRid=1987 (accessed January 25, 2010).

Find a Grave. "Wallis Simpson." www.findagrave.com/cgi-bin/fg.cgi?page=gr&GRid=4252 (accessed January 25, 2010).

"Foreign News: Viva L'Amore!" *Time,* August 16, 1937. www.time.com/time/magazine/article/0,9171,770784,00.html (accessed January 28, 2010).

"King Edward VIII & Wallis Simpson: In a Scandal That Rocked the World, He Gave Up the British Throne to Marry an American Woman He Felt He Couldn't Rule Without." *People,* February 12, 1996. www.people.com/people/archive/article/0,20102762,00.html (accessed January 25, 2010).

"Person of the Year 1936: Mrs. Wallis Warfield Simpson." *Time,* January 4, 1937. www.time.com/time/subscriber/personoftheyear/archive/stories/1936.html (accessed January 25, 2010).

Platinum Guild International. "King Edward VIII & Wallis Simpson." www.platinumguild.com/output/Page2014.asp (accessed January 25, 2010).

"Profile: Wallis Simpson." BBC, January 29, 2003. http://news.bbc.co.uk/2/hi/uk_news/2699035.stm (accessed January 25, 2010).

Rosenberg, Jennifer. "King Edward VIII Abdicated for Love." About.com: 20th Century History. http://history1900s.about.com/od/1930s/a/kingedward.htm (accessed January 25, 2010).

Scandalous Women Blog. "Wallis Simpson: The Woman Who Might Have Been Queen." December 17, 2007. http://scandalouswoman.blogspot.com/2007/12/duchess-of-windsor-woman-who-would-have.html (accessed January 25, 2010).

Socyberty. "Scandals That Rocked the World." http://socyberty.com/history/scandals-that-rocked-the-world/ (accessed January 25, 2010).

Steiner, Zara. "The Man Who Wouldn't Be King." Review of *King Edward VIII: A Biography,* by Philip Ziegler. *New York Times,* February 10, 1991. www.nytimes.com/1991/02/10/books/the-man-who-wouldn-t-be-king.html (accessed January 25, 2010).

Trex, Ethan. "5 Things You Didn't Know about Wallis Simpson." Mental Floss Blog, December 18, 2009. www.mentalfloss.com/blogs/archives/43397 (accessed January 25, 2010).

Trivia Library. "Famous Marriages: King Edward VIII and Wallis Simpson Part 1." www.trivia-library.com/b/famous-marriages-king-edward-viii-and-wallis-simpson-part-1.htm (accessed January 25, 2010).

"Wallis Simpson." www.divasthesite.com/Political_Divas/Wallis_Simpson.htm (accessed January 25, 2010).

Wikipedia. "Edward VIII of the United Kingdom." http://en.wikipedia.org/wiki/Edward_VIII_ of_the_United_Kingdom (accessed January 25, 2010).

Wikipedia. "Wallis, Duchess of Windsor." http://en.wikipedia.org/wiki/Wallis,_Duchess_of_ Windsor (accessed January 25, 2010).

20. CLARK GABLE AND CAROLE LOMBARD

"Clark Gable & Carole Lombard: He Was a Man's Man and She Was a Man's Woman, and To- gether They Soared beyond Stereotype. Then Fate Stepped In to Pull Hollywood's Golden Couple Apart." *People*, February 12, 1996. www.people.com/people/archive/article/0,2010 2771,00.html.

Datehookup.com. "The Romance of Gable and Lombard." www.datehookup.com/content-the -romance-of-gable-and-lombard.htm (accessed March 8, 2010).

Harris, Warren G. *Clark Gable: A Biography.* New York: Three Rivers Press, 2002.

Murphsplace.com. "Time Magazine—1939; Cinema—Boy Gets Girl." www.murphsplace.com/ lombard/time/time1.html (accessed March 8, 2010).

Murphsplace.com. "Time Magazine—1942; U.S. at War—End of a Mission." www.murphsplace .com/lombard/time/time-death.html (accessed March 8, 2010).

Murphsplace.com. "Time Magazine Articles—Gable's Death; Show Business—Hero's Exit." www.murphsplace.com/lombard/time/time-gable.html (accessed March 8, 2010).

Pioneer Saloon History Site. "Gable and Lombard—The Clark Gable & Carole Lombard story." www.pioneersaloon.info/history/history2.htm (accessed March 8, 2010).

Scandalous Women Blog. "Hollywood's Golden Couple: Gable and Lombard." February 22, 2009. http://scandalouswoman.blogspot.com/2009/02/hollywoods-golden-couple-gable -and.html (accessed March 8, 2010).

Shilcutt, Katharine. "Houston 101: Frankly, My Dear, I Don't Give a Damn." Houston Press Blogs, September 23, 2009. http://blogs.houstonpress.com/hairballs/2009/09/houston_101_ frankly_my_dear_i.php (accessed March 8, 2010).

Wikipedia. "Carole Lombard." http://en.wikipedia.org/wiki/Carole_Lombard (accessed March 8, 2010).

Wikipedia. "Clark Gable." http://en.wikipedia.org/wiki/Clark_Gable (accessed March 8, 2010).

21. DESI ARNAZ AND LUCILLE BALL

Answers.com. "Biography: Desi Arnaz." www.answers.com/topic/desi-arnaz (accessed October 15, 2009).

Find a Grave. "Lucille Desiree Ball." www.findagrave.com/cgi-bin/fg.cgi?GRid=50&page=gr (ac- cessed October 15, 2009).

Huver, Scott. "Legendary Lovebirds: Lucille Ball and Desi Arnaz." Hollywood.com, February 13, 2006. www.hollywood.com/feature/Legendary_Lovebirds_Lucille_Ball_and_Desi_Arnaz/ 1104111 (accessed June 9, 2010).

"Lucille Ball." *New York Times.* http://movies.nytimes.com/person/599102/Lucille-Ball/biography (accessed June 9, 2010).

"Lucille Ball & Desi Arnaz: Their Torrid Match Had to Burn Out, but Back in the Days When Desi Loved Lucy, They Set Off Sparks So Fierce, They Would Warm Future Generations." *People*, February 12, 1996. www.people.com/people/archive/article/0,20102764,00.html (accessed October 15, 2009).

McGrath, Douglas. "The Man behind the Throne: Making the Case for Desi Arnaz." *New York Times*, October 14, 2001. www.nytimes.com/2001/10/14/arts/television/14MCGR.html (accessed June 9, 2010).

Petrozzello, Donna. "The Sad Situation behind Lucy's Comedy." *New York Daily News*, April 29, 2003. www.nydailynews.com/archives/entertainment/2003/04/29/2003-04-29_the_sad_situation_behind_luc.html (accessed October 17, 2009).

Schindehette, Susan. "The Real Story of Desi and Lucy: Onscreen They Were the Irrepressible Ricardos; Off-Camera, Their Stormy Love Outlasted a 20-Year Marriage That Foundered on Celebrity and Success." *People*, February 18, 1991. www.people.com/people/archive/article/0,20114475,00.html (accessed October 17, 2009).

Wikipedia. "Desi Arnaz." http://en.wikipedia.org/wiki/Desi_Arnaz (accessed October 15, 2009).

Wikipedia. "Lucille Ball." http://en.wikipedia.org/wiki/Lucille_Ball (accessed October 15, 2009).

22. HUMPHREY BOGART AND LAUREN BACALL

Bacall, Lauren. *By Myself and Then Some*. New York: Harper, 2006.

Basic Famous People. "Humphrey Bogart Biography." www.basicfamouspeople.com/index.php?aid=1331 (accessed July 4, 2009).

Boeder, Laurie. "Three Great Screen Couples: Better Living through On-Screen Chemistry." About.com: Classic Movies. http://classicfilm.about.com/od/actorsanddirectors/a/Screen Couples.htm (accessed July 4, 2009).

Cagle, Jess. "To Have and Have Knot: Lauren Bacall and Humphrey Bogart Wed—A Recap of How the Screen Idols Met." *Entertainment Weekly*, May 24, 1991. www.ew.com/ew/article/0,314378,00.html (accessed July 4, 2009).

Cantrell, Susan. "The Show Goes On: Legend Lauren Bacall on Life, Acting, and Bogie." *Carmel Magazine*, 2009. www.carmelmagazine.com/archive/09sp/lauren-bacall.shtml.

Everything2 Database. "Lauren Bacall." www.everything2.org/index.pl?node_id=502055 (accessed July 4, 2009).

Hollywood & Los Angeles: Including Unique Information on Hollywood Stars, Celebrities and Tourist Attractions. "Final Resting Place of Humphrey Bogart." www.hollywoodusa.co.uk/GlendaleObituaries/humphreybogart.htm (accessed July 7, 2009).

"Humphrey Bogart & Lauren Bacall: The Tough-Guy Exterior Was Just an Act. And Their Movie Clinches Paled in Comparison to the Real-Life Ardor between Bogie and His Baby." *People*, February 12, 1996. www.people.com/people/archive/article/0,20102776,00.html (accessed July 4, 2009).

Hyena.com. "Humphrey Bogart." www.hyenaproductions.com/humphrey-bogart.aspx (accessed July 4, 2009).

Keeping, Susan. "Humphrey Bogart and Lauren Bacall Biographies: One of the Most Well-Known Celebrity Couples in Hollywood History." Suite101, October 11, 2008. http://celebrity-couples.suite101.com/article.cfm/humphrey_bogart_and_lauren_bacall (accessed July 4, 2009).

Klausner, Kim. "Lauren Bacall." Jewish Virtual Library: A Division of the American-Israeli Cooperative Enterprise. www.jewishvirtuallibrary.org/jsource/biography/bacall.html (accessed December 21, 2009).

Lane, Christina. "Humphrey Bogart." *St. James Encyclopedia of Pop Culture*, January 29, 2002. http://findarticles.com/p/articles/mi_g1epc/is_bio/ai_2419200117/ (accessed July 7, 2009).

Rich, Frank Kelly. "Three Drinks Ahead with Humphrey Bogart." *Modern Drunkard Magazine*, January 2005. www.moderndrunkardmagazine.com/issues/05_03/05-03-bogart.html (accessed July 4, 2009).

Sea Witch Manor Inn & Spa, Bewitched & BEDazzled B&B. "Humphrey Bogart." http://bewitched bandb.com/boghstar.html (accessed July 4, 2009).

Squidoo. "Humphrey Bogart, Hollywood Tough Guy." www.squidoo.com/bogie (accessed July 7, 2009).

Wikipedia. "Humphrey Bogart." http://en.wikipedia.org/wiki/Humphrey_Bogart (accessed July 3, 2009).

Wikipedia. "Lauren Bacall." http://en.wikipedia.org/wiki/Lauren_Bacall (accessed July 4, 2009).

Yahoo! Movies. "Lauren Bacall Biography." http://movies.yahoo.com/movie/contributor/18000 28466/bio (accessed July 4, 2009).

23. RONALD REAGAN AND NANCY DAVIS

BBC. "End of a Love Story." June 5, 2004. http://news.bbc.co.uk/2/hi/americas/265714.stm (accessed February 9, 2010).

Connelly, Sherryl, with Michelle Caruso. "Two Became One—And Now Stands Alone: Nancy's Always Been by His Side." *New York Daily News*, June 6, 2004. www.nydailynews.com/archives/news/2004/06/06/2004-06-06_two_became_one_-_and__now_on.html (accessed June 11, 2010).

Dowd, Maureen. "All That Glitters Is Not Real, Book on Nancy Reagan Says." Review of *Nancy Reagan: The Unauthorized Biography*, by Kitty Kelley. *New York Times*, April 7, 1991. www .nytimes.com/1991/04/07/us/all-that-glitters-is-not-real-book-on-nancy-reagan-says .html (accessed June 11, 2010).

Glaser, Gretchen L. "The Woman behind the Man." Young Ladies Christian Fellowship, September 7, 2004. http://ylcf.org/2004/09/woman-behind-man/ (accessed February 10, 2010).

Hancock, David. "His Fierce Protector: Nancy." CBS News, June 5, 2004. www.cbsnews.com/stories/2004/06/05/national/main621274.shtml (accessed February 10, 2010).

Reagan, Nancy. *I Love You, Ronnie: The Letters of Ronald Reagan to Nancy Reagan*. New York: Random House, 2002.

"Ronald Reagan & Nancy Davis: Faced with Their Biggest Challenge Yet—His Alzheimer's—the Former First Couple Look to the Future the Way They Always Have: Together." *People*, February 12, 1996. www.people.com/people/archive/article/0,20102780,00.html.

Schindehette, Susan. "Journey's End: Actor, President, Husband, Father: Friends and Family Remember the Storybook Life and Difficult Death of an American Icon." *People*, June 21, 2004. www.people.com/people/archive/article/0,20150369,00.html (accessed February 9, 2010).

Stritof, Sheri, and Bob Stritof. "Ronald Reagan and Nancy Davis Reagan Marriage Profile." About .com: Marriage. http://marriage.about.com/od/celebritymarriages/p/reaganronald.htm (accessed February 9, 2010).

"Sun Sets as Reagan Laid to Rest in California." MSNBC, June 12, 2004. www.msnbc.msn.com/id/5144264/ (accessed February 10, 2010).

White House. "Nancy Davis Reagan." http://georgewbush-whitehouse.archives.gov/history/firstladies/nr40.html (accessed February 10, 2010).

Wikipedia. "Nancy Reagan." http://en.wikipedia.org/wiki/Nancy_Reagan (accessed February 12, 2010).

Wikipedia. "Ronald Reagan." http://en.wikipedia.org/wiki/Ronald_Reagan (accessed February 9, 2010).

Wilson, Jeff. "Nancy at Reagan's Side until the End." *Albany Times Union*, June 5, 2004. www.timesunion.com/ASPStories/story.asp?StoryID=254575&TextPage=1 (accessed February 10, 2010).

24. RICHARD BURTON AND ELIZABETH TAYLOR

"A Love Too Big To Last." Excerpted from *Furious Love: Elizabeth Taylor, Richard Burton, and the Marriage of the Century* by Sam Kashner and Nancy Schoenberger. *Vanity Fair*, July 2010, 126–141.

BBC. "On This Day 10 October 1975: Liz Taylor and Richard Burton Remarry." http://news.bbc.co.uk/onthisday/hi/dates/stories/october/10/newsid_4089000/4089030.stm (accessed January 3, 2010).

Cagle, Jess. "Creatures of the Nile: Elizabeth Taylor and Richard Burton—The Actors Had Their Scene Together for "Cleopatra" 29 Years Ago." *Entertainment Weekly*, January 18, 1991. www.ew.com/ew/article/0,312989,00.html (accessed January 3, 2010).

Cahalan, Susannah. "'Furious Love': The Love Letters of Richard Burton and Elizabeth Taylor." Review of *Furious Love: Elizabeth Taylor, Richard Burton, and the Marriage of the Century*, by Sam Kashner and Nancy Schoenberger. *New York Post*, June 6, 2010. www.nypost.com/p/news/opinion/books/furious_love_the_love_letters_taylor_3RREnDd0ABuOMWMFVNDcGO (accessed June 11, 2010).

CNN. "Elizabeth Taylor: Loving Men and Being a 'Dame.'" www.cnn.com/2007/US/03/21/larry.king.taylor/index.html (accessed January 3, 2010).

"Dame Elizabeth Taylor 'Still Pines for Richard Burton.'" *Telegraph*, September 17, 2009. www.telegraph.co.uk/news/newstopics/celebritynews/6200148/Dame-Elizabeth-Taylor-still-pines-for-Richard-Burton.html (accessed January 3, 2010).

Devine, Darren. "Hollywood Star Elizabeth Taylor Still Has Photo of Burton by Bed." *Wales Online*, September 17, 2009. www.walesonline.co.uk/news/wales-news/2009/09/17/hollywood-actress-still-has-a-photo-of-burton-by-bed-91466-24710285/ (accessed January 3, 2010).

Everything2 Database. "Richard Burton." http://everything2.com/title/Richard+Burton (accessed January 3, 2010).

"'I Would Have Married Richard Burton a Third Time,' Says Hollywood Legend Elizabeth Taylor." *Mail Online*, September 16, 2009. www.dailymail.co.uk/tvshowbiz/article-1213880/Id-marry-Richard-Burton-time-alive-says-Hollywood-legend-Elizabeth-Taylor.html (accessed January 3, 2010).

Kamp, David. "When Liz Met Dick." http://davidkamp.com/2006/09/when_liz_met_dick.php (accessed January 3, 2010).

"Liz Un-Burtoned Again: Elizabeth Taylor Heads Home after Richard Burton, Husband and Lover for 15 Years, Asks for a Divorce before Her 44th Birthday." *People*, March 15, 1976. www.people.com/people/archive/article/0,20066251,00.html (accessed January 3, 2010).

Platinum Guild International. "Elizabeth Taylor & Richard Burton." http://platinumguild.com/output/Page2016.asp (accessed January 3, 2010).

"Richard Burton & Elizabeth Taylor: Through Two Marriages and 23 Years, the Lustiest of Couples Couldn't Live with—or without—Each Other." *People*, February 12, 1996. www.people.com/people/archive/article/0,20102761,00.html (accessed January 3, 2010).

Rogers, Lisa Waller. "Elizabeth Taylor: Burton Called Her 'Lumpy.'" Review of *How to Be a Movie*

Star: Elizabeth Taylor in Hollywood, by William Mann. http://lisawallerrogers.wordpress
.com/2009/11/05/elizabeth-taylor-burton-called-her-lumpy/ (accessed January 3, 2010).

Stritof, Sheri, and Bob Stritof. "Elizabeth Taylor and Richard Burton Marriage Profile." About.
com: Marriage. http://marriage.about.com/od/elizabethtaylor/a/liztaylorburton.htm (accessed January 3, 2010).

Wikipedia. "Elizabeth Taylor." http://en.wikipedia.org/wiki/Elizabeth_Taylor (accessed January 4, 2010).

Wikipedia. "Richard Burton." http://en.wikipedia.org/wiki/Richard_Burton (accessed January
3, 2010).

25. JOE DIMAGGIO AND MARILYN MONROE

"About Marilyn Monroe." www.english.illinois.edu/Maps/poets/g_l/grahn/monroe.htm (accessed June 15, 2009).

Berkow, Ira. "Sports of the Times: A Baseball Love Affair Suffering a Breakup." *New York Times,*
November 12, 1998. www.nytimes.com/1998/11/12/sports/sports-of-the-times-a-baseball
-love-affair-suffering-a-breakup.html (accessed June 15, 2009).

Biography.com. "Marilyn Monroe Biography." www.biography.com/articles/Marilyn-Monroe
-9412123 (accessed June 15, 2009).

Brady, Erik. "Ultimate Celebrity Had Air of Mystery." *USA Today,* March 9, 1999. www.usatoday
.com/sports/baseball/joed/joed14.htm (accessed June 15, 2009).

Creamer, Robert W. "A New Biography of Joe and Marilyn Is More Soap Opera Than Tragedy."
Review of *Joe & Marilyn: A Memory of Love,* by Roger Kahn. *Sports Illustrated Vault,* December
8, 1986. http://sportsillustrated.cnn.com/vault/article/magazine/MAG1065605/index.htm
(accessed June 15, 2009).

Doll, Susan. "Marilyn Monroe's Early Career." HowStuffWorks. http://entertainment.howstuff
works.com/marilyn-monroe-early-career.htm.

Doll, Susan. "Marilyn Monroe's Later Career." HowStuffWorks. http://entertainment.howstuff
works.com/marilyn-monroe-later-career.htm (accessed June 15, 2009).

Donner, Simon. "Joe DiMaggio." *St. James Encyclopedia of Pop Culture.* http://findarticles.com/p/
articles/mi_glepc/is_bio/2419200319/ (accessed June 15, 2009).

Find a Grave. "Joe DiMaggio." www.findagrave.com/cgi-bin/fg.cgi?page=gr&GRid=4701 (accessed June 18, 2009).

Find a Grave. "Marilyn Monroe." www.findagrave.com/cgi-bin/fg.cgi?page=gr&GRid=725 (accessed June 15, 2009).

Hoberman, J. "Korea and a Career—Marilyn Monroe." *Artforum International Magazine,* January
8, 1994. http://findarticles.com/p/articles/mi_m0268/is_n5_v32/ai_15143588/ (accessed
June 15, 2009).

Hoppe, Art. "Joe Di Maggio Weds Marilyn Monroe at City Hall." Virtual Museum of the City of
San Francisco. www.sfmuseum.org/hist8/jodimag.html (accessed June 15, 2009).

"Joe and Marilyn." Review of *Joe and Marilyn,* by Roger Kahn. *National Review,* January 30, 1987.
http://findarticles.com/p/articles/mi_m1282/is_v39/ai_4629830/ (accessed June 15, 2009).

"Joe DiMaggio—Marriage to Marilyn Monroe." http://sports.jrank.org/pages/1187/DiMaggio
-Joe-Marriage-Marilyn-Monroe.html (accessed June 15, 2009).

Lovetripper. "Marilyn Monroe & Joe DiMaggio Wedding." www.lovetripper.com/bridalstars/
wedding-database/marilyn-monroe-dimaggio.html (accessed June 15, 2009).

"Marilyn Monroe & Joe DiMaggio: What Becomes a Legend Most? A Goddess by His Side. Although Their Marriage Lasted Only Months, the Slugger and His Star Left Their Public Blinded by the Sight." *People*, February 12, 1996. www.people.com/people/archive/article/0,20102765,00.html (accessed June 15, 2009).

"Marilyn Monroe: The Legend." www.ncu.edu.tw/~wenchi/english/articles/monroe/monroe_bio.htm.

Mosca, Alexandra Kathryn. "Marilyn Monroe: The Sad Life and Untimely Death of America's Fantasy." www.qcc.cuny.edu/socialsciences/ppecorino/SS680/Funeral_Marilyn_Monroe.html (accessed June 15, 2009).

Scherman, Tony. "When Marilyn Married Joe." *American Heritage*, January 14, 2006. www.american heritage.com/articles/web/20060114-marilyn-monroe-joe-dimaggio-yankees-baseball-hollywood-arthur-miller-suicide-marriage-divorce_print.shtml (accessed June 15, 2009).

Schwartz, Larry. "Joltin' Joe Was a Hit for All Reasons." ESPN. http://espn.go.com/sportscentury/features/00014151.html (accessed June 15, 2009).

Shelden, Michael. "The Greatest Celebrity Match of Them All." *Telegraph*, May 3, 2004. www.telegraph.co.uk/culture/3616377/The-greatest-celebrity-match-of-them-all.html (accessed June 12, 2009).

"When Marilyn Married Joe." *Age*, May 12, 2004. www.theage.com.au/articles/2004/05/11/1084041400232.html (accessed June 15, 2009).

Wikipedia. "Joe DiMaggio." http://en.wikipedia.org/wiki/Joe_DiMaggio (accessed June 15, 2009).

Wikipedia. "Marilyn Monroe." http://en.wikipedia.org/wiki/Marilyn_monroe (accessed June 15, 2009).

Wilson, Mat. "Joe DiMaggio and Marilyn Monroe—Where's Shakespeare When You Need Him? Joe DiMaggio: Marilyn's Real-Life Hero." Der Keiler Newsgroup Archive. http://news groups.derkeiler.com/Archive/Rec/rec.arts.tv/2005-12/msg03245.html (accessed June 15, 2009).

26. PRINCE RAINIER AND GRACE KELLY

Barker, Dennis. "Obituary, Prince Rainier of Monaco: Europe's Longest Serving Monarch, Head of the 700-Year-Old Grimaldi Dynasty and Husband to the Late Movie Star Grace Kelly." *Guardian*, April 6, 2005. www.guardian.co.uk/news/2005/apr/06/guardianobituaries1 (accessed January 10, 2010).

"Grace Kelly & Prince Rainier III: When Hollywood's Princess Met the Prince of Monaco, She Traded Her Realm for His. The Result Wasn't Always a Perfect Marriage, but It Lasted Till Death Did Them Part." *People*, February 12, 1996. www.people.com/people/archive/article/0,20102778,00.html (accessed January 10, 2010).

Silvester, Christopher. "High Society: Grace Kelly and Hollywood by Donald Spoto: Review." Review of *High Society: Grace Kelly and Hollywood*, by Donald Spoto. *Telegraph*, June 12, 2009. www.telegraph.co.uk/culture/books/bookreviews/5514352/High-Society-Grace-Kelly-and-Hollywood-by-Donald-Spoto-review.html (accessed January 10, 2010).

Spoto, Donald. *High Society: The Life of Grace Kelly.* New York: Harmony Books, 2009.

Wikipedia. "Grace Kelly." http://en.wikipedia.org/wiki/Grace_Kelly (accessed January 10, 2010).

Wikipedia. "Rainier III, Prince of Monaco." http://en.wikipedia.org/wiki/Rainier_III._Prince_of_Monaco (accessed January 10, 2010).

27. JOHNNY CASH AND JUNE CARTER

Academy of Achievement. "Johnny Cash Profile." www.achievement.org/autodoc/page/cas0pro-1 (accessed March 20, 2010).

Anderson, Brett. "Unbroken: June Carter and Johnny Cash Celebrate Her New Album with Soulful Spirituals and Fried Green Tomatoes." *Salon*, May 18, 1999. www.salon.com/enter tainment/music/feature/1999/05/18/johnny_cash (accessed March 20, 2010).

BBC. "Johnny Cash's Wife Dies." May 16, 2003. http://news.bbc.co.uk/2/hi/entertainment/ 3033071.stm (accessed March 20, 2010).

Beard, Steve. "The Fevered Love of June and Johnny." *Thunderstruck*. www.thunderstruck.org/ june3.htm (accessed March 18, 2010).

Carr, Patrick. "June Carter Cash: The Den Mother of Country Music." *Slate Magazine*, May 20, 2003. www.slate.com/id/2083251 (accessed March 20, 2010).

Grand Ole Opry and Robert K. Oermann. "Johnny and June." Excerpt from *Behind the Grand Ole Opry Curtain: Tales of Romance and Tragedy*. 2008. www.hachettebookgroup.com/31935A 1DE04642D8989D13AF0C014CC3.htm.org/entry/June_Carter_Cash (accessed March 20, 2010).

Janzen, Daniel. "The Swan Song of Johnny Cash 1932–2003." *Flak Magazine*. www.flakmag.com/ opinion/cash.html (accessed March 20, 2010).

LaSalle, Mick. "Their Love Raged in a Ring of Fire—Johnny Cash and June Carter Held On in Good Times and Bad." Review of the film *Walk the Line. San Francisco Chronicle*, November 18, 2005. http://articles.sfgate.com/2005-11-18/entertainment/17399555_1_cash-s-voice -johnny-cash-sing (accessed March 20, 2010).

New World Encyclopedia. "Cash, June Carter." www.newworldencyclopedia.org/entry/June_ Carter_Cash (accessed March 20, 2010).

Ratliff, Ben. "June Carter Cash, a Fixture in Country Music, Dies at 73." *New York Times*, May 16, 2001. www.nytimes.com/2003/05/16/obituaries/16CASH.html?pagewanted=1 (accessed March 20, 2010).

Roberts, Glenys. "Johnny Cash: The Maniac in Black." *Mail Online*, September 1, 2007. www .dailymail.co.uk/tvshowbiz/article-479165/Johnny-Cash-The-Maniac-Black.html (accessed March 19, 2010).

Rolling Stone. "Johnny Cash Biography." www.rollingstone.com/artists/johnnycash/biography (accessed March 20, 2010).

Sedgewick, Augustin. "June Carter Cash Dies." *Rolling Stone*, May 16, 2003. www.rollingstone .com/news/story/5936388/june_carter_cash_dies (accessed March 20, 2010).

Shoji, Kaori. "A Ray of Love for Johnny Cash." Review of the film *Walk the Line. Japan Times Online*, February 17, 2006. http://search.japantimes.co.jp/cgi-bin/ff20060217a2.html (accessed March 20, 2010).

Silverman, Stephen M. "Country Legend June Carter Cash Dies." *People*, May 16, 2003. www .people.com/people/article/0,626055,00.html (accessed March 20, 2010).

Smolowe, Jim, and Steve Dougherty. "Fade to Black: A Sharecropper's Son, Country Hero Johnny Cash Walked the Line and Became a Legend." *People*, September 29, 2003. www .people.com/people/archive/article/0,20148218,00.html.

Stritof, Sheri, and Bob Stritof. "Johnny Cash and June Carter Cash Marriage Profile." About.com: Marriage. http://marriage.about.com/od/entertainmen1/p/johncash.htm (accessed March 10, 2010).

TV.com. "June Carter Cash." www.tv.com/june-carter-cash/person/86493/biography.html (accessed March 20, 2010).

Waxman, Sharon. "The Secrets That Lie Beyond the Ring of Fire." Review of the film *Walk the Line. New York Times*, October 16, 2005. www.nytimes.com/2005/10/16/movies/16waxm.html (accessed March 20, 2010).

Wikipedia. "Johnny Cash." http://en.wikipedia.org/wiki/Johnny_Cash (accessed March 20, 2010).

Wikipedia. "June Carter Cash." http://en.wikipedia.org/wiki/June_Cash (accessed March 20, 2010).

28. ARISTOTLE ONASSIS AND MARIA CALLAS

Blumenfeld, Bruno. "Moonlight and Mayhem: The Epic Romance of Onassis and Callas." Review of *Greek Fire: The Story of Maria Callas and Aristotle Onassis*, by Nicholas Gage. *New York Daily News*, October 8, 2000. www.nydailynews.com/archives/entertainment/2000/10/08/2000-10-08_moonlight_and_mayhem_the_epi.html (accessed March 16, 2010).

Burget, Estelle. "Callas, 30 Years On." Luxe-magazine.com, January 2008. www.luxe-magazine.com/46-2325-callas_30_years_on (accessed March 17, 2010).

France, Miranda. "Book Reviews: The Shipboard Romance." Review of *Greek Fire: The Love Affair of Maria Callas and Aristotle Onassis*, by Nicholas Gage. *Spectator.* www.spectator.co.uk/books/19179/the-shipboard-romance.thtml (accessed March 17, 2010).

Gage, Nicholas. *Greek Fire: The Story of Maria Callas and Aristotle Onassis.* New York: Knopf, 2000.

"*Greek Fire* Reviewed in the October 2000 issue of *W*." October 2000. www.nickgage.com/rv2.htm (accessed March 17, 2010).

"The Greek Love Triangle: Aristotle Onassis, Jacqueline Kennedy & Maria Callas." October 2002. www.irinasworld.com/irinasworld/love_stories.html.

Maslin, Janet. "Books of the Times: A High-Rent Romance Full of Mythic Minutiae." Review of *Greek Fire: The Story of Maria Callas and Aristotle Onassis*, by Nicholas Gage. *New York Times*, November 9, 2000. www.nytimes.com/2000/11/09/books/books-of-the-times-a-high-rent-romance-full-of-mythic-minutiae.html (accessed March 17, 2010).

Stassinopoulos, Arianna. "Maria Was a Weapon in Ari's Marital Battles with Jackie. Even after He Wed Jackie Kennedy, Onassis Held Maria Callas Fast, and Her Passion Sustained Him." Excerpted from *The Woman behind the Legend*. New York: Simon & Schuster, 1981.

Wikipedia. "Aristotle Onassis." http://en.wikipedia.org/wiki/Aristotle_Onassis (accessed March 16, 2010).

Wikipedia. "Maria Callas." http://en.wikipedia.org/wiki/Maria_Callas (accessed March 16, 2010).

29. ELVIS PRESLEY AND PRISCILLA BEAULIEU

ABC News. "Priscilla Presley on Life with Elvis: In '85 Interview, Priscilla Presley Talks about Her Romance with the King." http://abcnews.go.com/2020/story?id=123860&page=1 (accessed January 25, 2010).

Biography.com. "Elvis Presley Biography." www.biography.com/articles/Elvis-Presley-9446466 (accessed January 25, 2010).

"Elvis Presley & Priscilla Beaulieu: As Powerful and Disturbing as a Scene from Grand Opera, the Cloying Romance of the King and His Child-Love Became an American Cautionary Tale." *People*, February 12, 1996. www.people.com/people/archive/article/0,20102773,00.html (accessed February 6, 2010).

ElvisPresleyNews.com. "Elvis Presley Funeral." www.elvispresleynews.com/ElvisFuneral.html (accessed February 6, 2010).

Finstad, Suzanne. *Child Bride: The Untold Story of Priscilla Beaulieu Presley.* New York: Three Rivers Press, 1997.

Harris, Misty. "Burning Love Affair with Elvis 75 Years after His Birth." *Canada.com,* January 7, 2010. www.canada.com/story_print.html?id=2416489&sponsor= (accessed January 25, 2010).

Mahalo.com. "Priscilla Presley." www.mahalo.com/priscilla-presley (accessed January 25, 2010).

Nash, Alanna. *Baby, Let's Play House: Elvis Presley and the Women Who Loved Him.* New York: It Books, 2010.

Presley, Priscilla Beaulieu, with Sandra Harmon. *Elvis and Me.* New York: Berkley Books, 1986.

Rolling Stone. "Elvis Presley Biography." www.rollingstone.com/artists/elvispresley/biography (accessed February 6, 2010).

Romance 101. "Priscilla Beaulieu and Elvis Presley." http://rom101.com/storyview.jsp?storyid=463 (accessed February 6, 2010).

Stritof, Sheri, and Bob Stritof. "Elvis Presley and Priscilla Beaulieu Marriage Profile." About.com: Marriage. http://marriage.about.com/od/entertainmen1/p/elvispresley.htm (accessed January 25, 2010).

Turner Classic Movies. "Biography for Priscilla Presley." www.tcm.com/tcmdb/participant .jsp?spid=155139&apid=0 (accessed January 25, 2010).

Wikipedia. "Elvis and Me." http://en.wikipedia.org/wiki/Elvis_and_Me (accessed January 25, 2010).

Wikipedia. "Elvis Presley." http://en.wikipedia.org/wiki/Elvis_Presley (accessed February 6, 2010).

Wikipedia. "Priscilla Presley." http://en.wikipedia.org/wiki/Priscilla_Presley (accessed January 25, 2010).

30. JOHN LENNON AND YOKO ONO

Answers.com. "John Lennon/Yoko Ono." www.answers.com/topic/john-lennon-yoko-ono -classical-musician (accessed August 10, 2009).

The-Beatles-History.com. "Yoko Ono Biography." www.the-beatles-history.com/yoko-ono.html (accessed August 13, 2009).

Carucci, John. "Yoko Ono Displays John Lennon's Bloodied Clothes." Huffington Post. www .huffingtonpost.com/2009/05/12/yoko-ono-displays-john-le_n_202702.html (accessed August 10, 2009).

DeCurtis, Anthony. "Biography." John Lennon: The Official Site. www.johnlennon.com/html/ biography.aspx (accessed August 10, 2009).

Gilmore, Mikal. "Lennon Lives Forever: Twenty-Five Years after His Death, His Music and Message Endure." *Rolling Stone,* December 5, 2005. www.rollingstone.com/news/story/8898300/ lennon_lives_forever (accessed August 11, 2009).

"John Lennon & Yoko Ono: His Band Didn't Survive It, His Fans Couldn't Fathom It. But the Thinking Man's Beatle Found Love—and the Courage to Imagine—with a Strong-Willed Original Named Yoko." *People,* February 12, 1996. www.people.com/people/archive/arti cle/0,20102769,00.html (accessed August 10, 2009).

Jones, Ronald. "Yoko Ono." http://findarticles.com/p/articles/mi_m0268/is_n2_v37/ai_ 21230383/(accessed August 13, 2009).

Lyrics007. "John Lennon—God Lyrics." www.lyrics007.com/John%20Lennon%20Lyrics/God% 20Lyrics.html (accessed August 24, 2009).

Neumaier, Joe. "When John Met Yoko: November 9, 1966 at Indica Gallery." *Entertainment Weekly*, November 5, 1999. http://articles.absoluteelsewhere.net/Articles/john_met_yoko .html.

Notable Names Database. "Yoko Ono." www.nndb.com/people/087/000023018/ (accessed August 22, 2009).

Ryder, Caroline. "Yoko Ono." *Swindle Magazine*. http://swindlemagazine.com/isueicons/yoko -ono/(accessed August 22, 2009).

Sardone, Susan Breslow. "The John Lennon/Yoko Ono Bed-In: Visit the Suite Where 'Give Peace a Chance' Was Recorded in Montreal, Canada." About.com: Honeymoons/Romantic Travel. http://honeymoons.about.com/cs/canadiangetaways/a/johnyoko.htm (accessed August 10, 2009).

Sheff, David. "1980 Playboy Interview with John Lennon and Yoko Ono." John-Lennon.com. www.john-lennon.com/playboyinterviewwithjohnlennonandyokoono.htm (accessed August 10, 2009).

Wikipedia. "John Lennon." http://en.wikipedia.org/wiki/John_Lennon (accessed August 10, 2009).

Wikipedia. "Yoko Ono." http://en.wikipedia.org/wiki/Yoko_Ono (accessed August 10, 2009).

Wilson, Jack. "Yoko Ono Tells of Last Night with Lennon." FreeRepublic.com. www.freerepublic .com/focus/f-news/1848343/posts (accessed August 22, 2009).

Yannicos, Trina. "John Lennon and Yoko Ono's Honeymoon for Peace." Examiner.com. www .examiner.com/x-4732-Celebrity-Travel-Examiner~y2009m3d23-John-Lennon-and -Yoko-Onos-honeymoon-for-peace (accessed August 10, 2009).

31. PAUL MCCARTNEY AND LINDA EASTMAN

AllExperts Encyclopedia. "Linda McCartney." www.associatepublisher.com/e/l/li/linda_ mccartney.htm (accessed January 19, 2010).

BBC. "On This Day 12 March 1969: Paul McCartney weds Linda Eastman." http://news.bbc.co .uk/onthisday/hi/dates/stories/march/12/newsid_3607000/3607215.stm (accessed January 19, 2010).

BBC. "The Seven Ages of Paul McCartney." June 17, 2006. http://news.bbc.co.uk/2/hi/5087006 .stm (accessed January 19, 2010).

Beatles Bible. "Paul McCartney Meets Linda Eastman." www.beatlesbible.com/1967/05/15/ paul-mccartney-meets-linda-eastman/ (accessed January 19, 2010).

The-Beatles-History.com. "Linda McCartney Biography." www.the-beatles-history.com/linda -mccartney.html (accessed January 19, 2010).

Beatles Number 9 Fan Site. "The Story of Linda McCartney." http://beatlesnumber9.com/linda .html (accessed January 19, 2010).

Connor, Tracy. "All He Needs Is Love—and Paul McCartney Always Found It." *New York Daily News*, November 8, 2007. www.nydailynews.com/gossip/2007/11/08/2007-11-08_all_he_ needs_is_love__and_paul_mccartney-2.html (accessed January 21, 2010).

Fields, Danny. *Linda McCartney*. Los Angeles: Renaissance Books, 2000.

Gates, Anita. "Television Review: The Lovely Linda, Camera in Hand." Review of *The Linda McCartney Story* (CBS). *New York Times*, May 20, 2000. www.nytimes.com/2000/05/20/arts/ television-review-the-lovely-linda-camera-in-hand.html (accessed January 19, 2010).

Guntheranderson.com. "The Long and Winding Road Lyrics and Chords." http://guntherander son.com/v/data/thelonga.htm (accessed January 21, 2010).

Kozinn, Allan. "Linda McCartney, Photographer of Rock Stars, Dies at 56." *New York Times*, April

20, 1998. www.nytimes.com/1998/04/20/arts/linda-mccartney-photographer-of-rock-stars-dies-at-56.html (accessed January 21, 2010).

Lyrics Freak. "I Saw Her Standing There Lyrics." www.lyricsfreak.com/b/beatles/i+saw+her+standing+there_10026349.html (accessed January 23, 2010).

MACCA-Central: Unofficial McCartney Website. "Linda McCartney Was Nobody's Pushover." www.macca-central.com/news/?3243 (accessed January 19, 2010).

Morgan, Laura. "A Day in Their Life: Remembering Paul McCartney's Marriage—The Handsome Beatle Disappointed Millions of Hopeful Fans When He Wedded Linda Eastman." *Entertainment Weekly*, March 17, 2000. www.ew.com/ew/article/0,275682,00.html (accessed January 19, 2010).

Notable Names Database. "Linda McCartney." www.nndb.com/people/311/000045176/ (accessed January 19, 2010).

"Sir Paul McCartney on Linda." *Times Online*, April 6, 2008. http://entertainment.timesonline.co.uk/tol/arts_and_entertainment/music/article3666255.ece (accessed January 19, 2010).

Stritof, Sheri, and Bob Stritof. "Sir Paul McCartney and Lady Linda Eastman Marriage Profile." About.com: Marriage. http://marriage.about.com/od/entertainmen1/a/mccartneylinda.htm (accessed January 19, 2010).

Wikipedia. "Linda McCartney." http://en.wikipedia.org/wiki/Linda_McCartney (accessed January 19, 2010).

Wikipedia. "Paul McCartney." http://en.wikipedia.org/wiki/Paul_McCartney (accessed January 19, 2010).

32. PATRICK SWAYZE AND LISA NIEMI

Associated Content. "Patrick Swayze & Lisa Niemi—The Time of My Life—One Last Dance." www.associatedcontent.com/article/2207091/patrick_swayze_lisa_niemithe_time_of.html?cat=33 (accessed December 27, 2009).

Famous Hookups. "Relationship Details: Patrick Swayze & Lisa Niemi." www.famoushookups.com/site/relationship_detail.php?relid=2770&celebid=1006&name=Patrick_Swayze (accessed December 27, 2009).

Internet Movie Database. "Biography for Lisa Niemi." www.imdb.com/name/nm0001568/bio (accessed December 27, 2009).

Körzdörfer, Norbert. "Patrick Swayze and Lisa Niemi: Hollywood star Died in the Arms of the Wife He Loved." Bild.com. www.bild.de/BILD/news/bild-english/celebrity-gossip/2009/09/16/patrick-swayze-lisa-niemi/hollywood-star-died-in-wifes-arms-after-losing-cancer-battle.html (accessed December 27, 2009).

Oprah Winfrey Show. "Remembering Patrick: Lisa Niemi Talks about Patrick Swayze." www.oprah.com/oprahshow/Lisa-Niemi-Talks-About-Patrick-Swayze/1 (accessed December 27, 2009).

Stritof, Sheri, and Bob Stritof. "Lisa Niemi and Patrick Swayze Marriage Profile." About.com: Marriage. http://marriage.about.com/od/entertainmen1/p/patrickswayze.htm (accessed December 27, 2009).

Swayze, Patrick, and Lisa Niemi. *The Time of My Life.* New York: Atria Books, 2009.

Wikipedia. "Dirty Dancing." http://en.wikipedia.org/wiki/Dirty_dancing (accessed December 27, 2009).

Wikipedia. "(I've Had) The Time of My Life." http://en.wikipedia.org/wiki/(I've_Had)_The_Time_of_My_Life (accessed December 27, 2009).

Wikipedia. "Lisa Niemi." http://en.wikipedia.org/wiki/Lisa_Niemi (accessed December 27, 2009).

Wikipedia. "Patrick Swayze." http://en.wikipedia.org/wiki/Patrick_Swayze (accessed December 27, 2009).

Zurko, Roz. "Lisa Niemi Swayze and Patrick Swayze a Hollywood Love Story for over Three Decades." Associated Content. www.associatedcontent.com/article/2175417/lisa_niemi_swayze_and_patrick_swayze.html?cat=7 (accessed December 27, 2009).

33. PRINCE CHARLES AND CAMILLA SHAND

ABC News. "Most Fascinating Person: Camilla Parker Bowles." http://abcnews.go.com/Entertainment/story?id=1355896 (accessed January 31, 2010).

Anderson, Becky. "The Woman Always Close to Charles." CNN, February 11, 2005. www.cnn.com/2005/WORLD/europe/02/11/love.history/index.html (accessed January 31, 2010).

Barton, Laura. "When Fred Met Gladys: Charles and Camilla—A Love Story." *Slate Magazine*, April 7, 2005. www.slate.com/id/2116377 (accessed January 31, 2010).

BBC. "The Love Affair of Prince Charles and Camilla Parker Bowles." www.bbc.co.uk/dna/h2g2/a4158371 (accessed January 31, 2010).

Biography.com. "Camilla Parker Bowles Biography." www.biography.com/articles/camilla-parker-bowles-9542218 (accessed January 31, 2010).

Bowditch, Gillian. "The Love Affair That Has Spanned Three Decades." *Scotsman*, February 11, 2005. http://news.scotsman.com/princeofwales/The-love-affair-that-has.2602326.jp (accessed January 31, 2010).

British Royal Wedding. "Prince Charles and Camilla Parker Bowles." www.britishroyalwedding.com/royal-weddings/price-charles-and-camilla/ (accessed January 31, 2010).

CBS News. "From Laughing Stock to Love Story." October 31, 2005. www.cbsnews.com/stories/2005/10/31/listening_post/main996464.shtml (accessed January 31, 2010).

Enberg, Tanya. "A Royal Affair: Enduring Romance Suggests 'Other Woman' Might Just Be 'The One.'" *Toronto Sun*, November 5, 2009. www.torontosun.com/life/sexfiles/2009/11/05/11640531-sun.html (accessed January 31, 2010).

ExpressIndia.com. "5 Quotes from Prince Charles' Love Life." www.expressindia.com/news/fullstory.php?newsid=44686 (accessed January 31, 2010).

Farag, Prof. Talaat I. "Hunting the Fox Hunter." *Ambassadors Online Magazine: The Forum for Cultures and Civilizations* 8, no. 1 (2005). http://ambassadors.net/archives/issue18/opinions.htm (accessed January 31, 2010).

Gibson, Hirlen. "The Woman Who Won't Be Queen." *Time Europe*, February 13, 2005. www.time.com/time/europe/html/050221/camilla.html (accessed January 31, 2010).

Grice, Elizabeth. "Charles and Camilla, 1970s–1990s." *Telegraph*, February 11, 2005. www.telegraph.co.uk/news/uknews/1483283/Charles-and-Camilla-1970s-1990s.html (accessed January 31, 2010).

Hinckley, David. "Camilla Emerges." *New York Daily News*, August 30, 1998. www.nydailynews.com/archives/news/1998/08/30/1998-08-30_camilla_emerges.html (accessed January 31, 2010).

Kinsley, Michael. "Love, Royal Style." *Washington Post*, April 10, 2005. www.washingtonpost.com/wp-dyn/articles/A38724-2005Apr8.html (accessed January 31, 2010).

McAllister, J. F. O. "The 34-Year Courtship." *Time Europe*, February 13, 2005. www.time.com/time/europe/html/050221/story.html (accessed January 31, 2010).

MSNBC. "Prince Charles to Marry Longtime Lover Camilla." February 11, 2005. www.msnbc.msn.com/id/6945019/(accessed January 31, 2010).

Pearson, Allison. "Love in a Cold Climate." *New Yorker*, August 25, 1997. www.newyorker.com/

archive/1997/08/25/1997_08_25_124_TNY_CARDS_000379276 (accessed January 31, 2010).

"Profile: Camilla, Duchess of Cornwall." CBC News, April 18, 2006. www.cbc.ca/news/back ground/royals/camilla.html (accessed January 31, 2010).

Puente, Maria. "Prince Charles, Camilla Parker Bowles Marry." USA Today, April 9, 2005. www .usatoday.com/life/people/2005-04-09-royal-wedding_x.htm (accessed January 31, 2010).

Scandalous Women Blog. "How Do You Solve a Problem Like Camilla? The Life of the Duchess of Cornwall." July 17, 2008. http://scandalouswoman.blogspot.com/2008/07/how-do-you -solve-problem-like-camilla.html (accessed January 31, 2010).

Sky.com. "Charles and Camilla: A Love That Never Died." http://news.sky.com/skynews/Home/ Charles-And-Camilla-A-Love-That-Never-Died/Article/200503413318377 (accessed January 31, 2010).

Thomas, June. "Pity the Poor Prince: Charles is Atoning for the Sins of Rich, Middle-Aged Men Everywhere." Slate Magazine, April 7, 2005. www.slate.com/id/2116364/(accessed January 31, 2010).

Wendyharmer.com. "Charles and Camilla." www.wendyharmer.com/charlesandcamilla.html (accessed January 31, 2010).

Wikipedia. "Camilla, Duchess of Cornwall." http://en.wikipedia.org/wiki/Camilla,_Duchess_ of_Cornwall (accessed January 31, 2010).

Wikipedia. "Charles, Prince of Wales." http://en.wikipedia.org/wiki/Charles,_Prince_of_Wales (accessed January 31, 2010).

34. RENÉ ANGÉLIL AND CÉLINE DION

All Free Essays. "Celine Dion." www.allfreeessays.com/essays/Celine-Dion/878.html.

AOL Music. "Celine Dion Biography." http://music.aol.com/artist/celine-dion/biography/1003472 (accessed January 5, 2010).

Asianet Press Release. "Celine Dion and Rene Angelil Renew Their Vows." www.ryt9.com/es/ anpi/21447/ (accessed January 5, 2010).

"Celine Dion." www.angelfire.com/art/angel4ever/celine.html (accessed January 6, 2010).

"Celine Dion." www.facebook.com/celinedion?v=info.

"Celine Dion: The Story of a Star." http://destin.8m.com/bio.html.

"Celine Dion: The 'Ultimate Diva.'" CNN, October 22, 2002. www.cnn.com/CNN/Programs/ people/shows/dion/profile.html (accessed January 5, 2010).

Dion, Celine, with Georges-Hébert Germain. Celine Dion: My Story, My Dream. Translated by Bruce Benderson. New York: Morrow, 2000.

Iley, Chrissy. "'People Are Jealous': She's Sold More Records Than Any Other Woman and Has Just Made £125m from Her Residency in Las Vegas. So Why Do Critics Deride Her Music, Her Taste, Her Marriage? Celine Dion Talks to Chrissy Iley." Guardian, December 10, 2007. www.guardian.co.uk/music/2007/dec/10/popandrock1 (accessed January 5, 2010).

Internet Movie Database. "Biography for Céline Dion." www.imdb.com/name/nm0001144/bio (accessed January 5, 2010).

Lovetripper. "Celine Dion and Rene Angelil's Wedding." www.lovetripper.com/bridal/wedding -database/celine-dion.html (accessed January 5, 2010).

Sinatra, Ashley. "Celine Dion: A Brief Biography." Associated Content. www.associatedcontent .com/article/2364030/celine_dion_a_brief_biography.html?cat=33 (accessed January 6, 2010).

Szklarski, Cassandra. "Celine Dion's Love Story 'Inspirational.'" *Star*, October 2, 2008. www .thestar.com/article/510672 (accessed January 5, 2010).

Walters, Barbara. "Celine Dion's Return to the Spotlight: Diva Tells of Domestic Joys, Plans for Return to Spotlight." ABC News. http://abcnews.go.com/2020/story?id=123953&page=1 (accessed January 5, 2010).

Wikipedia. "Celine Dion." http://en.wikipedia.org/wiki/Celine_Dion (accessed January 5, 2010).

Wikipedia. "René Angélil." http://en.wikipedia.org/wiki/Rene_Angelil (accessed January 5, 2010).

Zaslow, Jeffrey. "'You Enter People's Lives': Some Critics Dismiss Celine Dion as an Over-the-Top Power Balladeer. But Millions Buy Her Albums and Tickets to Her Sold-Out Concerts." *USA Weekend*, September 11–13, 1998. www.usaweekend.com/98_issues/980913/ 980913celine.html (accessed January 5, 2010).

ACKNOWLEDGMENTS

In a book dedicated to love, the acknowledgments page has to begin with those whom I hold nearest and dearest. The first is my mother, Gilda Wagman, who always believed in me, even when all the signposts pointed to the contrary. Next is my husband, Joel (my "and the rest is history"), for making me, in the words of Fanny Brice, "a Sadie Sadie married lady." As she sang, "See what's on my hand / There's nothing quite as touching / As a simple wedding band." My most fervent hope is that for my daughter, Jordanna (Jordi) Geller, life will be the same as the three words that end classic fairy tales.

My most heartfelt thanks goes out to my three New York City fellow musketeers. Writing is my life preserver, and the first person who was instrumental in making this book a reality is my literary agent, Caren Johnson. I had, for the third time, the privilege of having Meg Leder as my editor. My publicist, Heidi Reicher, did her utmost on my book's behalf.

Lastly, *And the Rest Is History* could not have been possible without the iconic lovers whose turbulent affairs comprise this volume. Their grand passions, although often leading to heartbreak, make for grand stories.

And, in case anyone is feeling cynical about *amour* after reading these tales where the course of love ran anything but smooth, one can take hope from the case of Herbert and Zelmyra Fisher from North Carolina, who hold the record for the world's longest marriage. Herbert, 104, and Zelmyra, 101, have enjoyed eighty-six years of wedded bliss. A favorite shared pastime is sitting on their porch and counting cars. And, if that isn't heartwarming enough, the two tweeted love advice on Valentine's Day on their joint Twitter account: @longestmarried. Hence, in love, as in life, all things are possible, something that we must always believe, even against all odds.

POSTSCRIPT

There is a saying that "to say good-bye is to die a little," and it is with reluctance that I bid farewell to *And the Rest Is History*. I would like to end this volume of the romances of the ages with a love story that embodies Elizabeth Barrett Browning's quotation, "And, if God willeth / I shall but love thee better after death."

J. R. R. Tolkien met Edith Mary Bratt when the author, at age sixteen, moved into the boarding house in which she lived. Their favorite pastime was visiting Birmingham teashops, especially one that had a balcony overlooking the sidewalk. They would sit on the balcony and throw sugar lumps into the hats of those who passed beneath them. Romance inevitably followed. They are buried side by side, in a single grave, near Tolkein's beloved Oxford. Their headstone bears the names Lúthien and Beren, fictional lovers that Tolkein created for his Middle Earth fantasies.